E C O C I D E

Heedless or deliberate destruction of the natural environment by such actions as overexploitation of resources, dumping of pollutants, or an act of war.

"Once upon a time people did grievous harm to the environment without fully understanding the consequences of their actions. That defence is no longer available, and that sure knowledge we now have entails equally sure moral obligations. In this context, the idea of establishing the crime of Ecocide is both timely and compelling."

Jonathon Porritt, founder of Forum for the Future

"The problem in the past is that if you hold a company responsible [for environmental destruction], who sits in the dock? All the court can do is fine the company if it has transgressed. Who pays the fine? We do, because they pass the cost of the fine onto their customers – so it does not have very much effect, at all. But who is responsible? There are real people in the company and the object of the Ecocide Act is not just aimed at companies, it is aimed at individuals. Individual responsibility is the only way there will be any change."

Michael Mansfield QC, human rights lawyer

"Establishing a law to help end ecocide would signal a major breakthrough in the way we deal with crimes against the natural world. By ranking ecocide alongside genocide, crimes against humanity, crimes of aggression, and war crimes it would empower the courts to bring those responsible for environmental crimes to justice. So I am proud to endorse the End Ecocide Campaign and to be part of this global movement daring to imagine a better, fairer greener future."

Caroline Lucas, Green Party MP for Brighton Pavilion

ECOLIBRIUM NOW

The Earth in Balance
A Creative Tapestry in Support of Ending Ecocide

Ecolibrium Now is the work of a team of diverse individuals, all of whom are concerned about the health of the Planet and want to help establish an international 'Law against Ecocide' at the United Nations. This law will make all damage to, destruction of, or loss of ecosystems on the Earth the Fifth Crime Against Peace – The Keystone in the Arch of Environmental Protection.

FOREWORDS BY JONATHON PORRITT
+
MICHAEL MANSFIELD QC

Ecolibrium Now is published for the purpose of education and study and is not for profit.

The Book Group

Editor

Andrea Gear

Project Manager

Chris Stockdale

Book Team

Judy Barber
Jean Laurent Bos
Greg Dance
Chris Stockdale
Rob Mehta

Assisted by

Sabine Crittall
Ruth Davey
Trish Dickinson
Rowena Ewens
Peter Maynard
Jehanne Mehta
Adam Ormes Court
Edgar Vaid

Cover Image

Ruth Davey

Cover Design

Peter Maynard

Book Design

Chris J Bailey

Webmaster

Greg Dance

For more information about the Team and Contributors please look at the website, www.ecolibriumnow.com

This book includes contributions from Jonathon Porritt, Michael Mansfield QC, Michael Meacher, Fritjof Capra, Vandana Shiva, Maddy Harland, Patrick Holden, Rob Hopkins, Tony Juniper, Charles Eisenstein, Polly Higgins, Zac Goldsmith, Jane Davidson and Carol Ann Duffy (Poet Laureate), and many other outstanding writers, poets and artists. It also includes historical quotes, dating back to Plato (c428-348 BCE), which show that love and concern for the Earth are far from being a recent phenomenon.

First published in September 2015

Published by the *Ecolibrium Now* Book Group in association with *Resurgence & Ecologist* magazine.

ISBN 978-0-9931002-1-5
Printed by Imprint Digital.com

WWW.ECOLIBRIUMNOW.COM

ECOLIBRIUM NOW

CONTENTS

CONTENTS

JONATHON PORRITT

Foreword

TREEHUGGER.COM

Back in 1992, Al Gore wrote a hugely inspiring book called *Earth in the Balance*. It presented a not untypical balance sheet: the hellish trends and trajectories of doom and gloom, balanced (somewhat apprehensively, it has to be said) by a scattering of seeds of hope and pinpricks of positivity.

Twenty-two years on, *Ecolibrium Now* takes another look at that balancing act. I'd be kidding you if I said that it looks that much better in 2015 than it did in 1992. Those trends and trajectories (on pollution, injustice, accelerating climate change, loss of biodiversity etc, etc) are still heading in the wrong direction; and though it's true that many of those seeds of hope have now germinated and are generating amazing insights and benefits for individuals, communities and whole nations, the imbalance is still more than a little unnerving.

Many of the highly eloquent contributors to *Ecolibrium Now* have been seeking to correct that imbalance for decades. And on the whole, they're still baffled as to why so many people are so calmly participating in an act of mass suicide. How can it be that such an ugly, destructive, techno-centric and inhumane model of progress still dominates every corner of our lives?

Such a persistent blockage, operating on a global scale, might easily induce despair. But there's no giving way to despair in *Ecolibrium Now*. There is, however, anger, often deep, excoriating anger at the fact that so many people's lives are still blighted by false models of progress; so many species and habitats thoughtlessly put at risk through the 'denaturing' of the natural world; so many brave, loving individuals persecuted for their beliefs and their defence of the natural world.

And there's pain, deep pain at the cruel and careless way we abuse each other and the Earth. The still unfolding horror story of 'ecocide' is brought to life through a number of these essays; others invite us to explore the psychological and philosophical origins of ecocide, starting with that moment in human history where we chose to define ourselves as being separate from the rest of life on Earth. That 'ontological assumption of separateness' (in the words of American philosopher Willis Harman) underpins so much of today's dysfunctional politics and economics.

And then there's longing, a deep and poignant longing for the world we know is out there waiting to be born. The whole idea of *Ecolibrium Now* is all about that sustainable world in waiting.

But waiting can be so frustrating! So how can we speed things up? How can we change dominant mindsets and behaviours – through technology, community, spiritual practice, politics, and different forms of land use?

Underlying all that potential is the powerful idea that we need a New Story to make sense of our roles and responsibilities in the world today. It's now 35 years since Thomas Berry exhorted us to put the Old Story behind us and to elaborate a new story based on properly understanding our place in the cosmos and in the community of life on Earth. *Ecolibrium Now* is full of insights into what that new story might mean, and full of sparkling ideas as to how to tell that story in different ways for different purposes with different people.

I particularly love the practicality of all that. The new story has to come alive in practice as well as in the telling. For instance, we won't transform food retail in the UK by moaning about big food retailers; we'll do so by doubling the amount of food that is not sold in those 8,000 large supermarkets from 3% to 6%, multiplying the influence of community-supported agriculture all around the country.

And we won't become 're-enchanted with the natural world' simply by talking about the beauty and diversity of nature, but by getting our hands into the soil, by getting involved in practical actions to heal the multiplicity of wounds inflicted over so many decades.

A lot of this, as ever, comes down to personal responsibility – not just in how we live and how we spend our money, but in terms of how we feel and reach out to others. There's a lot of reaching out in *Ecolibrium Now*; as one of the authors puts it, 'empathy and compassion are very contagious'. And that means empathy across space, empathy across species, and empathy across time.

Here in 2015, our Earth is still in the balance. We have a bit of time – not much, but enough – to restore that balance. *Ecolibrium Now* reminds us of how best to use that time, and how to turn pain and despair into hope and action. That makes it a timely and inspiring contribution to the single most important debate that we're all involved in today.

Jonathon Porritt was the 'Founder Director' of 'Forum for the Future' and is currently a Trustee. 'Forum for the Future' has the mission to accelerate change to a sustainable future.

MICHAEL MANSFIELD QC

Foreword: Before It's Too Late

There's a PlayStation game called Ecolibrium which requires participants to create a perfect virtual ecosystem by growing flora and fauna to achieve a perfect equilibrium. However, the variables are somewhat limited and exclude the most important factors. Two of these relate to population growth and climate change. It is these pressures which create the major threats to the future of our planet. And as Polly Higgins has advocated in her previous books, as custodians of our planet, Mother Earth should be viewed as a living organism which we have a duty to represent and protect. Eradicating Ecocide would be a start.

But first it is necessary to recognise the underlying forces driving the various forms of Ecocide (GM crops is one form mentioned in this book.) Recently there have been two significant events relating to population and climate change. Both flag up the warning signs of ultimate meltdown. Both relate to the need for immediate and concerted action to eliminate the profligate abuse of our resources, often putting profit before people.

Naomi Klein in her recently published book *This Changes Everything* attributes the root cause to the ravages of Capitalism. Whilst this undoubtedly provides an entirely plausible analysis, changing the system cannot be achieved in time to stop what is soon to become an irreversible situation. Personal as well as political commitment to entirely practical measures must be paramount. We each need to re-examine our lifestyles and the constant demands we make upon the environment along with campaigning for governments to implement targets.

The first event mentioned above was the publication by Washington University of a scientific report containing the alarming prediction that global population growth was set to exceed previous predictions and would reach 11 billion by the end of the century. This has serious ramifications for the finite resources underpinning our planet. 'There is now a strong argument that population should return to the top of the international agenda. Population is the driver of just about everything else and rapid population growth can exacerbate all kinds of challenges' (*Guardian* Friday 19th September 2014).

This prognosis overturns the previous consensus that population growth would peak in 2050 at about 9 billion people, which has been the basis for policies formed by many institutions dealing with global problems. A prominent example is the Intergovernmental Panel on Climate Change.

By coincidence the second event was the People's Climate March two days later on 21st September, which preceded the UN summit on Climate Change on the 23rd. Currently it is anticipated that we are heading for a 4.5C temperature rise, twice the target levels canvassed over the last decade. Such a rise would result in serious flooding and submerged coastlines, scorched earth, heat waves and drought.

The poorest countries with large populations are likely to be the hardest hit. The National Oceanic and Atmospheric Administration in Washington revealed that June, July and August 2014 were the hottest months on record. However, the summit is only a small part of an ongoing process of tortuous negotiations which have yet to agree the level of cuts to greenhouse gas emissions – let alone their implementation. This has been trundling on for an unacceptable length of time dating back 50 years, and including well known summits in Rio, Kyoto, and Copenhagen. The focus of attention has been manmade emissions stemming from fossil fuels.

This is the background to Polly Higgins' courageous and determined initiative to ban Ecocide by making it the 5th international crime against peace, alongside better known ones like Genocide. The Rome Statute of 1998, which embodies the existing four crimes and established the International Criminal Court in the Hague, was intended originally to embrace Ecocide but this was vetoed at the last minute by countries with a vested interest in oil exploitation.

A definition of Ecocide has been proposed by Polly in her book *Eradicating Ecocide*: 'the extensive destruction, damage to or loss of ecosystems of a given territory, whether by human agency or by other causes to such an extent that peaceful enjoyment by the inhabitants of that territory has been severely diminished.' Some of the terms used are already employed in International law and are familiar to lawyers.

The most significant aspect of this proposal is its ambit of responsibility and liability. Like the other crimes justifiable at the ICC, it renders individuals liable to prosecution rather than corporate entities behind which individuals often hide their responsibility. An additional rigorous feature is the need for strict liability. It would not require the element of 'mens rea' commonly associated with the definition of crime. Put another way it is a crime of consequence. This hopes to concentrate the ultimate objective of the law in prevention, in a pre-emptive binding obligation.

In September 2011 this model was put to the test in a mock trial staged in the Supreme Court in Westminster. An indictment was framed to charge two senior officials involved in two different environmental disasters. The first was based on the 2010 events in the Deepwater Horizon oil spill in the Gulf of Mexico. The second concerned the longstanding extractive oil industry based at Athabasca Tar Sands in Canada, reputedly the largest energy project in the world. I performed the role of prosecutor. It was intended to demonstrate how such a prosecution would work and some of the key moments in the proceedings can now be watched on *YouTube*.

This possibility has particular relevance to the current declared policy of the UK Government to proceed with the authorisation of fracking (hydraulic fracturing). Potentially it is clearly capable of involving the commission of the crime of ecocide. The means of exploration and extraction of shale gas, a fossil fuel, employs intrusive land drilling, the possibility of earth tremors, huge quantities of fresh water, and the addition of chemicals (some of which are carcinogens and hazardous pollutants). The largest component of the whole operation is water consumption estimated to be in the region of 5 million gallons to drill and frack a well.

The most obvious and substantial risks to ecosystems and the peaceful enjoyment of inhabitants arise from the possibility of gas leaks and emissions (shale naturally contains radioactive materials), extensive pollution of ground water and fresh water sources, substantial depletion of the same resources, resultant damage to health through sensory, respiratory, and neurological complications.

Given the centrality of these issues to the survival of the planet they plainly take priority over the majority of other more parochial matters and demand a plan of action sooner rather than later. Every political candidate needs to be put on the spot with specific questions about their green positioning, their attitude to policies incorporating sustainability and ultimately what they intend to do about climate change.

Michael Mansfield QC is an English barrister and heads his own chambers. A republican, vegetarian, socialist, and self-described 'radical lawyer', he has participated in prominent and controversial court cases.

CHRIS STOCKDALE

Preface

This book arose from a World Café in Stroud, Gloucestershire, England, facilitated by Judy Barber and organised by her and Trish Dickinson to support Polly Higgins, who spoke about her work to bring in a law of Ecocide. I became a rapporteur for one table. When Polly came to that table I asked her about Fundraising. A subsequent visitor to the table, Jehanne Mehta, seeing the theme crayoned across the paper tablecloth, spoke about an American book†, and how that had garnered support and saved millions of acres of wilderness – could we not do something similar? On reporting this at the plenary session, I was challenged by Jean-Laurent Bos to take this up. Not being a writer or artist, I naturally declined, but I was further pushed and agreed that I could help to bring such a book about.

Thus it is with great pleasure, considerable relief, some concern, and a lot of hope that this book, the culmination of a huge amount of work carried out by the Team, has finally been presented to you, on behalf of the Mother of us all, our Planet Earth. The book is in three sections – Expose, Envisage, Evolve – although there is inevitably overlap. It is not a manual, a 'how to' book to save the Planet from ourselves. It is a compendium of pieces contributed by people who received and responded to our request for help.

Our wish is that the book will be entertaining, useful and inspiring. We hope it will encourage you to do whatever suits you and your locality to help us all help our ailing Earth.

For me, this is to support the EEE movement – End Ecocide England, End Ecocide Europe, and End Ecocide Earth. These are groups who are all working to bring about the adoption of 'Ecocide' as the Fifth Crime Against Peace at the UN, hence our three Es for Expose, Envisage and Evolve. For everyone what to do is entirely a personal matter, whether choosing to support the above, creating and managing Marine Conservation Zones, supporting Organic and Biodynamic farming, developing Permaculture, gifting a song into the global consciousness, donating time, artefacts or money to the great Earth Charities, drastically reducing one's carbon footprint or adopting green technologies. Of course, integral to all of this is achieving social justice, without which none of the above will succeed and nor will we as a species. It may simply be a choice to live a simpler way of life, 'living simply that others may simply live'.

On behalf of the team, I would like to apologise here to those whose work was submitted but does not appear, and to those who would have liked to have submitted work had we contacted them. For this and for all imperfections we are sorry. We have been a small volunteer group with limited resources and our competencies stretched to the edge. 'Day jobs' have had to be done and businesses run. Thank you to the contributors who have all been most fulsome in support. Thank you to Andrea Gear for being editor-in-chief and to the book group members not already mentioned. Finally, I would like to thank all the supporters not named who have helped in so many ways – and also you, for reading this far and for all you will achieve for us all.

On behalf of the Ecolibrium Now Book Team,
Chris Stockdale *Herefordshire, UK.*

† In Terry Tempest Williams' 'When Women Were Birds', she writes about her environmental group in Utah being sidelined by senators wanting to exploit millions of acres of Red Rock Wilderness for oil and gas. She and friends wrote to 25 poets, writers and historians asking for their 'best ever' descriptions of Utah wilderness. Within three weeks they had 20 articles and funds for a chapbook, 'Testimony – Writers of the West speak on behalf of the Utah Wilderness'.

Through sympathetic senators in Washington the book reached every senator, President Clinton and Vice President Al Gore. When the Red Rock Wilderness Bill was debated, senator after senator read from Testimony. It became a filibuster. Two million acres were protected. The Utah Public Lands Act died on the floor. President Clinton said, 'This little book made a difference'.

www.endecocide.eu
every hand helps
vote to end Ecocide

EXPOSE

This section tells us about what is happening that is damaging to our environment and risking the future well-being of life on earth, including ours. There is testimony to how strong feelings are and the scale of what needs to be exposed, not hidden.

Leaf Landscape: © ANNABEL WARD

Ecocide law, unlike any other law, has the capacity to disrupt what we perceive as immoveable. How can we possibly decouple from fossil fuels, from economics based on making money out of heavy extractive industries, from businesses that are threatening to sue governments that refuse to allow them to destroy their lands? And law holds this system in place.

The intent behind much of our laws is rarely based on the sacredness of life; all too often our laws are based on the supremacy of ownership and property – 'I own' has in many respects superceded the collective right to life. Yet, we are now waking up, blowing the horn.

Polly Higgins

22 Reasons for the Bedroom Tax

Because the Badgers are moving the goalposts.
The Ferrets are bending the rules.
The Weasels are taking the hindmost.
The Otters are downing tools.

The Hedgehogs are changing the game-plan
The Grass-snakes are spitting tacks.

The Squirrels are playing the blame-game.
The Skunks are twisting the facts.

The Pole-cats are upping the ante.
The Foxes are jumping the gun.
The Voles are crashing the party.
The Stoats are dismantling the Sun.

The Rabbits are taking the biscuit.
The Hares are losing the plot.
The Eagles are kicking the bucket.
The Rats are joining the dots.

The Herons are throwing a curveball.
The Shrews are fanning the flames.
The Field mice are sinking the 8-ball.
The Swans are passing the blame.

And the Pheasants are draining the oil from the tank –
but only the Bustards have broken the bank.

Carol Ann Duffy is Poet Laureate. She combines tenderness and toughness, humour and lyricism, unconventional attitudes and conventional forms, which has won her a very wide audience of readers.

STEVE McPHERSON

Plastic Landscape

This beach – this is the beach of both my child and adulthood. I have walked on these sands countless times. I have walked on this shore with all of those who I have loved. I still do with those who I love above all others. I have watched every time of day and every season change as waves endlessly break and the tide heaves and yawns over the chalk reefs and shifting sands. Here the sky's constant changing paints the sea, while clouds roll and blister over heavy cargo ships queuing on the horizon.

This beach – this beach is drenched. Drenched by the ebb and flow. Drenched in its geology and saturated in its history. On this beach I stand, walk, sleep and float, this is the beach of my day and my night. I find myself here. I find myself connected to my own history, connected to environmental history, connected through molecules of water in the shallows of my small and insignificant shore to the countless shores of others.

Sea becomes rain, rain becomes lakes. Lakes, rivers, aquifers become the water I bathe in, become the water I drink, become my sweat, my tears, my blood, my breath. Each molecule moving, drifting from one state to the next, in a continual process that passes through plant, animal and human animal. Coursing through the veins of each and expelled, evaporated or exhaled in particles to rejoin the cycle to rejoin the sea again. Water – life – life water.

This beach is a beach of gems, of treasures. This beach and cliffs are fossil, where embedded flint seams layer in memory. Sponges and urchins mark geological time whilst pyrites nodules bleed and stain iron their chalky white beds. Caught in the sun, burning coals against the weed, amber and copal occasionally dot the strand line. Degraded from long journeys from Baltic coasts, these resinous lumps move along the water's edge silently, and tumble into rivulets and marine vegetation. Some gems float, some sink.

29
Compose Character

This beach is confettied. Highly coloured plastic fragments flutter in squalls, and are picked up at the water's edge to be landed on the other side of the bay. Amongst my footsteps, glistening from the pulled tide and slowly crystallising in salt lie flotsam, things, items, stuff, debris, litter, objects, whatsnames, thingamajigs, doodahs and other lost bits and bobs. Surreptitiously and silently they have filled our lives and our homes, as they now do beaches all over the world. They slip off, and out of, into the tide – who slips them back onto and into the beach. From corner shops, cafés and supermarkets to sea and shore, objects and packaging's fluster and flag our over-consumption and needless want and waste.

Whilst most people believe to the contrary, or haven't even considered it, plastic is not an inert material. The growing list of leaching constitutes chemicals and plasticisers, endocrine-disrupters, carcinogens and hormone mimics, are a small nuisance in the convenient world of consumerism. The idea of plastic being toxic or harmful is, by most, as easily discarded as an empty wrapper or bottle. Easily ignored, easily thrown out of sight – out of mind – thrown away! Away into landfill, away into a gutter – into a river that flows away to the sea.

This beach is filled and moved on storms and churning spring tides, lifting and depositing natural and manufactured aggregates around the bay, whilst smoothing edges and dulling surfaces. Shards rise and fall, splinter in their thousands. Left in the environment they will sit in silt and sand for countless years. Until exposed, photo-degradation and the abrasive corrosive marine environment eventually reduces them into indistinguishable elements that only microscopes could reveal. Bit by bit they will become smaller, crumb by crumb, grain by grain until they blend with the sands. Already those poisonous grains fill beaks and stomachs, clog canals and bleed into the systems of living organisms, frequently condemning their hosts to slow starvation. Larger birds and mammals are virally mourned but where are those who will grieve over the plastic-filled stomachs of shrimps and sprats, left unseen like other wracked objects, lost on our shores?. This beach is a beach of treasures of the lost and dead. My booted feet are surrounded, and dead chalk, fossils, marine flora and fauna, fishing gear, waste, wood, and plastic are endlessly trapped and discharged in tide cycles. The brightly coloured plastic items are shattered, scarred and slowly patinated, to become contemporary archaeological artefacts that emerge alien against the natural pallette of a Kentish beach.

All world history has been formed in plastic. The dreams, fantasies, horrors, wishes and hopes of human beings have been moulded in this wonder material, whose resilience and permanence are its saviour and also its downfall. It has become part of our polluted land and seascape, and efforts of clean-ups usually result in moving this pollutant from one strained location to another, from the sea to the beach to the land. From it, gases will continue to rise, chemicals will leach into the soil, into our food and water supplies. Becoming the water I bathe in, the water I drink, my chemical sweat, chemical tears, blood and breath. Coursing through veins, transforming organs – cellular toxic plasticity.

We have an impact; the objects we consume have an impact. This beach continues through summers and winters. It sparkles in my dreams and waking when I feel its call. During those moments I search the beach, for objects, and for that which has been lost, and that which can be found. I sift and scour its surface while waves drum and dump in heart-beating rhythm. Water – life – life water.

Here I find myself and I find myself here often, caught in changing light and drifting through waves.

Steve McPherson is a writer, photographer, and installation artist.

HELEN MOORE

From Greenwash: A User's Manual

When it's that really tough
competitive edge you're after,
just front-load your business
into our new green
washing machine;

it takes all kinds –
and at high or low temperatures
will tackle the most stubborn
campaigns, offsetting your conscience
instantly – top results our guarantee!

Our washer uses only
the most charismatic of powders,
and will even take delicates,
like oil companies, airlines
and car manufacturers –

creating a soft-soap screen,
a turn-coat of iridescent suds,
in which your CEO can parade
transparent on the stock exchange.

Not that this
is the emperor's new clothes –
after a rinse with softener
(for that added shareholder comfort),
and plenty of extra spin,

your business will be newly laundered.
It can then be hung out to dry
(for that natural fresh-air scent) –
you secure in the knowledge
that it's had a cleaner,
greener type of wash.

Helen Moore is an award-winning eco-poet who publishes poetry, essays and reviews in a wide range of anthologies and journals, and regularly performs her poetry at literary events and environmental conferences around the UK.

"You wouldn't think you could kill an ocean, would you? But we'll do it one day. That's how negligent we are."
From 'Blood Hunt' 1995, Ian Rankin, writer

"Economists treat economics as if it is a pure science divorced from the facts of life. The result of this false accountancy is a wilful confusion under cover of which industry wreaks its havoc scot-free and ignores the environmental cost."
Vivienne Westwood, fashion designer

MATT HARVEY

They Say That Fish

They say that fish don't have a word for water
The same way birds don't have a word for air
That bricks, quite rightly, have no word for mortar
And angels, bless them, have no word for prayer

Most bees, when questioned, have no word for honey
The Oedipal don't have a word for Freud
The stinking rich don't need to carry money
The non-existent have no word for void

Though it may take us aeons to achieve it
– Perhaps just to conceive of it's enough
It's an effort, frankly, just to half-believe it –
Our world may one day have no word for love

Matt Harvey is a writer, poet, and enemy of all that's difficult and upsetting. His way with words has taken him from Totnes to the Wimbledon Tennis Championships via Saturday Live, the Edinburgh Festival and the Work section of the Guardian.

"Whether we or our politicians know it or not, Nature is party to all our deals and decisions, and she has more votes, a longer memory, and a sterner sense of justice than we do."
Wendell Berry, novelist, poet, environmental activist and farmer

---

"Unlimited growth assumes unlimited resources, and this is the genesis of Ecocide. To feed the increasing demands of our consumer-based capitalist system, humans have seen nature as a great resource for our personal pleasure, convenience and profit, and not as a living ecosystem from which all life springs. The move to commodify all of nature is the next step in its destruction. The earth is not ours to plunder. Nature has rights as surely as any that exist."
Maude Barlow, activist and author

KAREN EBERHARDT-SHELTON

What's the Point of More Growth?

The whole of civilisation has lost the plot. As I write (September 2013), hugely wealthy Ibrahim Ibrahimov (a construction tycoon) wants to build 50 artificial islands in the Caspian Sea south of Baku (capital of oil-rich Azerbaijan) and populate them with thousands of villas and apartments, 8 hotels, a Formula One racetrack, a yacht club, an airport, 150 schools, 50 hospitals, 5 university campuses, numerous parks, and plenty of shopping centres – along with the world's tallest building, the Azerbaijan Tower. Is he mad?

Ronald Wright, in his hugely informative little book, *A Short History of Progress*, states that, 'Civilisations often fall quite suddenly, because as they reach full demand on their ecologies, they become highly vulnerable to natural fluctuations.' Has Ibrahimov never heard of climate change, rising sea levels, extinction, pollution, diminishing natural resources, a global population that is already far too huge to sustain itself? Wright goes on to say that 'things are moving so fast that inaction itself is one of the biggest mistakes. The 10,000-year experiment of the settled life [when early agriculture took hold] will stand or fall by what we do, and don't do, now. The reform that is needed is not anti-capitalist, anti-American, or even deep environmentalist; it is simply the transition from short-term to long-term thinking. From recklessness and excess to moderation and the precautionary principle… Now is our last chance to get the future right.'

Ibrahimov, and so many others of his ilk, is heading in absolutely the wrong direction. It is this indulgence in excess, over-consumption, ignoring limits, and disregard for balance in the Earth's ecosystems that is precipitating the ultimate crash of all that we depend on for the continuation of our species. Every civilisation previous to ours has ultimately spun out of control and destroyed itself. We're next in the queue.

Bigger, taller, faster, newer, stronger, posher, more complex, cleverer… Is that what life is all about? What's the point of perpetual growth and development, economic or otherwise? Does it realistically improve our lives, make us better humans? Where is it all taking us? Where do we want it to take us, and why? Are we trying to prove something? Is it about superiority? If so, over what, to what end? Do individuals ever stop to reflect on this as they traipse about – consuming, wasting, borrowing, sullying the Earth in their daily routines?

Do politicians, the heads of huge companies, the oil barons, the controllers of commerce, the policy practitioners, the clergy, the architects of education, the roster of developers, the huge assortment of manufacturers and suppliers of their goods, etc. have any true inkling of what these combined stresses are inflicting on the global biosphere that has enabled us to breathe and be present for thousands of fertile years?

Do we want our children and their children to be around in the years to come? If we do, why are we messing it up for them and everything else? Why sacrifice the future to an overwhelmingly busy, wasteful and reckless now? If we want to protect future security, equilibrium, sustenance, and the ongoing marvel of life on Earth, why do we persist as though we have no real idea why it's absolutely vital to connect the dots to the Big Picture? It's all falling apart and we just carry on watching *Eastenders*.

Economic growth? Why??? More housing estates? Stop! 7 billion and growing. Why? Why? Why? Don't we care? Is there no gratitude? Don't we want to understand, learn, and change simply to make sure we wind up with a dear, sweet, pleasant next century, and the century after that, and hopefully on and on?

Karen Eberhardt-Shelton is a widely travelled writer, poet and photographer.

PETER ADAMS

The Pooh and the Wee End Up in the Sea

My rubbish goes in a bag in the bin
Then a bigger bag in a bigger bin
Then a lorry comes with rubbish men
Who chuck the bags and rubbish in.
Then they tip it on a tip –
In bulldozed mounds it hangs around,
The flapping bags like buried flags.

It rains and rains and gradually
The rain becomes a toxic tea
That flows, because of gravity
Down to its resting place, the sea.
The sea is the sump
For all the world's dumps,
All the rubbish round the globe
Is our ocean's toxic overload.
Discharges most unsatisfactory
Spewing out of every factory –
Think of it all –
The planet's too small!
How toxic the sea
That was once clean, must be!

And now let us trace
All the human waste
Down its sewers and pipes
Of all sizes and types.
Its noxious traces
Reach the same poisoned places.
The pooh and the wee
Both collect in the sea.
And the washing-up liquid
In the prawns and the squid.
And is fabric conditioner
A dolphin decommissioner?
Deodorant, shampoo,
They all must get through
And leave residue
In our seawater stew.
And the medicines we take
That we eliminate…

All this poison chemistry
Ends up in the poor old sea.
Our toxic potions
Are destroying the oceans.
And do we care?
We carry on and do the same to the air.
There's no away to throw rubbish to,
So what on earth are we going to do?
All the rubbish we throw
Has nowhere to go.

Peter Adams is a poet, writer and homeopath.

Pulp and Paper

Paper is my primary medium as an artist. My work with Feral Theatre often involves shadow puppets made of paper and card. Whilst researching our performance/ritual about the extinction of the Javan Tiger I came across Asia Pulp and Paper, a multi-national corporation regularly flouting environmental law in SE Asia. They 'accidentally' clear-cut ancient rainforest to manufacture paper products. They seem the perfect subject for this work.

Emily Laurens, theatre practitioner based in Wales.

ALICE OSWALD

Song of a Stone

there was a woman from the north
picked a stone up from the earth.
when the stone began to dream
it was a flower folded in

when the flower began to fruit
it was a circle full of light,
when the light began to break
it was a flood across a plain

when the plain began to stretch
the length scattered from the width
and when the width began to climb
it was a lark above a cliff

the lark singing for its life
was the muscle of a heart,
the heart flickering away
was an offthrow of the sea

and when the sea began to dance
it was the labyrinth of a conscience,
when the conscience pricked the heart
it was a man lost in thought

like milk that sours in the light,
like vapour twisting in the heat,
the thought was fugitive – a flare of gold –
it was an iris in a field

and when the man began to murmur
it was a question with no answer,
when the question changed its form
it was the same point driven home

it was a problem, a lamentation:
'What the buggery's going on?
This existence is an outrage!
Give me an arguer to shout with!'

and when the arguer appeared
it was an angel of the Lord,
and when the angel touched his chest,
it was his heartbeat being pushed

and when his heart began to break
it was the jarring of an earthquake
when the earth began to groan
they laid him in it six by one

dark bigger than his head,
pain swifter than his blood,
as good as gone, what could he do?
as deep as stone, what could he know?

Alice Oswald, poet, recipient of poetry awards (including the T. S. Eliot Prize in 2002). Her poetry is intimately attentive to the perils of ecological stress, and the human presence in her writing is often a component, rather than a dominant.

HELENA PAUL

GM Crops are Driving Genocide and Ecocide

The unfolding human and ecological disaster of GM agriculture in the Americas must send the EU a powerful message. We don't want it here, and we should stop buying the products of GM-driven genocide and ecocide abroad. We currently face a desperate, almost farcical push for GM crops in the UK and Europe, characterised by hyperbolic and inaccurate claims. So rather than taking those claims on trust, let's look at the impacts of GM crops in countries that have adopted them.

The cultivation of herbicide-tolerant crops in Argentina began in 1996 with GM soya and spread swiftly through the country. Powerful groups of investors helped drive GM soya production. Small farmers could not compete and many have left or been driven off their land, often into urban slums. People who remain in the countryside and small towns find themselves bombarded from the air with increasingly complex mixtures of chemicals intended to combat the problem of increasing weed and pest resistance. Although GM crops were promoted as a means to reduce levels of pesticides used, pesticide use in Argentina has increased massively from 34 million litres in 1990 to more than 317 million litres today.

In 2010, following years of mounting harm and protests, the Faculty of Medical Sciences from the National University of Córdoba called a first meeting for doctors working in the crop-sprayed towns in several provinces of Argentina. The physicians stressed that they have been serving the same populations, in general, for over 25 years, but what they found in recent years was quite unusual and strictly linked to systemic sprayings of pesticides.

For example, Dr Rodolfo Páramo, a paediatrician and neonatologist at the public hospital of Malabrigo, a Northern city in Santa Fe, highlighted the alarm he experienced when he found 12 cases of birth defects in newborns, out of 200 births per year in

2006. This situation is analogous with the four cases of stillbirths due to birth defects in the small town of Rosario del Tala, in Entre Ríos, both areas characterised by massive pesticide spraying.

Since that meeting, reports of illness caused by agrochemicals have continued to accumulate, along with evidence of failure to apply any rules about spraying, or to inform people about the dangers. Meanwhile GM crops continue to expand in Argentina, covering around 24 million hectares, some two-thirds of the total arable land available. Repression and displacement, often violent, of remaining rural populations, illness, and falling local food production have all featured in this picture.

Paraguay has lost nearly a million hectares and Argentina nearly two million hectares of forest since 2004 alone, with GM soya considered to be a major driver. The impacts include biodiversity loss, including many species found nowhere else, and displacement of indigenous peoples, some not previously contacted, plus impacts on soils and water, regional and local climate change and changes in rainfall. This is short-sighted destruction driven by short-term profits. And it is criminal – ecocide and genocide rolled into one.

Helena Paul, campaigner on issues including indigenous peoples' rights and tropical forests, oil exploration in the tropics, agricultural biodiversity, patents on life, genetic engineering and corporate power. This article was originally published by The Ecologist in 2014.

"Today we are faced with a challenge that calls for a shift in our thinking, so that humanity stops threatening its life-support system. Recognizing that sustainable development, democracy and peace are indivisible is an idea whose time has come"

Wangari Maathai (1940-2011), environmental and political activist

HEATHCOTE WILLIAMS

Cobalt Blues

In German folklore a kobold was a deadly sprite
That inhabited mines and could live inside rock;
Ugly and hunched it warned off human busybodies:
It would click and make an eerie, echoing knock.

In the sixteenth century some miners believed
They'd discovered a new precious mineral.
It looked like a glittering mixture of gold and silver.
They grew excited by the metal's potential.

But their digging it up led to their teeth falling out;
Their children were born with terrible defects.
They ascribed their misfortune to the mine spirits
And called the metal 'Cobalt' for its ill effects.

This was mankind's very earliest experience
Of his contracting a radiation sickness
Yet he recklessly revives such bad fairies
While ruthlessly ravaging earth's riches.

For he still ignores similar warning signals
Such as the clicks from a Geiger counter:
'Nuclear power is quite safe, for greed says so –
Never mind that it manufactures monsters.'

The cobalt bomb was known as the Doomsday Machine.
It was designed to extinguish all life on earth:
By its generating record levels of radioactivity
Human beings would be too sick to give birth.

Like the lion and the unicorn, man's death wish
And the life force, endlessly fight for the crown:
For their right to proclaim 'I'm king of the castle'
In civilization's all-consuming clone-towns.

Frackers are now ripping into the Celtic rainforest
And poisoning water with nucleotides;
They're over-heating the planet with cheap gas
Only to fuel an apocalyptic eco-cide.

Yet with manpower the Tarahumara run barefoot
For two hundred miles at a bound;
The radiant high which they get has no side-effects
And they're happy to leave metal underground.

Heathcote Williams is a poet, actor and award-winning playwright, perhaps best known for the book-length polemical poem 'Whale Nation' (1988), which offered a powerful argument for the newly instigated worldwide ban on whaling.

"If you talk to the animals they will talk with you and you will know each other. If you do not talk to them you will not know them, and what you do not know you will fear. What one fears one destroys."
Chief Dan George (1899-1981), author, poet and actor

"Wherever forests have not been mowed down, wherever the animal is recessed in their quiet protection, wherever the earth is not bereft of four-footed life – that to the white man is an 'unbroken wilderness'. But for us there was no wilderness, nature was not dangerous but hospitable, not forbidding but friendly. Our faith sought the harmony of man with his surroundings; the other sought the dominance of surroundings. For us, the world was full of beauty; for the other, it was a place to be endured until he went to another world. But we were wise. We knew that man's heart, away from nature, becomes hard."
Chief Luther Standing Bear (1868-1939), Lakota Sioux

NICOLA PEEL

Where Rivers Run Black

With my own eyes I've witnessed streams and rivers running black with heavy crude oil, butterflies coated in this toxic substance struggling to move their once multicoloured wings, dead fish floating on the current, and others contaminated but still alive, only to be eaten by indigenous people downriver.

Welcome to the Amazon, the ultimate edge, where the mountainous Andes meet the tropical rainforest. Since the 1960s the oil industry has been drilling here, yet few people are aware of this, or that ecocide and ethnocide take place in what once was paradise on a daily basis. Lago Agrio in northern Ecuador is the heart of the oil boom, its name, given by Texaco, appropriately enough meaning 'sour lake'. Shortly after Texaco's arrival, two local indigenous groups, the Tetetes and the Sansahuari, were reported to have disappeared forever, while the Cofan, Secoya, Siona, Kichwa and Huaorani have been affected deeply by the loss of their ancestral territory.

The Tagaeri and Taromenane are the two last known indigenous groups living in voluntary isolation in Ecuador. They have refused all contact with the outside world and are now threatened by the discovery of oil in their home, the Yasuni World Biosphere Reserve. Yasuni has been deemed the most biodiverse area on Earth, the jewel of our planet. But have you heard of it before? I believe that if we can't manage to save this place, then there's little else we can.

In the Amazon people have always drunk water straight from streams and rivers, but the difference now is the added hydrocarbons, heavy metals and radioactive substances which come courtesy of the oil industry. Children swim and play in these rivers, and their skin tells the story in rashes and lesions. In Ecuador doctors report the highest cancer rates and birth defects in the country.

But it's not just people's health that's affected by the contaminated water, air and earth, it's also their minds and souls. Their beloved homeland, where their ancestors have lived since time immemorial, has been taken from them. Deforested and contaminated, now in place of jungle grow towns, roads, oil wells, brothels and cheap motels. And where have the jaguars gone? They once roamed this land, along with the sloths and numerous varieties of monkeys. Brightly coloured birds now have nowhere to nest and the reptiles (once more abundant than anywhere else on Earth) have gone.

This addiction to oil knows no boundaries. Nothing and no one is sacred. The indigenous people are generously told they own only the surface of the Earth, while what's below belongs to the government. Once oil is discovered, the monster moves in, sucking out the ancient sunlight, which has remained in darkness for millennia. Like a drug addict's syringe, it perforates the body, sucking out this valuable liquid.

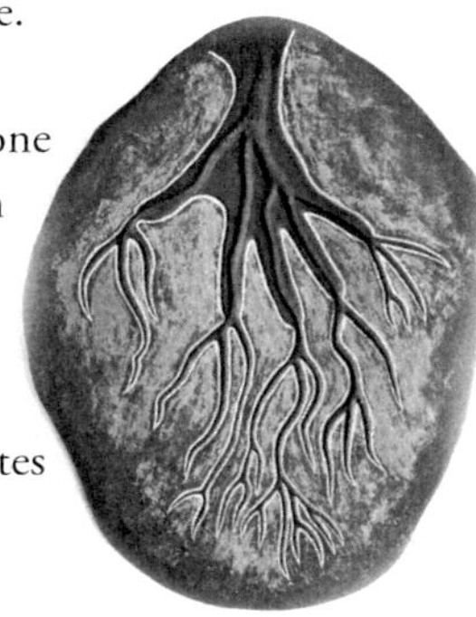

IMAGE: VARDA ZISMAN

For years local people were protesting, shouting loudly, trying to protect their homes and children, but their voices went unheard. That had to change. In 1994 under the banner of Frente de Defensa de la Amazonia (The Amazon Defence Coalition), 30,000 affected individuals united. They filed a class action lawsuit against Texaco (now Chevron) for deliberately dumping 18 billion gallons of toxic waste directly into the environment and spilling roughly 17 million gallons of crude oil. Texaco had also left hazardous waste in 916 open pits dug out of the forest floor, and many of these pits continue to leak into the water table or overflow in heavy rains, polluting rivers and streams.

After 21 years, this David and Goliath case was won by the Ecuadorian people. Chevron Texaco was ordered to pay $8.6 billion and make a formal international apology. They chose not to, so the judge raised the fine to $19 billion. Of course Chevron appealed, but again they lost. And so it seemed that justice had been served, the Earth and the people had won, and it was time to clean up the toxic wasteland left by this irresponsible corporation. However, Chevron then filed a civil lawsuit under the Racketeer Influenced and Corrupt Organizations Act (RICO) saying the trial was a fraud. The case continues.

When the law of Ecocide comes into being this will be a different story. But for now the other main oil industry players are supporting Chevron as they know that failure to win the case could set a dangerous precedent for further actions. Valiantly continuing to engage in this battle is Pablo Fajardo, an Ecuadorian lawyer raised in poverty and of native Cofan descent. He became CNN Hero of the Year and recipient of the Goldman Environmental Prize; nevertheless his ongoing work is often unpaid, unrecognised and largely unsupported.

How can this be? Perhaps because very few people know what's going on. After every screening of my documentary film *Blood of the Amazon*, I ask the audience to raise their hands if they've heard about this ecocide. On one occasion, out of an audience of 200 people, only 4 raised their hands.

It's now time for corporations to be held responsible for their actions and for everyone to understand the power they have as a consumer. The Chevron Texaco trial shows that their refusal to apologise cost them $10 billion, but they clearly thought it was worth this cost as the negative publicity would affect their public image, consumer demand and shareholder support. But their refusal has also ensured that people have yet to hear about one of the largest environmental disasters in history.

If people had heard, would it make a difference? Are people prepared to change? If a Chevron or Texaco garage is most convenient to where they live, would they actually go the extra mile to avoid it, or better still decide to give up their car? When does our conscience kick in and help us decide to boycott the large multinational corporations behind the ecocide we're all facing?

It's not just heavy crude oil that threatens the Amazon. Palm oil, the so-called 'clean green biofuel' is another threat. Millions of acres have been deforested and burnt for re-planting with oil palms. Scientists estimate around 15-17% of annual carbon emissions – more than all the cars, buses, trains and aeroplanes in the world – are caused by the burning of tropical forests.

And there seems to be no limit to the size of these 'farms'. As far as the eye can see tropical rainforest once teeming with life has been replaced by monoculture. The multitude of life that once lived there has been driven out, made homeless or burnt. This oil, which governments seem to think is an answer, only replaces one destructive oil with another. International food giants also use palm oil in their food. Cheap, mass produced junk food, both unnecessary and unhealthy for humans, is also driving the death of the Amazon.

How much more of this burning and destruction can the planet stand? We live in a world of cause and effect, supply and demand. Whatever we ask for is given. So let's ask for a healthy world. Support small businesses, question our lives and reconsider what we demand. Let's think more globally about how our shopping habits are affecting the lives of those on the other side of the planet. Let's be more compassionate and tell these companies it's time to treat others as we wish to be treated ourselves, and together move towards a fair and just world for all.

Nicola Peel is a film-maker and environmentalist in the Ecuadorian Amazon, who has documented ecocide with her film 'Blood of the Amazon', and continues to directly help the indigenous people she meets. www.eyesofgaia.com

JOHN BURNSIDE

Swimming in the Flood

Later he must have watched
the newsreel,

his village erased by water: farmsteads and churches
breaking and floating away

as if by design:
bloated cattle, lumber, bales of straw,

turning in local whirlpools; the camera
panning across the surface, finding the odd

rooftop or skeletal tree,
or homing in to focus on a child's

shock-headed doll.
Under it all, his house would be standing intact,

the roses and lime trees, the windows,
the baby grand.

He saw it through the water when he dreamed
and, waking at night, he remembered the rescue boat,

the chickens at the prow, his neighbour's pig,
the woman beside him, clutching a silver frame,

her face dislodged, reduced to a puzzle of bone
and atmosphere, the tremors on her skin

wayward and dark, like shadows crossing a field
of clouded grain.

Later, he would see her on the screen,
trying to smile, as they lifted her on to the dock,

and he'd notice the frame again, baroque and absurd,
and empty, like the faces of the drowned.

John Burnside, award-winning Scottish poet and novelist, whose work explores fundamental spiritual and ecological issues about the nature of our dwelling on earth. This poem, from the book 'Swimming in the Flood' is reproduced with permission from the author and Random House Group Ltd.

"Earth provides enough to satisfy every man's needs but not every man's greed."

Mahatma Gandhi (1869-1948), independence leader

"We must protect the forests for our children, grandchildren and children yet to be born. We must protect the forests for those who can't speak for themselves such as birds, animals, fish and trees."

Qwatsinas, Hereditary Chief Edward Moody (1951-2010), Nuxalk Nation

---

"The 'control of nature' is a phrase conceived in arrogance, born of the Neanderthal age of biology and philosophy, when it was supposed that nature exists for the convenience of man. The concepts and practices of applied entomology for the most part date from that Stone Age of science. It is our alarming misfortune that so primitive a science has armed itself with the most modern and terrible weapons, and that in turning them against the insects it has also turned them against the earth."

From 'Silent Spring' 1962, Rachel Carson (1907-1964), marine biologist and conservationist

What Is to Be Done?

I certainly want to pay heartfelt tribute to the work of Polly Higgins whose relentless determination to see Ecocide made the fifth Crime Against Peace under the International Criminal Court (ICC) Rome Statute has been a profound inspiration to us all.

On that specific point, I would only comment that, whilst I think Polly Higgins has dealt adequately with the objection that individual intent must be proved by advancing the concept of 'presumptive responsibility', the other main objection still has to be faced, that the four other crimes against peace – war crimes, crimes against humanity, genocide and crimes of aggression – focus on destruction of human life. I wonder whether your definition of ecocide could be strengthened to encapsulate the following requirement which would make it easier to win the 13 majority (86 votes) of an ICC Assembly of States Parties review of the Rome Statute. I would propose:

'Ecocide is the crime of degrading the environment to such a degree as to threaten the loss of life for humans and other species on a mass scale whether locally, regionally, nationally or globally, either now or in the future.'

That is justified in my view by two main considerations.

- It is not just that frequency and ferocity of climate upheaval is increasing, it's rather the imminence of certain thresholds/ tipping points which unleash potentially catastrophic feedback mechanisms – e.g. the warming of Siberian permafrost which could release billions of tons of methane which is 20 times more toxic than CO_2; dieback of the Amazon which will transform the world's greatest rainforest from an absorber of CO_2 into a desert that generates it; collapse of the West Antarctic ice sheet which will raise sea levels by 7 metres which will wipe out several regions and cities of the world.

- Biodiversity is being destroyed at 100 to 1,000 times the rate in historical and palaeontological record, and given interconnectedness of the world's food supply, the cumulative destructive impact on species, including humans, is incalculable.

So what is to be done to confront this environmental and socio-economic impasse? What is clearly needed is a new economic paradigm based on true-cost accounting, a huge five times increase in renewable energy and big incentives for energy conservation and energy efficiency.

It is not all doom and gloom – there are three positive drivers:

- China has several low-carbon zones operating and President Obama is determined to push through a new climate change bill and is tightening emission standards for power stations especially coal, and California, the world's twelfth largest economy, is pushing through electrification of cars.

- Breakthrough for competitive renewable energy is gaining traction and gathering speed – independent estimates expect solar will be cheaper, without subsidy, than alternative means of generating electricity almost everywhere by 2020.

- The sheer savagery of climate upheaval. I've just returned from the Philippines where typhoon Haiyan, the fourth most violent storm in history, killed 6,000 people at Tacloban. The drought in Russia in 2012 destroyed a quarter of the grain harvest. The United States has suffered 25 extreme weather events since 2011. Extreme weather worldwide now kills and costs over £1.5 billion per year.

So, how to break the deadlock?

Possibly a coalition between G20 and leading companies and cities that are greening and wrestling with transition to a low-carbon landscape. This may be the best means to begin to break the stranglehold of unbridled markets driven by financialised capitalism. (Indeed the biggest problem for the Left is the abject failure of radical and progressive forces across the world to come up with a plausible alternative ideology to market fundamentalism after the biggest financial crash for a century and the longest recession since the 1870s.) Then a deep-rooted and wide-ranging social movement to carry it through to being implemented. That must include a reassertion of democratic governance when power at present has shifted sideways to banks, the big corporate and the over-dominant media.

But again, it is not all bleak –

George Osborne and the Eurozone are clearly trying to help us with their catastrophically perverse policies of prolonged austerity. The latest polls show the public is now more up in arms about tax avoidance than any other abuse of corporate power. There is even some glimmer of recognition that the ultra-rich might even make a fair contribution to tax when the Sunday Times records Britain's richest one thousand increased their wealth since the crash by a cool £190 billion.

But none of this will get very far unless gatherings like this go out and tap festering resentment and eagerness for radical change that lies just below the surface, and that is the task for all of us.

Michael Meacher is a long-standing Labour Member of Parliament and former Minister of State for the Environment (1997-2003). This article is a lightly edited transcript of a talk given in February 2014.

IMAGE: DENNIS GOULD

RESIST much

OBEY little

1819 Walt 1892

Whitman

ART NOT OIL COALITION

Performance as Perforation

Moments before a Shell-sponsored classical concert at the Royal Festival Hall, a small choir launches into a gospel song recast as a litany of Shell's destructive practices; many in the audience applaud. The BP-sponsored Vikings Live exhibition at the British Museum is invaded by Vikings bearing BP logos on their shields, only to be evicted by a group of onlookers, some part of the performance, others inspired to join in. A wind turbine blade, 16.5 metres long, is carried into the BP-sponsored Tate's Turbine Hall as a gift to its permanent collection. A BP-sponsored live relay of a performance at the Royal Opera House is presaged by a group of immaculately drilled dancers who enact the trampling of the BP logo with Taylor Swift's *Trouble* as their soundtrack.

These are just some of the ways that 'Art Not Oil' has mobilised and protested against Big Oil cultural sponsorship since 2004, with exhibitions in community spaces, campaigns, online galleries and communications with artists and employees of sponsored institutions. Since then it was a Rising Tide UK campaign, until 2013, when it became a coalition of the various UK-based groups using diverse creative means to see an end to such sponsorship.

Made up of BP Out of Opera (BOOO), Liberate Tate, London Rising Tide, Platform, The Reclaim Shakespeare Company, Science Unstained, Shell Out Sounds & UK Tar Sands Network, the Art Not Oil Coalition tries to expose Big Oil cultural sponsorship for what it truly is; an attempt to neutralise our potential collective disgust and disquiet about the way fossil fuel industries perpetuate and exacerbate inequality, as well as threatening the living systems of this planet.

All the performances given as examples above date from 2012-14, and there does now seem to be a bubbling up of energy on this issue, along with a real sense that fossil fuel sponsorship is becoming increasingly unpopular – a lightning rod, even, for ever-greater discontent at the way we are still gunning our engines with disaster surrounding us, lulled in part by highly polished high art... But what room would there be for art of any kind on a planet ravaged by ecological collapse?

If climate change and the myriad ecological crises that we face demand dramatic, creative responses, then perhaps cultural spaces like museums, theatres, concert halls and galleries provide the perfect setting. Of course, it's the fact that companies like BP, Shell, Exxon and Total have decided to pump a few paltry gallons of their oceans of profit into these London-based spaces that has been the main reason for their movement into the front line of climatic dissent. But the groups that make up the Art Not Oil coalition are passionate about putting creativity at the heart of their activism, and about dismantling the line between protest and performance.

They do this partly because they sense a need to sidestep people's inbuilt preconceptions and prejudices about protest, to creep under the radar of expectation in order to elicit a deeper, perhaps more heartfelt response. However, the motivation also wells up from a less strategic, more instinctive desire to fuse together the making of art and the making of change. This is, no doubt, one reason why so much of the group's work is about trying to persuade other artists that to divorce one's creativity from the world around us, including its political make-up and its ecological state, is a terrible mistake, and a rejection of a golden opportunity to transform that world for the better.

Some artists argue that it's not possible to make effective art that is also concerned with our collective well-being (or lack of it), but while it's true that there are examples of frustratingly didactic, clunky or preachy politicised art, throughout history there have been many really powerful pieces that work beautifully on a variety of levels. Coming closer to the present day, Liberate

Tate's wind turbine wing donation – known as The Gift – managed to work as a beautifully choreographed piece of citizen action, a moving performance, not to mention a witty nod to the many energy solutions that lie (so often unused) at our feet.

The groups and individuals that make up the Art Not Oil Coalition are part of a movement that will see an end to oil sponsorship of the arts. But they won't mothball their voices, their bodies or their imaginations when that comes about, because this is the way they love to create positive change, and because there is always going to be more change needing to be made.

The Art Not Oil Coalition has, since 2004, mobilised against sponsorship of the arts by oil companies.

"Should you err, the animals will begin to disappear, one by one, forever, from the face of the earth; and the air in your settlements and fortresses will become dangerous to breathe; the seasons will be reversed and your climates turned on end; the animals you eat will bring sickness and death upon you; and you will no longer rule the earth. I find myself in favour of the animals, for they have been sorely tested and abused."

From 'The Animals' Lawsuit Against Humanity' c950,
Sufi Muslim petition

"Until we consider animal life to be worthy of the consideration and reverence we bestow upon old books and pictures and historic monuments, there will always be the animal refugee living a precarious life on the edge of extermination, dependent for existence on the charity of a few human beings."

Gerald Durrel (1925-1995), naturalist, zookeeper, and conservationist

DAVID DONALDSON

Message from the Bottlenose Whale which Died in the Thames, London during January 2006

Do you understand? It wasn't a wrong turning I took
Somewhere south of Foulness Point. For this
Now is how it is for us of the deeps and the wild
And the polar ice: circumscribed, dwindling,
Beached, for lack of what we need to live.

Thank you for the attention. The special barge,
The lifting gear. It was all well meant. And those
Thousands of you crowding the rails to see:
Jonah's whale, itself turned prophet, headed for
The dead-end reaches of your city, great Nineveh!

Thank you for your concern, your touching pity,
Your fervent wishes for me to live my way
Back to the ocean's freedom and a happy ending.
How relieved you would have been! How
Pleased that your best efforts had succeeded.

But it wasn't to be. Do you understand? Your gear,
Your expertise, your heart-felt well-meaning wasn't
Enough, was of no avail. You are killing the Earth
With that draining deadness of disconnection you call
'Thinking'. Your shallow measures lack all reality:

Standards of living, unending growth as if we did not
Exist. What will it profit you, in owning the world,
To lose it? You are blind and deaf to real inflation –
The spiralling costs of Love. I died in your midst
In spite of your best endeavours. Remember me.

I showed you what is.

IMAGE: SABINE CRITTALL

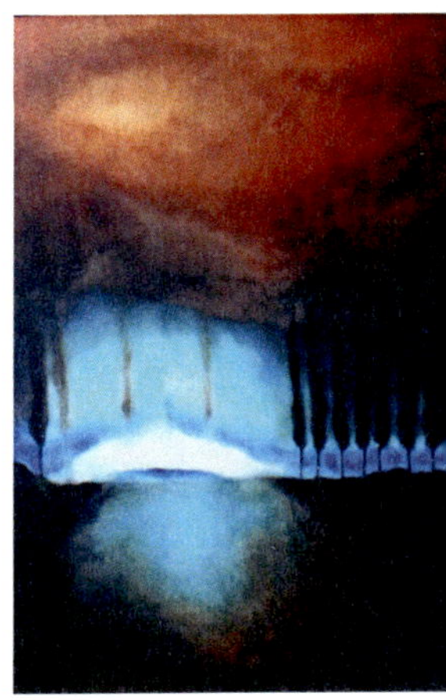

David Donaldson is a poet, for many years a Steiner teacher, and author of 'The Voices of the Wells' (2012) from which this poem is taken.

JO WOOLLEY

The White Lion

The first time I saw a white lion was at evening time when the sun was setting in the Timbavati region, at the heart of the Kruger to Canyons Biosphere area, South Africa. It was gilded with a golden light which seemed to emphasise the power and majesty of the being I gazed upon – the sight was incomparable.

To be there and to bear witness to nature's grandeur personified by this awe-inspiring creature was a profound and utter privilege. Nothing had prepared me for the sheer size, strength and palpable power of this king of the beasts. Truly, that first evening the lion looked almost surreal, the stuff of legends, mythic in its proportions and in the unique signature of its extraordinary snowy colouring. The Shangaan tribe, local to that region, and indigenous tribes all over Africa, recognise white lions as sacred animals which are gifted to us by the Great Spirit; they are angels in leonine form.

I spent six weeks with the Global White Lion Protection Trust (WLT) in autumn 2012. I can testify to the fact that they are extraordinary animals filled with the power of Light and a purity of unconditional Love that emanates tangibly from them. They are not easy creatures to be around for a sustained time, as standing in the intensity of such light-bearers naturally brings up our own shadows which need to be acknowledged and dealt with. It was a roller-coaster experience that had me both crying with joy and weeping with heartfelt pain. But it was transformative – the effects of which continue to work within me to this day.

How tragic therefore, that though lions are endangered animals, the white lion has no protection whatsoever – and their survival hangs in the balance. They originated only in this region, and despite (the still legal) trophy hunting, and other artificial removals over six decades, white lions continue to recur here naturally.

WLT's work has included the scientific reintroduction of three white lion prides integrated with golden lions from the region and returned to their ancestral homeland, to restore nature's balance. As white lions may be legally hunted in the neighbouring areas of Timbavati, about 4,400 acres of ancestral heritage lands have been secured as a Protected Area for them. It has taken monumental efforts, and more support is needed to extend these protected borders.

How many there are in captivity around the world is anyone's guess – responsible studbooks are not kept. Worse still, they are being bred in cages on hunting farms, hand-reared and petted by tourists, only to be shot by trophy hunters in captivity. The vile practice of 'canned hunting' is still legal in South Africa, despite the fact that white lions are on the brink of extinction, and despite the fact that local tribes regard them as sacred animals integral to our own well-being and survival!

The only place on Earth where they occurred is this Timbavati region, which in the ancient Shangaan language means: 'Place where the star-lions came down', and the knowledge that links this 'Starbeast' to the ancient Egyptian mystery of the Sphinx is explained in *The Mystery of the White Lions* by Linda Tucker, whose personal story is as extraordinary as her conservation work. Her wake-up call came when she and a group of friends found themselves surrounded by a pride of twenty-four angry lions at night, in an open-topped vehicle which had broken down in the middle of the bush. They were rescued by a Shangaan Medicine Woman, who walked on foot through the lions with a baby on her back to get into the vehicle. This African lady, Maria Khosa, was known as the 'Lion Queen of Timbavati'.

When Maria was eventually tracked down three years later, she revealed to Linda that she was her successor, and was required to commit her life to protecting the white lions. As they were being destroyed by trophy hunters and removed from their sacred heritage lands, she told Linda to watch for a sign. In 2000 a white lioness cub was born on Christmas Day in Bethlehem – a South African town notorious for its canned hunting farms and for its gold mining associations. A five year battle ensued which eventually resulted in Marah (mother of Ra – the sun god) being returned to the wilds of Timbavati where her offspring now roam freely.

But that was only the start of an extraordinary story and mission which is still unfolding, as since then Linda has presented appeals, at international congresses and parliaments in South Africa and Britain, for a prohibition on captive breeding/canned hunting malpractices. The white lions are in desperate need of an international law to protect them from the obscenity of canned hunting farms, from poachers who know the very high price their carcasses fetch, and from zoos and circuses where the lions become mere spectacles to satisfy human curiosity and ego.

The Law against Ecocide that Polly Higgins is advocating acknowledges the intrinsic power of nature beyond that of commercial, objectified commodity. Such a law would also recognise the rights of cultural heritage and how this is very often threatened as a result of environmental desecration and annihilation of specialised flora and fauna in unique ecosystems. If ratified internationally, it could move swiftly to ensure legal protection for the white lion, and make hunting them illegal, a crime against us all, which would carry very heavy financial penalties for anyone found to be responsible and involved in this heinous practice.

The lion itself is a world heritage icon – a symbol used world-wide to denote qualities of courage, bravery and responsible leadership. Additionally, the lion, at the apex of the food chain, has a critically important ecological role. Conserving it protects the whole of the food chain and the interrelated web of species fanning out beneath and around that leonine apex. The Law against Ecocide needs to be brought into place as quickly as possible to protect lions in general but most pressingly, to prevent white lions from becoming extinct in the wild, and brutally treated as a commodity in captive killing camps. How sad and reduced our world would become if we lost this marvellous animal's treasured presence in our natural world, only to be found in books or myth and legends.

The Law against Ecocide would enable us to step into proper stewardship of this precious Earth. It would empower us globally and personally and allow us to begin to express those iconic qualities exemplified by the White Lions: Love, Truth, Justice, Freedom, Dignity and Creativity – qualities that Nelson Mandela represented and wanted to bring into being for all people. The international Law against Ecocide has the capacity to bring about a new age of unity – a vision made famous by Martin Luther King's 'I have a dream' speech. The lions need us to take charge of our rights. The White Lions need an International Law against Ecocide to protect them now. Together, we can make this become our living reality; and thereby ensure a beautiful future for us all and for future generations.

Jo Woolley is a poet and writer (author of 'The Witen Lord' trilogy), who has been involved in environmental activism for many decades, encouraging the perspective of interrelationship between all beings, as a teacher, as a wordsmith and as a counsellor.

JEHANNE MEHTA

Prologue

If you are afraid to fall,
everywhere is edge
and crumbling:

the puddle
where the rubble
of the old road rises;

the newness
about to unfurl,
at the turning of this year
all at once,
beyond expectation;

the speckled depths in the eyes
of friends
when words threaten to open the
gulfs of the heart.

Nowhere is safe now;
we could tumble through anywhere,
without warning,
slipping into adjacent landscapes
we have always inhabited,
but with closed eyes,
between breaths.

Everywhere
we are threatened
with awakening.

Jehanne Mehta is a poet and song writer for the Earth, the Soul, and the Spirit. From 'Heart of Yew: Poems Inspired by the Spirit of the Yew'.

IMAGE: CHRIS DRURY

"Quote from Tolkien's 'Lord of the Rings': '...here nothing lived, not even the leprous growths that feed on rottenness. The gasping pools were choked with ash and crawling muds, sickly white and grey, as if the mountains had vomited the filth of their entrails up on the lands about. High mounds of crushed and powdered rock, great cones of earth fire-blasted and poison stained, stood like an obscene graveyard in endless rows, slowly revealed in the reluctant light. They had come to the desolation that lay before Mordor: the lasting monument to the dark labour of its slaves that should endure when all their purposes were made void; a land defiled, diseased beyond all healing – unless the Great Sea should enter in and wash it to oblivion. "I feel sick," said Sam. Frodo did not speak.'

Later, entering Morgul Valley, Frodo observed that 'Earth, air and water all seem accursed.' And closer still to Mount Doom they found 'a huge mass of ash and slag and burned stone,' where 'the air was full of fumes, breathing was painful and difficult...' Do we not see such blighted industrial wasteland today in Eastern Europe and Russia, and could we not easily find its equivalent in 'the West': radio-active deserts; poisoned rivers and even seas; clearcut and slashed and burned acres that were once rainforest, richest in life anywhere on the planet, smoking, reeking cities, where life by contrast, is cheap? All this has a name, by the way, The Greek 'Oikos', which gives us 'eco', means home or abode; the Latin 'caedere', to kill; hence, ecocide. (And the combination of Greek and Latin only confirms that no good can come of it.)"

From 'Defending Middle Earth' 2004, Patrick Curry,
eco-philosopher, author, and lecturer

"Images waver on the unsettling side of neutral, emitting a subliminal dysphoria without immediate or apparent reason. Is, for example, what appear to be gnomon-surmounted hub-caps, set out with regimented precision in an overall cast of lurid green, an aquatic art installation at Tate Modern? No – perhaps only a nuclear industry insider would know that what we are looking at are canisters containing waste which 'will be toxic for millions of years'. Or, has the grass-fringed lagoon in northern China been photographed during the restfulness of a contemplative oriental dawn? No – the pink tinge is the result of preservative contamination from a nearby tofu plant. And, are those images which quietly scream from the page 'look at this ecocide', rendering the text largely supplementary, or even superfluous? Examples include a log yard near Winnipeg, in which two thirds of the aerial view is packed solid with thousands of tree trunks from the old growth boreal forest – their ignominious destiny to be turned into pulp for newsprint. Or here we see the ravaged tracts of Canada's Athabasca tar sands. This scene could effortlessly double as a graphically realistic film set for a scarred and blasted post-apocalyptic waste-land, with industrial-scale tipper trucks malevolently carting off their spoils like voracious aphids."

From a review of Peter Essick's 'Our Beautiful, Fragile World' 2013, Edgar Vaid, book and film reviewer for *Resurgence & Ecologist*

"This we know; the Earth does not belong to man; man belongs to the Earth. This we know; all things are connected like the blood which unites one family. All things are connected; whatever befalls the Earth, befalls the sons of the Earth. Man did not weave the web of life; he is merely a part in it. Whatever he does to the web, he does to himself. We do not inherit the earth from our ancestors; we borrow it from our children."

Chief Seattle (c1780-1866), Suquamish tribe

"You cannot escape the responsibility of tomorrow by evading it today."

Abraham Lincoln (1809-1865), 16th President of the United States

---

"We need the tonic of wildness. At the same time that we are earnest to explore and learn all things, we require that all things be mysterious and unexplorable, that land and sea be indefinitely wild, unsurveyed and unfathomed by us because unfathomable. We can never have enough of nature."

From 'Walden' 1854, Henry David Thoreau (1817-1862), writer, poet, philosopher

---

"In nature there are neither rewards nor punishments – there are consequences."

Robert G Ingersoll (1833-1899), lawyer, political leader and orator

---

"The mountains of things we throw away are much greater than the things we use. In this, if no other way, we can see the wild and reckless exuberance of our production, and waste seems to be the index."

From 'Travels with Charley: In Search of America' 1962, John Steinbeck (1902-1968), author

'Smokey Mountain',
Phnom Penh,
Cambodia
2006-2009

Nigel Dickinson, a British photojournalist and filmmaker, focuses on the environment, marginalisation, identity and culture. 'Smokey Mountain' series won Critical Mass, Solo Exhibition Award in 2011.

© NIGEL DICKINSON www.nigeldickinson.com

ENVISAGE

In this section more lights are shone on what is happening around the world. There is a movement towards hope, towards envisaging what could be.

Single Leaf: © ANNABEL WARD

The hornblowers of our time are those who stand up and speak out, yet the law as it stands today protects those who are causing the harm. Those who speak out risk the wrath of those who seek to destroy, not those who seek to give support. Now more than ever we have a shrinking democratic space.

**Do we fight or do we create a new space?
A new space based on life-affirming principles is also a space where we face the harm and give it a name. That takes courage too. When we do that we disrupt the seemingly immoveable. A law against Ecocide would achieve this.**

Polly Higgins

"Here is your country. Cherish these natural wonders, cherish the natural resources, cherish the history and romance as a sacred heritage, for your children and your children's children. Do not let selfish men or greedy interests skin your country of its beauty, its riches or its romance. To waste, to destroy our natural resources, to skin and exhaust the land instead of using it so as to increase its usefulness, will result in undermining in the days of our children the very prosperity which we ought by right to hand down to them amplified and developed."

Theodore Roosevelt (1858-1919). 26th President of the United States

---

"When we became farmers and gardeners, we took on the responsibility of thinking ahead because we had the power to change the environment for all the rest of the lives on Earth. Now we have acquired more power – fossil fuel power, electrical power, nuclear power. The greater the power we can harness the greater the responsibility. Therefore we have to recognise certain limits to what we should do, and to draw clear lines between what will endanger the future of our race and its neighbours on this our one world."

From 'A good Going On' 1989, Lawrence D Hills (1911-1991), horticulturalist, journalist, and writer

---

"The catastrophic degradation of environment, destruction, damage or loss of ecosystems is happening on a mass scale every day as more and more carbon emissions are emitted by the ever increasing industrial output in our world. The best way to overcome it is to adopt Polly Higgins' proposed Law of Ecocide for the safety of future generations."

Vijay Mehta, Chair of Uniting for Peace

GABRIEL BRADFORD MILLAR

Breathing Earth

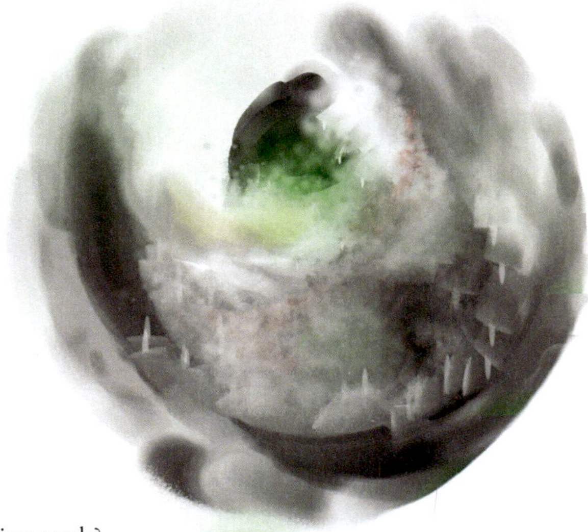

IMAGE: SABINE CRITTALL

Am I ready
to greet the breathing earth?
She's ready.
Past ready.

How shall I reply
to the passionate planet –
vermilion in the west
and the hill brooding indigo?

Green ground in the morning,
generous and strong,
rosebay willow herb,
fat apples and mallow?

I am plagued by the gravity
of this sacred charge
to praise her,
state her case.

Gabriel Bradford Millar is a renegade poet and co-founder of Celebration of the Word.

JULIE BROMILOW

Wild Wales

I roll up my tent when there's enough light to see my rucksack. Ducks take to the air and circle the water-field before leaving for the coast, reversing the journey they made the night before when the sky was pink. A hare startled in its journey across the field shrinks low and lower till it can't be seen among the divots. There are wet leaves in the grass, yellow toadstools in the nook of the kissing gate, skitter-pheasants crashing through sycamores and on the path is a stoat with a wren in its mouth. Pink television light wobbles through a dark window but it's hours before I see a person – far below me on a beach, jogging with abandon, snatched song tossed up the cliff by the wind. It will be hours more before I see builders on a roof, and more again before I speak to anyone; to order coffee in a beach café.

Things were different when George Borrow walked around Wales in 1854. He was a spirited English gentleman who talked with people he met along the way, astonishing them with his accomplished use of Welsh. His book *Wild Wales* is an account of his journey and what impresses me most is the sheer number of people he met every day. Stone breakers, Irish fiddlers, millers, masons, tree fellers, gypsies, drovers and knitting women all populate his pages with merry dialogue.

My journey is quieter. I too am English, walking 1,027 miles around the edge of Wales, but have yet to meet anyone knitting by the side of the road. I cook breakfast on beaches and in fields, camp in the dunes, lie on headlands to watch Atlantic grey seals, and follow roads bordered with ragwort, campion and scabious that tremble in lorry spray. Of course there are people, but I sometimes walk for hours and days without meeting any at all. George Borrow would stop and chat with reapers about poetry and religion, but farmland here is barely populated now. The people I meet are mostly clustered round beauty spots, walking their dogs, not working on the land. By tents and car radios, kids and dads scrag for causeway crabs, anglers are out on the Flintshire coast and boys throw stones in the sea. A Criccieth winkle digger fills hasty buckets with a fork, racing the tide, and sherry faced hunters with straw in their jumpers tumble from a barn at Carmel Head. No one offers to show me their bible or asks if I'm here to buy hogs, but a salesman in Penygroes does come to inquire, as I sit on my rucksack, if I've any need for Sky TV. When dusk falls I imagine crossing meadows in the summer dark with George Borrow returning the 'nos da' greetings of home-bound folk, but I'm not pining for a lost time. Life was hard for the Irish refugees, the urchins and quarrymen, the lime kilns were acrid, Swansea valleys 'full of blast and smoke' and in truth; I'm not much good at knitting. Sheep subsidies and grain imports did away with the oats, and supermarkets killed the Pembrokeshire cauliflower trade, but long before George Borrow went roaming, forests covered the hills. Times have changed, and they'll change again.

Research shows how we might respond to environmental challenges by changing again, the way we use land, with fewer grazing animals and more crops for human food and energy. If this were to happen we'd have a more diverse countryside than we do today, with agriculture pushing into towns and cities, and an increase in wildlife and rural jobs. Farming would be less intensive, and people would once again work in the fields and woods. Peat carts and bibles won't replace cars and television, but there might be people enough to stop and talk to.

I pause to adjust my rucksack. Sheepdogs swirl in a field. There are bryony berry ropes in the hedge and lingering harebells on muddy paths. Smashed orange beech leaves litter the lanes, cashmere clouds soften the hills, there are crabapples crushed on the road. And far away in the distance there's a man on a tractor, tossing hay to his sheep.

Julie Bromilow worked within sustainability education. This essay was originally published by Resurgence & Ecologist in 2013 and was a winner of their nature writing competition.

ALFRED RUSSEL WALLACE

The World of Life

SARAH GILLARD

This variety and beauty, even the strangeness, the ugliness, and the unexpectedness we find everywhere in nature, are, and therefore were intended to be, an important factor in our mental development; for they excite in us admiration, wonder, and curiosity – the three emotions which stimulate first our attention, then our determination to learn the how and the why, which are the basis of observation and experiment and therefore of all science and all philosophy.

These considerations should lead us to look upon all the works of nature, animate or inanimate, as invested with a certain sanctity, to be used by us but not abused, and never to be recklessly destroyed or defaced. To pollute a spring or a river, to exterminate a bird or beast, should be treated as moral offences and as social crimes; while all who profess religion or sincerely believe in the Deity – the designer and maker of this world and of every living thing – should, one would have thought, have placed this among the first of their forbidden sins, since to deface or destroy that which has been brought into existence for the use and enjoyment, the education and elevation of the human race, is a direct denial of the wisdom and goodness of the Creator, about which they so loudly and persistently prate and preach.

Yet during the past century, which has seen those great advances in the knowledge of Nature of which we are so proud, there has been no corresponding development of a love or reverence for her works; so that never before has there been such widespread ravage of the earth's surface by destruction of native vegetation and with it of much animal life, and such wholesale defacement of the earth by mineral workings and by pouring into our streams and rivers the refuse of manufactories and of cities; and this has been done by all the greatest nations claiming the first place for civilisation and religion!

And what is worse, the greater part of this waste and devastation has been and is being carried on, not for any good or worthy purpose, but in the interest of personal greed and avarice; so that in every case, while wealth has increased in the hands of the few, millions are still living without the bare necessaries for a healthy or a decent life, thousands dying yearly of actual starvation, and other thousands being slowly or suddenly destroyed by hideous diseases or accidents, directly caused in this cruel race for wealth, and in almost every case easily preventable. Yet they are not prevented, solely because to do so would somewhat diminish the profits of the capitalists and legislators who are directly responsible for this almost worldwide defacement and destruction.

From 'The World of Life' 1910, Alfred Russel Wallace (1823-1913), naturalist, explorer, geographer, anthropologist, and biologist.

MARTIN SPRAY

Living with the Microcosm

'There was always', John Ruskin noted, 'more in the world than men could see, walked they ever so slowly; they will see it no better for going fast.' If you go slowly enough, you see more today than Ruskin did in the nineteenth century, not least amongst living things. This is largely because of the incredible number of things 'discovered' since he wrote.[1]

Yet before we even have chance to learn of them, our prevailing techno-centric, consumerist, globally engulfing, and unromantic culture seems to be doing its best, willy-nilly, to delete what it can of 'unwanted' things – on the assumption that even if they aren't harmful they'll probably be of no damned use. To us, that is. Thus far we're doing quite well at eradicating the bigger ones (although there is still plenty of work to be done), but we have hardly started on the little ones!

When most of us think of shadowy, ill-defined terms such as wildlife and biodiversity, we probably have in mind 'nice' things like badgers, roses and butterflies, polar bears and orchids (and equally charming aquatic creatures). In the gloom of the un-nice side are such troubles as rats, locusts, tapeworms, and miscellaneous 'weeds'. Going slowly through woods, or fields, in the mountains, through the park, even down the High Street, we can demonstrate some progress with our project to remove what we don't want of the useless un-nice. It is as though we are trying to minimise the diversity around us at several scales.

I believe that terms such as biodiversity and wildlife apply most importantly to beings that science has seen only 'through a glasse darkly', and still has to describe properly let alone explain.

Moreover, when we speak about rather vague concepts such as 'habitats', 'communities' and 'ecosystems', we tend to imagine tropical rainforest and African plains, or the cultural landscapes of fields and hedges, riverbanks, and ferny, sunken lanes (and equally charming aquatic views). And as often as not we think of these to make in our minds picture-backdrops to ourselves. The composition as a whole is what matters; and, so far as we can, we make our (private or group) environment beautiful – like a picture, in the tradition we are used to.

The beauty we seek is a conventional, cultural aesthetic, not necessarily taken straight from Nature. Trees and birds and butterflies 'fit'; mosses, millipedes and beetles are nondescripts; slugs, worms, moulds, things upsettingly suspected in festering corpses, and things unknown in our own aching guts, even the dowdy caterpillar that perforates a pot-plant's leaf before becoming a fascinating moth… such things we would prefer not to share 'our' planet with, and we busy ourselves trying to zap them, or pretending they aren't there. But they are. And they are due our gratefulness, if not our love.[2]

It is explicable but unfortunate that there is a mismatch between our sentiment for (say) the tiger and our scorn for (say) the earthworm. We may not want to share a habitat with a tiger; but even as it springs on us it is a beautiful thing, and we gladly give money to keep it on some other person's patch. There is an even greater mismatch between our enthusiasm for finding out all we can about bigger things, and a willingness to have an extraordinary ignorance about little ones.

Ours is a culture (like many others) in which facade is important, and in which a thing that isn't human-made or human-controlled is commonly said to have small value, which makes it relatively easy for us to reject or destroy it. The 'ugliness' of much of Nature, its unreasonableness and ridiculousness, and its inclination to try to do what we do – that is, live as it wants – we deem 'problems' that we feel the need to solve.

I do understand that malaria makes Plasmodium protozoa, and

their mosquito transmitters, a huge problem; but most germs and bugs leave us alone; and in some cases science tells us to put them back, as we actually need them! 'Problem' is a mistaken presumption. Indeed, such presumptions seem a general handicap of adult minds.[3] I think this clash between Nature and norm is an example of something similar:

> *In the wind that blew last night*
> *peach blossoms fell, scattered in the garden.*
> *A boy came out with a broom*
> *intending to sweep them away.*
> *No – no, do not sweep them away.*
> *Are fallen flowers not flowers?* [4]

Beauty, moreover, is so often in the eye of the status-holder, that there can be dangers from allowing it to be the essential consideration of our dealings with fellow beings.[5] Though there is still more in the world than we can ever see, if it does come to our notice we often reject it. And, as often as not, because of that it is seen as a problem or enemy. We think in stereotypes.

> *Oh, don't mistreat the fly!*
> *He wrings his hands,*
> *he wrings his feet.* [6]

But… flies and flower-petals are enormous things. It is the normally invisible world of micro-organisms that sustains the landscape.[7] Although not as photogenic as orchids, tigers and butterflies, nor as cute as dolphins and pandas, and seldom inspiring great literature, it is some of those very minuties that are thought to be in the driving seat for Life's exploration of planet Earth. Remember that most photosynthesis is in single-celled marine algae, a spoonful of soil might contain over 5,000 kinds of bacteria,[8] that worms, mites and insects in soil outweigh the cows in the field above, and that neither those cows nor the insects can digest cellulose, but must rely on their gut communities doing so. Would it not therefore be a sad mistake to think that if these micro-organisms aren't harmful they'll probably also turn out to be of no damned use?

If you want telling evidence for the importance of little things, look in the mirror. If you are healthy, you should find at least something from scalp yeasts to eyebrow mites to athlete's foot fungus, gut nematodes, and a gut 'fauna and flora' that help you digest food. If ill, there may be others. While we rejoice that leprosy and black death are off our list pro tem, it is sobering to think that trying to eliminate all of these things may be a mistake, and that medics are beginning to put some of them back! [9]

But look closer. Is it not sobering, too, to hear that 'we ourselves are ecosystems. What we call our "selves" are not individuals but whole communities living in symbiosis?'[10] Look closer! Some 10% of 'you' (by weight) is bacteria. We've known about what at first was thought to be a small class of lifeforms for not a lot more than a century; we quickly learned of their roles in diseases, decomposition, nitrogen fixation, etc. They have been found everywhere from hot rocks a kilometre below your feet to the cells throughout your body. Biologists now say there are different types of 'bacteria' – as different as plants are from animals. Closer still… A few decades ago, we realized that mitochondria, the power-houses in our cells, like the chloroplasts in plants, are remarkably like engulfed but semiautonomous microbes. And, as if that wasn't complex enough, now we are told that much of the 'human' genome actually looks like donations from eons of invading viruses.[11]

Are they part of us? Our very 'selves' seem to leak like sieves! Every one of us is GM. You are far more intimate with little things than with any mere human.

Martin Spray is an environmental philosopher, and editor/writer for 'Ecos – A Review of Conservation'.

Notes

1. Estimates of species on earth range from 3 to beyond 100 million; one of the problems is the difficulty of defining just what a 'species' is.

2. A huge question of language looms over this sort of statement. 'Love of Nature', and love of individual aspects of Nature, are usually assumed to be poetic uses of language. The more clearly such love is intended to be of the same nature as human-to-human love, the more science – the more 'Western' culture generally – wants to distance itself from the usage. Yet when some people say such things as 'I love Nature / this cat / that worm / this stone', that is just what they mean. I have tried to explore some aspects of this in 'Also he loved a tree', Ecos 28(1) 27-40, 2007.

3. I am reminded of the understanding in Zen that a naive, 'uneducated' person sees many possibilities where an 'educated' person sees but one.

4. Anon., in Peter H. Lee (1974) Poems from Korea, London: Allen & Unwin.

5. See Robert Dixon (1995) The Baumgarten Corruption. From sense to nonsense in art and philosophy, London: Pluto Press. See also Crispin Sartwell (2004) Six Names of Beauty, London: Routledge, which discusses the meaning of 'beauty' in several cultures, from English to Navajo.

6. Japanese: Kobayashi Issa, 1763-1827.

7. An up-to-date view of the significance of micros is Nicholas P. Money (2014) The Amoeba in the Room, Oxford.

8. Note also that the North Carolina State University Belly Button Biodiversity study identified about 1,400 different strains of bacteria in the navels of 95 volunteers. The majority were previously unknown to science. http://web.ncsu.edu/abstract/science/wms-belly-button-biodiversity/.

9. A lighthearted and informative general look at our intimates is Robert Buckman (2003) Human Wildlife. The life that lives on us, Baltimore: Johns Hopkins University Press.

10. Quoted from a very interesting paper by Daniel C. Fouke (2011) Humans and the soil. Environmental Ethics 33(2) 147-162.

11. E.g. Frank Ryan (2010) I, virus: Why you're only half human. New Scientist 27 January, 32-35, and online. His Virolution, Collins (2009), looks in detail at viruses and the human genome.

IMAGES: © RUTH DAVEY

Giving the world a helping hand – *End Ecocide* events in Stroud.

MIRIAM DARLINGTON

Rough Meadow

If I look out of my window, in the distance, I can see the field. It curves away down to the river and out of sight. In the early morning, its contours seem to hold the form of something misty, carrying light through purple vetch and cotton grass. You might think there was a body hidden there, its flanks showing through, the field's flesh swelled with summer. But recently a sign has been stuck high in the hedge declaring 'Site Acquired for Development'.

Sometimes when loss fills the air the feet take precedence. I want to pace out this place before it changes, and as I walk along the lane its lush June growth gets to me. From the feet up, with its drenching green, its raw tang of fox, the field penetrates my senses. Wood pigeons, rooks, warblers and wrens mingle with the hum of distant traffic. The field opens out its secrets.

They say there are more birds in suburbia now than in the farmland that surrounds it, but rough grassland is a particularly special habitat, and although not as pretty as wildflower meadow, it supports many more species. I find them here in the between-land, their startling jizz enlivening the borders of town, giving this field its pulse, flitting between its hedges and the gardens and greens of the houses. The sun rises each day and the hedges buzz into life, their green veins meshing with the human settlement, nourishing it.

I stop at the moth-quiet movement of something white. Against the grasses and dew, it stands out, its light wings flitting gently on the edge of my vision; a barn owl. It is quartering the field, this way and that, searching for voles and mice.

Further on, above rough stone walls an old window gapes into a quiet grey world. Normally I would simply walk past, but this time something makes me want to look inside, into the muffled interior. Scattered with downy white feathers, it must be the owl's roost. I step back, fearful of disturbing anything, but then pause. Something else is in here, something alive, beyond the mice, flies and jackdaws. A strangeness of hissing prickles in my ears. My cochleae ring with its scratchy, rattlesnake presence. Hunched and awkward in a corner, a little face with two dark, watery eyes stares. An owlet… an owlet has fallen. I look up; two more, just visible, are still huddled safe on their ledge.

What should I do? Leave it? Let nature take its course? Get help? It would not last another night down there on its own, while the foxes have cubs to feed.

We want so much to do our bit, to give a helping hand. It's so easy to feel overwhelmed with the guilt of it all: climate change, the Pacific Garbage Patch, fracking, HS2. Here was something to actually do. If I succeeded, I would feel bountiful, righteous. I would walk home in glory.

It had been a bad winter and they had not all made it, the owls. Many had been found dead, starved or died from the cold. The owlet deserved to live.

I approached as softly as I could. The owlet cowered. It fell backwards as I bent down and grasped its warm body. The wriggly, scratchy legs caught in my shirt. A coating of snowy down remained all over its body like an extravagant thermal body-warmer. It smelled of rotting mouse and bird latrine. My human hands felt awkward and wrong, clasped around this fierce, wild thing.

I climbed, grabbing at tufts of bales, my fingers stretching for holds in the stone wall. Pressed against my body the young bird wriggled, its sweaty warmth seeping through my shirt.

I untangled the claws from me, pushed the fallen owlet back with the others and let go. Heart thumping, I thudded to the floor and retreated out into the sunlight to watch. Soon, the adult came silently swooping back.

Grief takes us to these moments. We might put ourselves in quiet places, or walk along tracks in a ritual of healing. But often words fail us.

This rough, overlooked field was not particularly attractive, perhaps it was unloved, but it all depends on how you look, on how you see it. To an owl, this rough place is home, food; a place to live. The tussocks and thistles support a vast range of invertebrates; the dead grasses left to rot each year form a litter layer in which field voles can thrive. Without this, there is no owl.

'Rough' is from the old English *ruh* and has associations with unevenness, something uncomfortable, hostile, or unfinished. Rough is the opposite of comforting. 'Rough' is scruffy; it is where ruffians come from, and crudeness, and anything undesirable.

Rough grassland is an edge-land that often has no value. No monetary value, that is. Until the developers come to develop. However, to the complex ecosystem it supports, it is of unimaginable value. It is the very scruffiness of it that supports so many exquisite forms, the most iconic of which is the white owl whose wings speckled with hues of gold dust, copper and ashes I had just seen and held. This owl is diminishing rapidly in our intensely farmed land, as our desire for profit and cheap food and fashionably converted barn complexes have by increments chased it away.

Later, I felt I might have dreamed the owlet. But the memory of the frail heartbeat, and the feathers that I had picked up confirmed that it had been real. I placed the ghostly bouquet of stray plumage in a small vase, and it seems to me that this small thing has left me as changed as if I had been spoken to by the creature itself. This owlet has made an altar of my workspace.

These days, in a world where the priorities of wildlife conservation are often in conflict with rapacious human encroachment, the owl acts like a talisman. Its presence in areas designated for development means that the habitat and therefore the animals must be mitigated for, or even protected and conserved.

Our Paleolithic ancestors had a different understanding of animals' importance. They scratched images of owls on to the walls of caves, perhaps to guide initiates through the dark or to teach mastery of some sort. Humans evolved alongside these creatures; they had something to teach. They nourished our soul and spirit, and they fed our imagination.

Framed in high resolution on our TV screens, owls present a paradox. They appear as savage as they are fascinating. In captivity, their reptilian gaze coolly suggests that our mortal existence is of little significance to them. Are we allowing ourselves to forget the old kinship, to reduce them to a consumer item, fetishised as a collectible emblem of cuteness? Viewed adoringly on YouTube, made into a pleasant, harmless image, they might become a fashion accessory. In compulsive acts of ownership, owl toys are obsessively hoarded and displayed.

Where, amongst all this, is the real owl?

When I look at the huge oak standing in the middle of the field, I long for an owl's-eye view of the world. High in the branches of a tree, looking at human encroachments, what might an owl say, if it could speak? What does an owl hear?

The barn owl's hearing is so accurate it should be called 'ear-sight'. This super sense is due to the asymmetrical placing of its ears; with one opening at the level of its forehead and one at the level of its nostrils, its auditory accuracy is almost as precise as bats' echo-location, so acute that they can locate prey in total darkness. Their old reputation for possessing a dark side might stem from the fact that they use their hunting tools as savagely as any top predator, and their scruffy young have been discovered standing on a bed of slaughtered voles, which the devoted parents catch ceaselessly and store in case of lean times. And if the owl can predict one thing, it is that there will be lean times.

In its rough grasslands the barn owl will always have a rough time. Beauty and roughness. This is how it is for raptors. They take their chances in a rough world. On the days that my hands still pulse with the memory of the owlet in the field, I remember that there is a great deal we can do, and are doing, to help the owls. Farmers can leave uncultivated field margins; we can protect rough pasture and provide sheltered nest-boxes for them; we can conserve their nesting sites and provide habitat for their prey. We can stop using rat poison that is found in ninety per cent of barn owl bodies.

The roof of the barn has caved in now, and the adults have flown away to find new roosts. The field will be developed and one hundred houses built for human families. The days that I feel the owl-warmth glow in my hands, I remember to make small gestures towards their survival, mindful to slow down, to speak for them when I can, as they cannot speak for themselves.

Miriam Darlington is a poet and author of 'Otter Country: In Search of the Wild Otter', Granta, 2012. She teaches Creative Writing at Plymouth University. She is working on a new book about owls.

JOHN MacPHERSON

Shoals

The beach was envious of the fish

Envious of their sleek silver darting

Through the dark depths of the ocean

So one day conspired with companions

Moon and sun

To shape and tug and swell and move and shift, then pull

Back

Revealing

Just briefly

The glistening gleaming shapes of sand and gravel

Darting silverlit into the depths of my imagination

Shoals

John MacPherson is a professional photographer and writer, born and living in the Highlands of Scotland. He has had a life-long interest in the natural world and the effect it has on people. www.john-macpherson-photography.com

IMAGE: JOHN MacPHERSON

ROBIN MAYNARD

Reflections on a Butterfly Cabinet

My father, a keen amateur naturalist, died some years ago and on a recent trip down to my mother's home I finally took the time to sift through the various items he'd bequeathed me. Being the 'environmentalist' amongst my siblings, these amounted to his modest, but broad-ranging natural history library, various fishing rods, boxes of flies and curious home-made lures (many more successful at attracting moths in the loft than they ever had fish in a river!), and a cabinet containing his collection of butterflies and moths gathered through his childhood and the early part of mine.

That cabinet jolted me from my obvious musings on the changes between the countryside's rich and diverse mosaic of my father's childhood to today's monotone green and yellow blocks – jolted me into the realisation that though lifeless, the moths and butterflies he'd methodically arrayed held a coded message. The purpose-built display cabinet of recycled English oak had twelve drawers, six each side with removable glass panes for adding other impaled specimens to the regimented rows already pinned to the cork lined base, and exuded a sickly sweet smell of the lethal moth balls my father had placed in each drawer – with no apparent sense of irony – to protect his specimens from attack by… moths.

The majority of the specimens are British species 'collected' from North Staffs where he grew up, and then later from Devon and Flintshire, where we lived through my childhood and into my teens. 'Collected' is, of course, a euphemism – the butterflies were netted alive on the wing or for the moths drawn down from the night by the seductive glare of a paraffin lamp illuminating a sheet smeared with a sticky concoction my father boiled up from cherry tree resin and sugar. Whichever their method of capture, both butterflies and moths met a common fate from the cyanide infused plaster of Paris set in a kilner jar.

IMAGE: © KATHY LEWIS

My introduction to the diversity and beauty of nature, the stirring of my instinct and increasingly present urge to be outside amongst and in nature, and the painful awakening of my more adult consciousness of the threats to and vulnerability of that natural connection all started with death. What startled me awake from my superficial skimming was finding myself staring at Death itself – the first specimen pinned at the top left corner of the first drawer being a Death's Head Hawk Moth (*Acherontia atropos*) – more a visitor from the Continent than truly a native British species, although it does breed here.

What pricked me alert was the realisation that my father must have made a conscious decision to pin that specimen precisely there in its primary, conspicuous place. For that drawer and its specimens were out of order with the overall meticulous design and classification of the cabinet – British butterflies followed in the next five drawers, ordered in their families. Then the right-hand drawers returned to moths – with the last two marked up as 'Foreign', reserved for the exotic species he'd purchased overseas. He must have placed the Death's Head Hawk Moth there deliberately – not a perverse, mocking message as from the fictional serial-killer, Hannibal Lecter, of *Silence of the Lambs* – but rather a coded acknowledgement of the contradiction and his innate, growing unease of killing something he loved.

My father was given the cabinet on his 12th birthday in 1935. The collection stops at the end of the 1960s, when I too was 12. Over those 35 years, we had caught, poisoned and pinned some 240 specimens – with the native numbers boosted by those bought-in exotics. The ghostly Moon moths (*Actias selene*) and huge Atlas moths (*Attacus atlas*) were like pins in the map of his wartime postings through India and the Far East. Something stopped us both, seven years on from the publishing of Rachel Carson's seminal *Silent Spring*. It was also on the eve of the environmental movement's birth that Carson's book gestated – and which I became part of fifteen years later, when I first began working for Friends of the Earth. It was not any social stigma attached to being a butterfly collector, although the collecting of birds' eggs had been made illegal in 1956 two years before I was born – but simply an awareness that there weren't as many butterflies or moths about.

It had always been an unspoken rule that we didn't collect 'too many' of any one species. When he was a boy and still well into my childhood, collecting butterflies and moths, if not birds' eggs was seen as a perfectly respectable hobby, marking one out as a 'naturalist'. Not today, as this contemporary comment on a conservation organisation's website makes plain: 'Why would you have a cabinet full of dead butterfly specimens? Many "collectors" will strongly argue their case, but in general, their behaviour is one of selfishness, greed and obsession. No collector could ever claim to be helping wild butterflies by killing them in their prime – often before they have a chance to mature and lay their eggs for future generations.'

As intended, those words hit home. But I can't characterise my father's love and knowledge of nature or my own as being nurtured and motivated merely by selfishness, greed or obsession. Nor do I want to taint those archetypal summer childhood memories of chasing through a meadow – nothing of 'special scientific interest', just the common-place farmer's field next door or along a woodland ride with butterfly nets in pursuit of a Silver-studded Blue, Meadow Brown, Purple Hairstreak or Silver-washed Fritillary.

But then there are very few wildflower and herb-rich meadows left for children to chase through and butterflies to flutter over – as the tired but true statistic which I've repeated, written, typed, stencilled onto banners too many times to remember tells us: '97% of our wildflower meadows lost since 1945'. Not 'lost' – but destroyed, drained, ploughed up and re-sown with monochrome mixes of non-native grasses, predominantly ryegrass. The Silver-studded Blue, and many of the fritillaries are no longer commonly or even occasionally found, but listed as 'vulnerable', 'endangered' and even if described as being of 'less concern' as to their numbers and distribution, still sit on the 'Red List' – the annex and waiting room leading to extinction as inevitably as the 'killing jar'.

Three-quarters of British butterflies are in decline – with 4 out of our 56 native species becoming extinct over the past hundred years. Of our much more numerous native moth species (2,400 plus), 62 have become extinct and the 'catch-rates' recorded by the Rothamsted field station have fallen by a third since the close of the 1960s; the point at which my father made the unspoken decision to halt our unconsciously 'selfish, greedy and obsessive' pastime.

Apart from the Death's Head Hawk Moth, one specimen of a Clifden Nonpareil moth or Blue Under-wing, described as 'the Victorian collector's classic all-time favourite' and the 'Foreigns' – our cabinet contains no butterflies or moths that at the time or until very close to the time we stopped, would have been considered anything other than 'common' or 'frequently found' – beautiful, exquisite, extraordinary in their detail and specific arrays, but not national rarities, scarcities or even regionally remarkable. Yet when comparing the contents of the butterfly cabinet to the official Red List – of the 30 or so species pinned in semi-immortality, three-quarters are on that list, and a third are described as 'threatened' or 'near threatened'. The yellow and orange Garden Tiger moths, which my boy's mind conflated as half World War One fighter plane, half leopard, regularly drawn down from the night on a lighted flare-path into our moth-trap, have suffered a 92% decline.

The blame for these nose-dives in the range and number of Garden Tigers and many other species of butterfly and moth should not be laid at the door of dead amateur naturalists or boys past or present bearing butterfly nets (ideally today, digital cameras rather than killing jars), but rather with the post-war and subsequent policy makers and their agribusiness advisers. It was they who set in train the wholesale destruction and dismantling of the type of mixed-farming that created the rich mosaic of habitats which supported such plentiful wildlife (and the farming community too), alongside and inherent in the production of crops and livestock, a past plenty that could stock a million such butterfly cabinets as the one I inherited without compromising nature's capacity to replenish herself.

Robin Maynard is a campaigner on farming, food, the environment, and population.

MICHAEL WEILER

People, Honey and Bees

SELBY McCREERY

Every child knows that when they see a bee on a flower it is collecting honey. But fewer and fewer people have really experienced the mystery of the little 'honey maker'(formerly Apis mellifica, now called Apis mellifera) or even looked into it in detail. But observing the processes carefully enables us to learn something of the production of honey and ultimately of its significance for bees and people.

It is not obvious that flowers contain a small amount of sweet fluid that is as clear as water. Only when the flowers are pulled apart do we really experience and comprehend what the bees do when they penetrate deeply into them. If we watch bees active in various flowers we will realize that their body shape is optimal for such activity. In order to discover that bee abdomens contain a crop in which nectar is collected and which is big enough to carry a significant amount, we first have to dissect them. And it takes many more observations to show that individual foraging bees are in no way directly self-motivated in their activity on the flowers.

A bee on her foraging flight usually visits flowers of the same kind (e.g. apple blossom) in a small area, until her crop is full.

Then she flies back to the hive. There she transfers the nectar to the house bees and soon flies off again. In doing so she flies to flowers of the same kind in the vicinity of the previous place as long as they are yielding nectar. Thus honeybees are constant in their preference for a particular flower species. Only when the source runs out – that is, when the secretion of nectar by the flowers visited so far decreases – are the bees then stimulated by the dances of other foragers in the hive to fly to a new, more attractive source of forage.

In the course of the year the foraging zone of a particular colony changes. Whereas the flight radius remains rather short in spring, at the beginning of the availability of main nectar sources such as fruit blossom, dandelion, rape and later, with the woodland forage or that of arable flowering crops (e.g. phacelia), it soon increases to 1,500m, which corresponds to an area of $7km^2$, or at times even to 3,000m, almost $30km^2$ or more.

The flight radius is dependent on the strength of the colony, weather conditions and the attractiveness of a particular source of forage. The latter is predominantly dependent upon the flower density, the nectar yield of individual flowers, the sugar content of the nectar and whether this is easy to get at in the flower. The more favourable these factors, the more bees fly to particular sources of forage, even if they are further away.

From 'Bees & Honey – from Flower to Jar'. Michael Weiler has been a beekeeper for over thirty years and runs courses and conferences on ecological beekeeping in Germany and the UK.

JAY RAMSAY

Bee Lines

The golden bees are making sweet honey
From all my old failures
– Antonio Machado, transl. Robert Bly

In a rough grass patch by a leaning silver birch
these boxes left as if in mid-move
two raised on a wooden frame, two down beside
half-abandoned to the rain, private, unnoticed –
bees hovering at the lip landing and crawling
in at each box's tiny post box aperture;
and all the air between wild hedge, and landing
trailing with bees constantly arriving…
each secret hive of honey massed
each box like dynamite running sweet inside
as they ferry their pollen; all knowing
their being and purpose, no doubting
all in their community, their meaning
to be the honey they are making…
as we drift apart in our separate lives
dreaming, desolate, violent, unsatisfied.

Jay Ramsay is a poet who believes that poetry has a unique, catalytic role in our culture.

Lessons from the Honey Bee

The story starts in a small village in rural England, built from the local warm-coloured stone. As is still common in such villages, there is a pub and a village grocery shop. The latter is now run as a communal effort and sells, amongst the packets of mass-produced breakfast cereal, surplus produce from villagers' vegetable gardens. The proceeds no doubt help keep the roof on the church, or maybe the village hall. What is most uncommon is that, next to the grocery shop, is a butchers of the sort that disappeared from most villages generations ago. Yet here it has held on. A conversation with the butcher soon shows why. This is a village that has a deep sense of itself, its place and its function.

On the shelves of the shop are jars of honey, labelled with the name of the butcher. Enquiry reveals that the beekeeper is not the butcher, as might be thought, but someone in a neighbouring village. The name, however, is there to show connection; the honey comes from the fields behind the shop. It is explained with pride that these fields have been sown as wild flower meadows. They are cut once a year for late hay, thus ensuring that the bees have access to the flowers throughout their blooming period. This year, the meadows have not been cut at all, and bees are still pollinating the late flowering plants. Thus occurs a mutual exchange; pollination, the gift of life for a flower, in return for nectar, the gift of life for a bee.

The discussion turns from meadows to modern industrial farming: 'What is being sprayed on the fields?' asks the butcher. 'It smells when I drive past; what is it doing to our children? Is it in that honey?' Thus the bees, through the vehicle of honey, show the connectedness of fields and food. What we sow, we reap.

Individual bees fly over many miles in search of nectar and pollen, which is taken back to the hive to nourish and sustain what we term the colony. But here again the bees have a lesson;

this is not a colony in the normal sense. Colonists chose to live together but may, if called upon, live apart. Bees are not like that. An individual bee cannot survive on its own. Living together is not an option, it is an absolute essential. The bee that we see on a flower has, at that moment, the appearance of a free-living creature. However, at the same time it is part of, and totally dependent on, the greater being that we term the colony. A better term is Bee (in German: *Bien*), with a capital letter, to reflect the unity that is the true bee organism.

This organism is composed of many tens of thousands of individual bees, that take as their outer skin the hollow of a tree, or a beekeeper's hive. Within that skin the bees build a skeleton of waxen comb and, in this, rear the next generation of individual bees. The Bee is thus a creature that constantly renews itself, in just the same way as a mammal renews the cells of its body over time.

How many of your cells have died and been replaced while you read this? The cells within your body are all connected, physically and physiologically. So it is with the Bee. Connections abound within the skin of the hive such that each individual bee know at all times the overall state of the hive. They know when the hive is needful, they know when it is sated, when it is safe and when under attack.

The next generation of bees is reared in the comb at a temperature of 35°C, close to mammalian body temperature, and fed bee milk. Such are the similarities between the physiology of the Bee and that of mammals that some physiologists refer to the Bee as a mammal made up of insects. That is another lesson of the Bee; things are not necessarily what they seem.

The Bee reproduces by swarming. Like an amoeba splitting in two, a cadre of bees leaves the hive with a mother queen and swirls in the air. Normally, flying bees return to precisely the spot that marks the hive entrance; move the hive and the bees return to where the entrance was before the move. Yet, in the moment that the swarm issues from the hive, many tens of thousands strong, the individual bees lose completely their attachment to their old hive and become a creature steadfast in its mission of finding a new home.

This creature swirls in the air, its body many yards wide and many feet high. After a few moments, the swarm begins to contract and coalesce on a nearby branch, until a cluster of bees, perhaps several feet long, has formed. From there scout bees seek out a new home and, when one has been found, the swarm debates its suitability. If it is deemed acceptable, the swarm will once again take to the air and travel to its new abode, led by the scout bees that have found it. This new home may be several hundred yards, or even a mile or more, from the old one. Once installed, the bees immediately start to sweat wax from their undersides to build the all-important bones of their new body – the comb within which the young will be reared and their precious food of pollen and honey will be stored.

One can wonder during this process where lie the boundaries of the creature we are observing? In the old hive the Bee has a defined skin: the walls of the hive, just as it is in the new hive, which is gradually filled with waxen comb. But what happens in between? Where are the boundaries of the Bee then? In concrete terms they cease to exist. One can stand in the middle of a swarm of 20,000 bees, right in its heart, the bees all around. The individual bees will not touch you, they navigate around you, yet they form a single coherent whole.

This is most clearly demonstrated when a beekeeper 'hives' a swarm – takes the cluster from the branch and tips it gently onto a sloping plank leading up to the entrance of a new hive. The swarm does not take to the air but sends a few bees to investigate the hive entrance. If it is pleasing, the whole swarm flows uphill into the new hive; demonstrating in the most dramatic fashion the unity of the organism that is the Bee. Nature is a unity too, and we are just a part. The Bee tells us to remember this in all we do.

An Anonymous Beekeeper (Natural Beekeeping Trust).

"If the bee disappeared off the face of the earth, man would only have four years left to live."

From 'The Life of the Bee' 1901, Maurice Maeterlinck (1862-1949), playwright, poet, and essayist

CLEO MUSSI

STEVE TAYLOR

Beyond Separateness: The Psychological Origins of Ecocide

Since European peoples began exploring and colonising the world in the 16th century, they have curiously observed 'indigenous' peoples and written accounts of their cultures. But what about the other way round? What have indigenous peoples made of the 'developed' peoples who have studied them, and whose culture has conquered theirs?

In 1932, the psychologist Carl Jung met a Native American chief, Mountain Lake, in New Mexico. When Jung asked him what he thought of the European people who had conquered his country, he gave a damning assessment: 'The whites always want something. They are always uneasy and restless. We do not know what they want. We do not understand them. We think that they are all mad.'[1]

Other indigenous peoples have shared Mountain Lake's bemusement. Many believed that the Europeans' lust for possessions was a kind of madness. As the Sioux chief Sitting Bull said, 'The love of possession is a disease with them… They claim this mother of ours, the earth, for their own and fence their neighbors away.'[2]

Perhaps most of all, however, indigenous peoples have been shocked by the Europeans' lack of connection to – and lack of reverence for – nature. As one of the most acute observers of the differences between the European and Indian worldviews, Chief Luther Standing Bear, wrote 'Indian faith sought the harmony of man with his surroundings; the other sought the dominance of surroundings… For [the Indian] the world was full of beauty, for [the White man] it was a place of sin and ugliness to be endured until he went to another world.'[3]

Indigenous peoples generally feel a strong sense of empathy and kinship with nature, and perceive natural phenomena as alive. In contrast, Europeans have generally seen nature as little more than a supply of resources to be exploited. Many of us appear to perceive natural phenomena as objects with no inner life or being. We have no sense of empathy with them – how could we have, since as far as we're concerned they have no being to empathise with? And since they are just objects with no interior, there's no reason why they should have any value for us, except as resources.

One of the European concepts which indigenous peoples like the Native Americans and Australian Aborigines found most difficult to understand was that of the ownership of land and natural resources. Ownership implies a position of superiority and dominance. Since we European peoples know that we are conscious and alive ourselves, and perceive natural phenomena as not being alive and conscious, we feel that we're superior to nature, as a master is to a slave, and so feel entitled to dominate it.

But indigenous peoples' sense of the sacredness and alive-ness of nature means that they could never take this attitude. Even as communities, they rarely see themselves as owning land or natural resources in the sense that we understand the term. As the anthropologist Colin Scott notes, to the Cree Indians 'no one, not even the Creator, owns land'.[4] At the most, they might see themselves as looking after it on behalf of the Great Spirit. This attitude often worked in European colonists' favour, since many Native American groups saw the idea of selling areas of land as an absurd joke, and let the Europeans buy them for almost nothing.

The psychological roots of Ecocide

Why do we have a different relationship to – and a different perception of – nature? This question is important because, in addition to the political and social factors involved, ecocide is a psychological problem. In fact, I would argue that it is primarily a psychological problem, which cannot be completely transcended until human beings in general develop a different way of relating to and perceiving the natural world.

In my view, there are two main psychological factors which have given risen to ecocide. The first is our 'over-developed' sense of ego, or intensified sense of individuality. You could argue that this is the essential difference between Western so-called 'civilised' peoples and tribal indigenous peoples: our stronger and sharper sense of ego. Most indigenous peoples don't seem to exist as personal, self-sufficient egos to the same extent that we do. Their sense of identity extends beyond their own bodies and minds and includes their community and their land.

For example, as the anthropologist Silberbauer noted of the Gwi people of the Kalahari Desert in Africa, 'Identity was more group-referenced than individual. That is, a person would identify herself or himself with reference to kin or some other group'.[5] While according to Boydell, the indigenous peoples of Fiji have a concept of 'the self-embedded-in-community [which] contrasts with the Western value of individualism with its idea of the self as separate and separating from others'.[6]

This is part of the reason why many indigenous peoples feel such a strong attachment to their land. The Fijian anthropologist Ravuva, for example, notes that the Fijian's relationship to their vanua or land is 'an extension of the concept of self. To most Fijians the idea of parting with one's vanua or land is tantamount to parting with one's life'.[7] However, our heightened sense of individuality creates duality and separation. It 'walls us off' within our own egos. It means that we perceive nature as something 'other', that we see natural phenomena as objects which we are entitled to use for our own devices.

The second factor is our 'de-sacralised' vision of nature, our inability to sense the 'aliveness' or 'being-ness' of natural phenomena. As children, we perceive the world around us with intense and vivid perception, and the natural world does appear alive to us, but as adults, our vision of the world becomes de-sensitised and automatic. We 'switch off' to the vivid 'is-ness' which we experience as children. The phenomenal world becomes a shadowy, one-dimensional place. In Australian Aboriginal terminology, we lose the ability to 'enter the dreaming' of natural things. And again, this encourages us to treat natural phenomena as objects. It means that we don't have any qualms about abusing and exploiting the natural world, tearing up its surface in search of resources and polluting it with our waste.

Healing the pathology

This might seem to be a pessimistic way of looking at our predicament. If the fundamental problem is a psychological one, then the only sure way of ensuring our survival as a species would be for us to undergo a psychological shift – specifically, to transcend our sense of separateness and regain a sense of connection to nature and a 'sacralised' vision of the natural world. And how could a shift like this take place?

However, I believe that this shift is already taking place. The last few decades have seen major cultural changes which are perhaps too close for us to see the full significance of. Particularly in Europe and the US, there have been many cultural developments which suggest that, collectively, we may be slowly moving beyond 'ego- separateness'. These include a healthier and more open attitude to sex and the human body, a general increase in empathy and compassion and an increased recognition of the rights of others – manifesting itself, for example, in more humane forms of punishment for offenders, and increased concern for the welfare of animals. Of course, we still have much further to go in these areas, and it might seem that, right at the moment, we are regressing in some ways.
But if you compare present day European culture to 200 years ago – when life was much more brutal and empathy and

compassion were very rare – it's clear that there is a general positive trend.

I believe that the massive upsurge of interest in 'spiritual development' – in Eastern traditions such as Buddhism and Yoga and practices such as meditation – is part of this trend too. And of course, the wave of environmental concern is part of it too. Over the last few decades a more reverential attitude to nature has developed, a sense of connection to our environment, a gradual return to the empathic and respectful perspective of indigenous peoples. We are beginning to recapture a shared sense of being with nature, and a sense that natural phenomena possess their own being or subjective dimension. (See my book *The Fall* for a fuller discussion of these developments.)

Is there enough time for this shift to manifest itself completely? After all, it's still really only a minority movement. It hasn't yet brought the kind of sweeping changes that we need. The isolated ego still holds sway, with its alienation from nature and desire to dominate the world. It's still pushing the human race towards ecocide. Nevertheless, I'm cautiously optimistic. As the threat of ecocide intensifies, so will the urgency for change. Crisis is often the spur for transformation – the more severe the crisis, the greater the transformation. And what crisis could be more severe than ecocide?

Steve Taylor PhD is a senior lecturer in psychology at Leeds Metropolitan University, and the author of several books on spirituality and psychology, including 'The Fall', 'Waking from Sleep' and 'Back to Sanity'.

References

1. Jung, C. (2002), The Earth has a Soul: the Nature Writings of C.G. Jung. Berkeley, CA: North Atlantic Books, p.42

2. In Wright, R. (1992), Stolen Continents. Boston: Houghton Mifflin, p.304

3. Chief Luther Standing Bear. (2011). Retrieved 3/7/2011 from http://www.firstpeople.us/FP-Html-Wisdom/ChiefLutherStandingBear.html

4. Scott, C. (1997). 'Property, Practice and Aboriginal Rights among Quebec Cree Hunters.' In Ingold, T., Riches, D. & Woodburn, J. (Eds.). Hunters and Gatherers, Volume 2: Property, Power and Ideology. Oxford: Berg, p. 40.

5. Silberbauer, G.B. (1994). 'A Sense of Place.' In Burch, E.S. & Ellanna, L.J. (Eds.), Key Issues in Hunter-Gatherer Research, Oxford: Berg, p. 131.

6. Boydell, S. (2001). 'Philosophical Perception of Pacific Property: Land as a Communal Asset in Fiji.' Pacific Rim Real Estate Society, Jan, 2004, p. 21.

7. Ravuva, A. (1983). Vaka I Taukei: The Fijian Way of Life. Java: Institute of Pacific Studies, University of South Pacific, p.7.

JULIAN ROSE

The Denaturing of Nature

There can be no more certain way to decimate life on Earth than through the act of setting in reverse the natural expansiveness of nature. Yet that is exactly what has been happening for the past two centuries, through the relentless eradication of farm and forest biodiversity in a fixated, tunnel vision pursuit of specialisation and profit.

Witness the fresh food market: so reduced has the range of edible vegetables available to the modern shopper become, that just seven varieties now constitute approximately 90% of green foods sold in post industrial Northern European and North American supermarket chains. In spite of supermarkets boasting global food sourcing policies that are supposed to offer almost limitless choice, less than one hundred years ago highly localised food growing offered a far wider range of fruits and vegetables.

The same goes for breeds of cattle, pigs, sheep and hens. A once great diversity of breeds has now been reduced down to a few well known lines owing to the superstores' rapacious demand for 'perfect conformation', standardisation and increasing sterilisation of the means of production.

It is almost impossible to comprehend the levels of destruction that have accompanied this merciless march of 'progress'. And this is how it is still hailed today, by the scientific and agrochemical specialists who feed through their apocalyptic dreams of genetically modified, pesticide-soused, super crops to the government officials and barley barons who collude to keep the agricultural industry on its road to Armageddon.

So where did it all start?

It is safe to say that the commencement of an industrial revolution in the British Isles around 1750 played a critical role in setting in motion, for the first time, the production of food as a 'commodity'. There arose a major industry with global outreach and a big-earning export market. Up until this point, farming was largely a family affair in which the first priority was to feed the household and only then was any surplus taken to the market.

The industrial revolution's rapacious demand for raw materials set in motion the first phase of a crushing ecocide which has now become the number one destroyer of flora and fauna throughout the World, denying much of humanity the opportunity to nourish and self-heal for free.

With the onset of the process of industrialisation came a new mindset – one that saw diversity as 'competition' and nature as something 'to be conquered'. Suddenly, thousands, if not millions, of years of expanding evolutionary biodiversity was stalled and then set in reverse. The ever changing cornucopia of the countryside became relegated to a backcloth and playground for those who were to make their fortunes at its expense.

In the UK, this coincided with the inauspicious land grab known as 'the enclosures', which over a period of some one hundred and fifty years, succeeded in ignominiously ejecting indigenous peasant farmers from the land; replacing them by 'yeoman' farmers and science oriented agri-industrialists favouring the development of higher yielding crops, more meaty animals and the specialised approach of the laboratory scientist. This led on to seed 'hybridisation' in an all out drive for maximum yields which eclipsed the broader concerns of ecology and biodiversity, essential in maintaining the overall equilibrium and balance of nature.

The trusteeship of the land was thus terminally shifted away from those who best understood its secrets and depended upon them for their daily nourishment. A growing sense of alienation between man and nature took root, accompanied by the rapid acceleration of a process of widespread biological regression.

Tragically, this reductionist farming model was expanded into areas of the world that never had an industrial revolution – a model which, to this day, is still hailed by its backers as the most 'efficient' way of supplying mass produced foods to an expanding global population. This system relegates the farmer to second place and proudly promotes the mechanised and technologically dependent farm and the bag of synthetic nitrate fertiliser as saviours of humanity.

A farm tailored to a pharmaceutical formula for the maximum propagation of hybridised laboratory crops and seeds presented a seductive package for the new breed of farmer spawned by this brave new world. After all, they were being offered a seed and chemical package whereby one could virtually overrule the vagaries of nature and produce uniformly regimented crops and animals to pre-planned formulae.

But at what cost?

The hybridisation and commercialisation of seeds, which got going around 1850, could only perform according to its laboratory creators' promises when accompanied by a precise application of synthetic nitrate – a product fabricated by extracting nitrogen from the atmosphere using oil as the main fuel for activating this process. It steadily replaced the free nitrogen provided by such crops as peas and beans that had earlier formed the foundation of crop rotation farming practices.

Synthetic nitrate stimulates the crop in the same manner as we are stimulated by a dose of white sugar. The resulting 'luxury uptake' directly enters the root of the plant entraining it to acquire its sustenance directly from an artificial source and bypassing the need to draw upon the mineral mix common to all naturally fertile soils.

As a result the DNA of the plant stem cellulose is weakened making the plant particularly susceptible to pest and disease attacks. Owing to this anomaly, government and industry trained laboratory technicians have, for the past century, been developing and manufacturing a vast range of synthetic, toxic substances capable of killing-off the pests, fungi and weeds that would otherwise have devastated their nitrate-weakened monocultural crops.

The combined agrochemical/pharmaceutical industry that stands behind the millions of tons of toxic sprays that still souse our fields has grown into a massive transnational powerhouse which has merged with hybrid and genetically modified seed manufacturers to take a controlling influence over food and farming operations worldwide.

For decade after decade, this suicidal cabal has been wiping out all but the most resistant native flora and setting back the ecological stability of the planet by hundreds, if not thousands of years.

In spite of the advent of organic agriculture and the (endangered) existence of mixed crop and livestock farms that use few chemicals, around 90% of post industrial arable land is still the battleground of a war employing a vast arsenal of toxic weapons of mass destruction. The war is led by names like Monsanto, Cargill, Dupont, Pioneer, Syngenta, Archer Daniel Midland, BASF, Bayer – to cite just a few.

A typical commercial arable farmer today has a choice of approximately three thousand chemical mixes to choose from in planning his annual crop protection regime. Every one of these has a direct and deleterious effect on farmland soil, insects and flora – but also beyond the farm – on the air we breath, as well as the rivers, streams and the seas into which these microscopic synthetic hydrocarbons make their innocuous way.

Let us not hesitate in stating that this is a criminal activity far exceeding the sporadic acts of so-called 'terrorism' that we are constantly warned to be on our guard against. In fact we could, and I believe should, hold up this barbaric war against nature as the supreme act of terrorism, for it goes right to the beating heart of all sentient life forms in an indiscriminate act of destruction that can readily be likened to the act of waging war.

In fact, as if to ram home the point, post World War Two pesticides and nitrates were derived directly from nerve gasses and explosive munitions surplus to the military requirement of the time.

Overseeing the continuation of this 'war theatre' and encouraging its further expansion, are the corporate backed agencies that pressurise national governments to adopt their vindictive 'free trade', 'no frontier' policies. The World Trade Organization sits firmly at the head of this table, expounding the rules of global trading and pushing its ambitions on largely unresisting parliamentary committees of governments around the world. The United States, the European Union and the various other quasi-democratic trading blocks, simply reinforce this globalist agenda and are amongst the chief protagonists of a corporate dictatorship which threatens to overwhelm all that tries to go in another direction.

It is our special responsibility to recognise this and to face up to the challenge that it presents.

We live on a planet whose glorious resilience is manifest day in day out in spite of everything that is thrown at her. This World is our garden and only we can ensure that it is nurtured back into an environment worthy of that name. Halting the march of ecocide is therefore the single greatest contribution we can make to life on Earth. It is an action born out of honour for the wellspring of Life itself – and there can be no greater incentive than that to get up and get going – and not rest until the job is done.

As an organic farmer and environmental activist, I have been part of the resistance to this 'war on nature' for most of my working life, often on the front line. Throughout this time I have witnessed, both on my farm and on holdings all over Europe and beyond, ecological and environmentally benign land management practices that demonstrate, without doubt, that copious amounts of highly nourishing foods can be grown and distributed without declaring war on nature.

We are now tasked with using these templates to bring about a revolution in planetary management. A revolution which will reverse all continuing acts of ecocide and rejuvenate, nourish and sustain our unique home for generations to come.

Sir Julian Rose is a pioneer organic farmer, writer, international activist, and social entrepreneur.

ROSE FLINT

Another World Is Possible

MAXINE RELTON

Another world is possible.
We can dream it in, with our eyes
open to this Beauty, to all
that Earth gives each of us, each day
those miracles of dark and light –
rainlight, dawn, sun moon snow, stormgrey
and the wide fields of night always
somewhere opening their flower –
stars – thus, this! Another world is

possible. With river and bird
sweet and free without fear, without
minds blind to harmony, to how
we can hold. We have been blind too long
spoiled greedy children of Earth,
life of rocks and creatures
slipping out of our careless hands.
We must stand now and learn to love
as a mother loves her child, each
cell of her, each grain of her, each
precious heartbeat of her that is
ourselves, our path and our journey
into our dream of future, where
another world is possible
cradling this one in its arms.

Rose Flint is a poet and art therapist.

Ecocide, the Cosmos, and Psyche

The phrase 'We know not what we do' occurred to me once again when I watched a programme on the reappearance of the earth's soil after the recent floods in the south of England. From a house which had been deeply flooded we looked out of the back window – and found an enormous cracked hole encompassing the whole previous garden, through which the owner's car had disappeared. The owners explained that there had been deep mining years ago under the house, which they had not been aware of, and the weight of the water had pushed down the intervening soil in the night through to the mining tunnels. The car had gone too, though luckily for them the house remained – a personal tragedy, and very salutary. Both present floods and earlier mining are the responsibility of people, digging out and overcrowding the natural landscape, layer upon layer, with unexpected results. Who is responsible? How can the earth and life be protected?

There is a Sufi petition, now in the form of a beautifully produced book, a thousand years old, written first in Arabic by Muslims, translated into Hebrew at the request of a medieval Christian king, and now in English. It is called 'The Animals' Lawsuit Against Humanity' and protests at the cruelties of their lives. In the twenty-first century Introduction the editor comments that modern 'man' is now routinely enabled to utilise, dominate and destroy all other creatures. This book asks what are the rights of animals; and what is and could be the goal of human justice and care vis-à-vis the rest of creation?

This Sufi book is of course spiritual, asking specifically spiritual questions about justice, and this is what I want to draw attention to. The questions are raised through a deep consideration of justice. However, it could also be argued that the moral questions raised by our treatment of other people, others species, lands and even outer space filled with our discarded machines, are also deeply spiritual questions. They are about the relationship of 'Psyche' (the human) to 'Cosmos' (the earth), and they are about unwarranted power.

What can human justice do to moderate our worst ecological excesses? A recent one is the practice of 'fracking', producing yet more polluting energy for human profit. Human populations in many countries are burgeoning, from the 2 billion of the 18th century worldwide, to the expected 9 billion towards the end of the present century – all intent on a higher standard of living for humans. Prophecies for the future of this century are dire, for people, for land, all for animals – humans are overcrowding the earth.

The culture that sprang up so strongly in seventeenth century Europe – particularly in England and France – was of a trade built on profit – a relentless capitalist science based on experimentation with the natural world, and the striving for 'more' involving the expanded 'new world'. 'The short term and the bottom line are all' in our modern society, writes cultural historian Richard Tarnas. It is the human psyche that has to shift from the consciousness based on our consumerist, business, individualist culture to a more transpersonal level. A different sense of reality is needed – this would need a new re-alignment of Cosmos and Psyche, of the earth and the human.

Tarnas points out in his massive study, that modern people tend to think that 'apart from the human being, the cosmos is entirely impersonal and unconscious'. However, there are still throughout the world, many people and some cultures, who experience the earth as alive and conscious. But this is hardly the view of the majority of those who have power. The God worshipped by most major religions speak to a God who is transcendent, male, all-powerful and entirely human centred.

There is, however, hope in our growing understanding of the

nature of the earth, based on recent work in geology, ecology and astronomy. Ecocide recognised as a crime would be a wonderful start. But beyond that, knowledge of the earth as a being needs to be deeper, more universal, so that we ALL appreciate her ways in the depth often experienced by early peoples. This requires that we as individuals need to experience the universe from a sense of awe, and to enable us to do that, we must grow in spirit. Then at last we might as a species recognise deeply that the natural world works in ways that are independent of human values. A spiritual, transpersonal understanding would be able to incorporate indigenous experience with modern investigation, recognising that the laws of nature are not the same as ours.

Until the nineteenth century it was widely believed that the earth was about 6,000 years old – we now know its age to be about 4. 5 billion years. As Michael Colebrook once wrote, 'we are the first generation of people who know that the universe has a history and that we, along with everything else, are participating in a very long and utterly marvellous story'. The human race emerged about 150 thousand years ago, so we have existed for only a tiny part of the earth's existence. Only now are we learning more about its nature and our place in the universe.

Modern geology has dug deep into understanding the development of the earth and her creatures, spelling out through fossils and rocks the long history of experimentation in billions of species. Through the books and films made very recently by Richard Fortey, Iain Stewart, Stephen Jay Gould, we can now begin to imagine the amazing beginnings of life on earth at the bottom of the oceans, the development of the first immobile life, the experimentation with hardly believable life forms uncovered in the fossils of, say, the Burgess Shale. We know now that there have been five major extinctions of life forms through the five billion years of life's history on the earth, the last one being the meteorite that killed the dinosaurs 65 million years ago.

All the writers emphasise that 'the earth' is not 'a thing', an object, but a process in a universe of processes – which of course include the lately arrived human species. All these writers have a sense of the communality of life in all its diverse forms. The sense of the connectedness of the earth, and indeed of all creation, requires a leap of understanding in modern humans from 'the short term and the bottom line' of today's societies into a world appreciated now by only a small but growing number.

James Lovelock's naming the earth as 'Gaia', a living being, has brought Cosmos and Psyche into a possible common orbit. People have now been able to see the earth from the edge of our solar system, as a tiny dot, and from the moon as a whole living being. Edgar Mitchell, one of the first astronauts, writes of his first glimpse. 'Suddenly, from behind the rim of the moon, in long, slow-motion moments of immense majesty, there emerges a sparkling blue and white jewel, a light, delicate sky-blue sphere laced with slowly swirling veils of white, rising gradually like a small pearl in a thick sea of black mystery. It takes more than a moment to fully realise this earth… Home.'

Humans have insufficient power to kill the earth herself, even with all the nuclear weapons stored up. But what we could do is mangle and corrode her beauty and complexity. What we need is a world where such a thing would be inconceivable – and that needs a massive shift in today's psyche. Justice would be a start – and then what we need is the experience of spirit and love.

Dr Jean Hardy has been a university teacher for most of her working life. She is an author of several books, including 'A Psychology with a Soul' (1987, 1996) and 'A Wiser Politics' (2011).

Culturecide

Let's face it – we campaigners are pretty much completely baffled as to why so many people are calmly participating in an act of mass suicide. Why won't they listen? Don't they understand? Are they in denial? Don't they care?!

Well, one not-very-widely acknowledged reason springs to mind, and that's how WE frame the debate. It's for good reason that many environmental campaigners get labelled as nature worshipping tree huggers who care more about the extinction of some rare and obscure double-jointed sub-species of Amazonian tree frog than they do about people's day to day lives. We're perceived as more interested in polar bears than people, because, all too often, that's the rhetoric we use, and it's the way we put the argument forward.

We need to start acknowledging that the biosphere will survive almost anything we throw at it. It's already done so through several mass extinction events, and although we're capable of fundamentally and radically altering it, we can't 'destroy' it. It will recover from whatever we do to it, as it always has as a result of natural catastrophes. We might think it's deplorable to behave that way, but as an argument in its own right, it doesn't constitute a day to day concern for most people, and it smacks of demanding guilt from them about how they are harming the poor innocent planet.

What does interest them is what sort of quality of life their children or grandchildren will experience, and it's that we should emphasise. Not that we'll wipe ourselves out and become extinct as a species (that's actually not very likely, particularly within the next few hundred years) but that in the very short term we'll destroy our culture and civilisation as a result of a radically altered climate. If people like this lifestyle, then let's start emphasising that it is what's going to go down the pan first,

POLYP.ORG.UK

'TRASH'

unless we make it sustainable in the short term, never mind the long term.

You all know the arguments – destructive social stress as a result of mass migration from flooded coasts leads to war… climate driven food shortages lead to even more poverty and urban conflict… and so on. But why do we emphasise these arguments so infrequently? Why aren't they the first thing we say, and then afterwards we can talk about the polar bears and double-jointed tree frogs as well?

In fact, shouldn't the main message be that if we alter the environment in a radical way, the first casualty, in the short term, will be democracy itself, as social upheaval and chaos opens the door to rigid dictatorships or military rule? That way, ecological concerns can be framed in terms of the human right of the next two generations to live in stable democracies – a far more effective appeal than one to the semi-sacred 'rights' of the biosphere. Where are the flyers and posters asking 'Why carefully save for your child's future if ignoring climate change and ecological destruction NOW will result in them becoming adults in a world full of fear and suffering?' (But with snappier wording, I hope.)

This approach would also allow us to neatly tackle one of the main sources of inertia and resistance to real action… the wealthy elite who directly profit from ecologically harmful activities. They're no fools. They know that the social and economic impacts of climate change will affect them the least. They can afford more expensive food or the cost of relocating inland to gated and guarded communities, leaving the rest to suffer the consequences of mass upheaval.

Let's start emphasising that their sabotaging of green initiatives is because it's they who don't care what happens to the majority of citizens. They accuse us of putting green concerns first, when it's them putting green pieces of paper before people. Let's pull the rug out from under their argument that it's they who want to provide a happy and comfortable life for everyone through growth, and throw it back at them.

But we can only do this when we put people first. We have to emphasise that a stable environment is what supports stable, just and democratic human civilisations, no matter how much we personally may care about nature as an issue in its own right.

The majority of people we need to appeal to live in cities, not gardens of Eden, and their concerns are about jobs, safe communities and what happens to their children. If we want them on side, let's change how we talk about the issues, so it actually means something to them.

Polyp is a political activist and cartoonist.

JOHN PARRY

Five Men in a Boat: A Salutary Tale for Today

A yacht belonging to a multi-millionaire, sailing in a remote part of the Pacific from Santiago in Chile to Tahiti, sank suddenly having struck a large floating object. This was a sea container washed overboard from a cargo ship thought to have contained a large quantity of expanded polystyrene bowls and beakers destined for fast food restaurants. Though waterlogged, the container was still afloat, but had been barely visible. Everyone on the yacht drowned except five men who had been on deck and were thrown clear, together with a small dinghy.

The five consisted of: the Mate who was the navigator, a deckhand who was the oarsman, an accountant, a barrister and a plump banker. In the morning, they discovered, hidden by the millionaire owner who was to meet the yacht on arrival in Tahiti, two heavy hold-alls, one full of gold bullion, the other sealed packs of bank notes in three different currencies. 'In

BANKSY

addition to the predicament we are in' said the Mate, 'we now have the bloody responsibility of looking after the boss's cash!'

The sea was choppy and water was coming over the sides of the dinghy almost as fast as it could be baled out and the Mate said that one or the other of the hold-alls must be dumped. The two crew members then noticed that the lawyer, accountant and banker had gone to one end of the boat and were talking quietly. The Mate demanded to know what they were discussing. The accountant said that if some of the treasure could be saved there seemed to be a good chance the two crew members would get a handsome reward. 'Or a job for life!' said the deckhand optimistically.

Using his knowledge of finance, the accountant offered to put a few hours into calculating the individual value of the two hold-alls so as to advise the crew which one to throw over the side. The lawyer then mentioned that there was a risk that the millionaire whose money it was that had been dumped would sue the crew to compensate for his loss. However, being legally skilled, the lawyer offered to make a careful record of why the decision had had to be taken and this could be used in their defence.

Of course to do this would take several hours and he would need to charge for his time as well. The Mate said, 'All well and good but what if the sea gets even rougher and both heavy hold-alls have to be dumped so there will be no possibility of a reward given to the crew?' The reply by both the accountant and the lawyer was that as professional men they would not be sharing in the profits and so would still have to charge for their time which in that event would presumably come out of the crewmen's wages.

This neat move, emerging from the collusion between the two professionals, meant that they would still be earning fees while sitting in the boat, which was being rowed and steered by their 'clients'! The snag was that before the professional work could begin, both accountant and lawyer needed to know that they would be certain to get their fees paid. The plump banker then spoke up. He said he could draw up documents for the Mate and deckhand to sign by which his bank would provide a loan to the crewmen to guarantee that the lawyer and accountant would get their fees. However, this would be on the basis that the bank, which would consider the 'venture' to be high risk, would need to cover its exposure by having their homes on shore pledged as security. Such security was vital because the bank's policy would not allow it to participate in the equity of an enterprise of this sort.

The Mate and the deckhand exchanged glances and then put the lawyer and the accountant over the side (the decision to do so taken on purely financial grounds). Later when the three remaining men ran out of food, they ate the banker, applying the reasonable parameters of a) who was least important for the navigation and handling the oars and b) who was the best source of life-saving nutrition. When the two seamen finally reached Tahiti and handed the valuables over to the multi-millionaire, because they had been through such an ordeal, he had been advised that they would no longer be fit for work and so he had to pay them off. Also, under the terms of their Contracts of Employment, they were responsible not only for the safety of the yacht (which was thankfully insured) but also for delivery of all valuables carried on board. Therefore, on legal advice they were not entitled to any reward either.

The fictitious anecdote has close parallels with real situations where professionals involved in legal and financial services are both averse to risk but unscrupulously greedy for reward and will take advantage of the vulnerability of others caught up in perilous situations. This involves a short-term focus, which puts in jeopardy a fair and reasonable outcome making people act for themselves, completely disregarding the interests of others.

It also illustrates, following the advice of professionals, how multi-millionaires can avoid paying a penny more for anything than they have to – which is how they become filthy rich in the first place. For professionals, the lesson that needs to be learned is that if all you care about is securing your fee, the eventuality may reveal itself far more painfully than what you might lose by being fair minded and taking account of the interests of others. And if the men in the boat had cooperated and thought out innovative solutions, they might have tied the hold-alls to the floating sea container and the three professionals could have learned how to catch fish.

John Parry, MBE.

"The fact is that no species has ever had such wholesale control over everything on earth, living or dead, as we now have. That lays upon us, whether we like it or not, an awesome responsibility. In our hands now lies not only our own future, but that of all other living creatures with whom we share the earth. This last chapter may have given the impression that somehow man is the ultimate triumph of evolution, that all these millions of years of development have had no purpose other than to put him on earth. There is no scientific evidence whatever to support such a view and no reason to suppose that our stay here will be any more permanent than that of the dinosaur."

From 'Life on Earth' 1979, David Attenborough, broadcaster and naturalist

The Environmental Impact of Drugs

The connection between hard-partying celebrities – from A-list to F – and the Revolutionary Armed Forces of Colombia (FARC) might not be immediately apparent to most. But then the free-market makes strange bedfellows of us all. The twin desires to usurp the existing Colombian power-base on the one hand, and maintain the illusion of bright-lights, big-city careers on the other, have colluded to throw the spotlight on a largely ignored form of ecocide.

As controllers of the majority of Colombia's cocaine production for more than a decade, FARC has been responsible for the slash and burn of more than two million hectares – an area the size of Wales – of both pristine primary- and secondary-growth Amazon rainforest, in the most biodiverse (per sq km) country in the world. As controllers of a large majority of the public's imagination, celebrities who either openly or clandestinely take cocaine are helping ensure that the Colombian coca farmers who work for FARC stay in business.

Life in the spotlight comes with certain responsibilities, however. When it comes to the potential impact of celebrities' brazen promotion of drug-taking, their 'lifestyle' choices and their ignorance of the environmental consequences of their actions, they must be held to account. Especially since their use perpetuates the destruction of still more rainforest through the influence they have on young people.

Examining the environmental consequences of recreational drugs presents many opportunities for teachers and pupils to be more creative in how they explore the role of drugs in today's society. What if children were asked, for example, to consider the impact of cocaine use on the recently discovered gold frog, the size of your fingernail, whose habitat of just 42 acres is in the remote mountains of Colombia? Or the recently discovered

Gorgeted Puffleg hummingbird, which only lives on some 1,200 hectares in the cloud forests of south-western Colombia and is predicted to disappear within two years? With these facts at their fingertips, might at least some children view drug-promoting celebrities in a different, less deferential light?

Making the environmental consequences of recreational drug use more widely known would also offer governments and drug education charities a chance to challenge the excuse of many users that since they are not dependent, somehow their use harms no one and so it's okay to continue. Might we imagine a future society in which Earth jurisprudence was firmly established within the legal framework, and where cocaine-snorting celebrities might be heavily fined, or even banned from performing?

Though it may sound far-fetched, the trial of Greenpeace protesters, acquitted last September of causing criminal damage to Kingsnorth power station, sets an important precedent. The judge ruled that the protest was reasonable given the potential future harm to the environment that the coal-fired power station could cause. By the same token, the use of recreational drugs on its current scale also constitutes genuine future harm to people and ecosystems.

Nick Kettles is an ecologist and writer. This article was originally published by The Ecologist in 2009.

MIKE TOWNSEND

Two Planets: Are We Serious?

JOHN PLAYFOOT

It's time to stop kidding ourselves. Progress towards a sustainable economy is way too slow. Our reliance on voluntary actions and incremental models for change are not delivering the necessary pace or depth of change. New models of business success and shared prosperity are within reach, but will require a more radical shift in our mindsets and behaviours. Are we prepared to do what it really takes, to cross the Rubicon and make an authentic transition to a truly sustainable model of commerce, where people, planet and business can thrive and prosper? It is surely time to think more creatively and generate the conditions necessary to deliver a real and lasting impact.

We need two planets by 2030, to maintain our current life styles.[1] Two planets by the year 2030! This simple but significant phrase echoes around my mind each day, unsettling my inner peace. We know we are living way beyond our means, yet progress towards a green and sustainable economy – despite some good work by a few leading lights – is still way too slow.

There is lots of talk, lots of noise. More and more companies are reporting on CSR (corporate social responsibility), and there are more events and articles, although the latest surveys reveal little meaningful progress across a range of metrics.[2] And of course, this is not just an environmental lament; our dwindling supply of natural resources and ecosystems will ultimately mean economic decline, with severe financial consequences for all. The numbers are staggering. Environmental damage caused by human activity in 2008 was estimated at $6.6 trillion, equivalent to 11% of global GDP.[3] And this is just for starters.

Translating this into each of our companies – and we should – how many business models are resilient enough to withstand a loss of 11% or more in sales, each year? Not many. And let us remind ourselves that this is not some far-off, distant and nebulous challenge – it is already here. More than half of small business owners in the US believe climate change will adversely affect them, with nearly one in five admitting that extreme weather events have already affected their operations.[4]

Small steps, small impact

Our response, in virtually all cases, is inadequate. Far too many companies are taking small, incremental steps towards addressing critical sustainability issues that will impact on their bottom lines, as well as all our shared future.[5] We are massively underestimating the scale of the challenge, as well as the type and quantum of solutions required. And let's not kid ourselves; there is a world of difference between slick communications and delivering genuine business transformation.

We also appear to have a crisis of leadership: most CEOs admit they are struggling to make the business case for long-term investments.[6] The problem, they believe, is that key influencers – such as consumers, governments and investors – are failing to provide them with the incentives and the signals they so badly need. Of course, we can all too easily point towards the activity or inactivity of others. But the truth is, we are all to blame. We know we are plundering the planet, so why are we not making more holistic and rational choices in our businesses?

The issues are complex and the challenges are huge. But, clearly, we are deploying the wrong model for change, in dealing with the situation at hand – our apparent reliance on voluntary actions and incremental improvements is not delivering the real shift we need to see. Are we really serious?

It is unfortunate, but we have to recognise that change at this scale does not often come through individual choice. Real change is harder than that. Even the mighty Unilever, bolstered with its hugely effective marketing machine, admits that it is struggling to influence consumer behaviour.[7] It is one thing trying to persuade people to buy more sustainable products, but it is quite another challenge to influence how these products are used in practice – of course, the more hand-washing in warm water we promote, the more energy will be consumed – we somehow need to ensure greater levels of clean energy for all, in supporting this.

It is hard to deliver a true impact, especially when our infrastructure and systems of business and economy don't yet add further support or reinforce these broader shifts.

All change!

The obvious often gets overlooked. But, when we think about changing the system, should we not look to adopt more systems thinking? In this case, perhaps we should be thinking more creatively on the conditions necessary to deliver real and lasting change? Polly Higgins draws a strong parallel between our current need for protecting the planet, with the movement that eventually led to the abolition of slavery in the 19th century. She reminds us of the three enabling conditions that William Wilberforce himself identified: we need to pull the current subsidies; outlaw the problem; and then establish the right incentives in the opposite direction.[8]

We badly need regulation. Ray Anderson, the self-confessed former plunderer of the planet, turned sustainable business evangelist, had it right when he said, 'Damn, some day people like me will be put in jail!'[9] And while Ray is sadly no longer with us, his insight might become a reality, perhaps sooner than we think.

But, we need good regulations – that deal with causes not just symptoms. And we certainly don't need another round of tick-box compliance legislation. Our regulations also need to be consistent – just look at the carbon trap the UK is walking towards, as we simultaneously enshrine carbon reduction targets alongside the duty to maximise fossil fuel production.[10] Go figure.

So, what laws will we need?

The proposed law of Ecocide looks like a good place to start, positioned as an international crime, over and above all other laws – to prevent mass damage, destruction to, or loss of our ecosystems. Some of the current Ecocide hot spots around the planet include the Alberta Tar Sands in Canada, the Pacific Trash Vortex, oil pollution in the Niger Delta, and the Lusi Mud Volcano in Indonesia.[11]

The plan is to end the era of Ecocide by 2020 and, thanks to the Eradicating Ecocide Campaign; this proposal could become an achievable reality – if two-thirds of member states agree to amend the Rome Statute and make Ecocide the Fifth International Crime against Peace.[12] Companies will certainly have to fully integrate environmental risks into their corporate strategies and decision-making, which should, therefore, deliver a major shift in corporate behaviour. Although, from where we are today, the power of vested interests working against this proposal should not be underestimated.

Rethinking capital

Back to our conditions for change – we should also focus on developing the right subsidies, including suitable financial incentives.

A key problem to date is that virtually all our business models have tended to exploit the natural world. Track back through each value chain and, somewhere down the line, our sources of income and profit are derived from over-utilised natural resources and energy, the exploitation of people, and leaving behind our waste, emissions and other pollutants. Thanks to outdated economic thinking, particularly in terms of our treatment of so-called externalities, our natural assets do not appear on traditional balance sheets and can, therefore, be invisible in our decision-making. Out of sight really does mean out of mind.

It may be that the emerging concept of Natural Capital provides a suitable mechanism for engaging with the true cost of conducting our businesses.[13] If we can assign pounds and dollars to nature, perhaps we can start valuing – if not fully appreciating – our natural world, and as a result start modifying our behaviours towards more sustainable business decisions. Building on this concept at business level, Environmental, Social and Governance (ESG) metrics are likely to become increasingly important within investment decisions – to better inform both business executives and investors on the interactions between different forms of value and capital, and where financial risks may lie. With the right accounting standards in place, then businesses will surely have to act in a more holistic and responsible manner?

But, before we rush into solutions mode, there is also a danger that we may be missing the point. It could also be argued that these frameworks seek to impose monetary and market values on to the natural world, in an attempt to integrate nature and sustainability within a capitalist framework. A case of, if we can assign pounds and dollars to nature, it becomes worth something.

This philosophy is probably well intended, but might also have some limitations. We might wish to reflect on the true value of natural assets – the ecosystems that support our world are so fundamental that they are in fact beyond monetary value. The reality is that there will be serious consequences for human existence if we undermine our habitat beyond certain thresholds, and no amount of financial wizardry can resolve this fundamental dependency. As John Ruskin wrote – 'There is no wealth but life'.

Perhaps there are simpler, more effective incentives. As Paul Polman recently reminded me, taxation is also an important instrument. Should we consider shifting from our current emphasis on taxing people and labour, towards a more appropriate tax on resources? In any case, rather than trying to force-fit the natural world into our more recent man-made construct of capital, perhaps we should put the horse back in front of the cart, and develop an economic model that better aligns with and supports our natural world.

This leads us to a further condition for change – the need for a new operating system for business, within which the primary purpose of business is to serve life.

Real wealth and purpose

When redesigning our system of business, we could start by reframing our ambitions for wealth. David Korten urges us to recognise the difference between real living wealth and phantom financial wealth – a very interesting and insightful division – and worthy of much reflection.[14] Money, he reminds us, is simply a number entered on an accounting ledger – it has no intrinsic value, and can disappear in an instant, as we have all seen during and since the financial crisis.

Real wealth, on the other hand, has intrinsic value. We can think about fertile land, healthy food, knowledge, productive labour, pure water and clean air, or physical infrastructure – they all add true value, enriching our lives, each day. This is where the notion of the Purpose Economy comes to the fore – supported by business models centred on generosity, creativity and resilience – based on need, rather than greed. In all honesty, how many of our current business models contribute real value by enriching people and the planet?

Purpose is certainly becoming a big issue. The recently launched GameChangers 500 (GC500) aims to provide the antidote to the Fortune 500, by creating a new list to profile the world's top purpose-driven organisations that are maximising their positive impact, rather than just maximising their profit.[15] Unilever has been considering shifting its aim from being 'the best at marketing in the world' towards being 'the best marketing for the world'. A small change on the surface, but the implications are huge. By opening our minds to the very real needs out there, thinking through our position and role in helping to transform our world, the opportunities for business with real purpose are almost endless.

Of course, when we start exploring our purpose we open the lid on an underlying and unresolved tension – is our primary aim to satisfy the interests of people and planet, or to maximise returns to shareholders? We can perhaps seek to optimise the returns we make, while delivering on our purpose, but in reality it is unlikely we can aim to maximise profits at the same time. We cannot serve two masters.

The problem is that many of our business operating systems are geared towards the rather narrow view of shareholder primacy – that business is solely about making profits for the benefit of shareholders – and that we should do whatever it takes to maximise profits, so long as we comply with the rules of the game.[16] Sustainability and purpose will always come second, within this framing of business.

Thankfully, the notion of shareholder primacy is being challenged. According to the findings of the international Sustainable Companies Project, there is nothing in company law that requires us to maximise shareholder returns, it is only the social norm of shareholder primacy that drives us to behave in this way.[17] And where does this social norm come from? Well, of course, our infatuation with shareholder primacy is also one of the key tenets underpinning our entire model of capitalism. That is how this system works.

This leads us to one further and fundamental condition for change – we need to tackle capitalism's fundamental faults – including our insatiable desire for growth and consumption, short-termism, and our dysfunctional financial systems – and to imagine what a viable and sustainable economic system could look like. Only with the right underpinning economic system can we hope to deliver on the promise of sustainable prosperity.

Change the system

This challenge has inspired the Sustainable Economy Project – an initiative born out of a desire to create a better economic system.[18] Thankfully, we have found much cause for hope. There is already a huge amount of good work going on around the world, with a range of initiatives creating a surprisingly cohesive and consistent picture of people and businesses migrating towards a more sustainable economic system. One can really get a sense of a quiet revolution, already happening.

There now needs to be widespread and active participation in order to make the most of what could be a tipping point in the transition towards a sustainable economy. Action is centred on eight projects for change – including new models for business success and new financial and banking systems – bolstered with a passion to encourage the type of economic activism that will help achieve this aim.

Engagement is taking place at a number of levels, including online communities, but also through a global network of Sustainable Economy Hubs, established in some of the more progressive business schools and universities, that are already exploring pathways for systemic change. The network of progressive academic institutions – which already includes Business School Lausanne, Exeter Business School, University of Oslo and the University of Technology, Sydney – has a major role to play in forming the new economy, expanding their remit to act as catalysts for proactive change in each region, shifting the business–economic conversation and creating a shared agenda for change within business and political communities.

Time to get serious...

Business as usual really is not an option. We have to develop more radical and lasting solutions. We also have to select a more robust model for change, giving much more thought to how we can shape the right conditions that will enable a truly real and lasting impact.

We know we need good regulation and the right incentives. But, we also need the right operating system for our businesses, focused on purpose and creating living wealth – sustainable prosperity. This will involve a necessary shift away from shareholder primacy – a major challenge. Of course, the power of vested interests may yet sink us. But we can be sure, our old model of economy is dying out – let us hope that this becomes extinct before we do. Are we serious enough for our planet? I sincerely hope so.

Mike Townsend is CEO of Earthshine, lead author of 'A Journey in Search of Capitalism 2.0' and Convenor of the Sustainable Economy Project. He is also a regular contributor for Sustainable Business magazine, 2-degrees Network, Edie.net, The Guardian, The Ecologist and Huffington Post.

JUDY BARBER

References

1. WWF (2012), Living Planet Report 2012, London: WWF.

2. Makower, J. et al (2014), State of Green Business 2014, San Francisco: GreenBiz.

3. UNEP (2010), Universal Ownership: Why environmental externalities matter to institutional investors: PRI Association and UNEP Finance Initiative.

4. Perella, M. (2014), American SMEs Already Feeling Harmful Effects of Climate Change, Edie.net, 27 July.

5. Ceres (2014), Gaining Ground: Corporate Progress on the Ceres Roadmap for Sustainability, Boston: Ceres & Sustainalytics.

6. UN (2013), Global Corporate Sustainability Report: United Nations.

7. Knowles, V. (2014), Unilever struggles to engage with consumers to make sustainable choices, 2-degrees Network, 30 April.

8. Higgins, P. (2012), Ecocide is the Missing 5th Crime Against Peace, TEDxExeter Talk, 1 May.

9. Dean, C (2007), Executive on a Mission: Saving the Planet, New York Times, 22 May.

10. Monbiot, G. (2014), The UK is making it a legal duty to maximise greenhouse gas emissions, The Guardian, 26 June.

11. Top 10 Ecocide Hotspots, Eradicating Ecocide website: http://eradicatingecocide.com/overview/10-ecocide-hotspots/

12. The Rome Statute is the governing document, which sets out the existing international Crimes Against Peace. Ecocide was to be included in earlier drafts, until it was removed in 1996. Source: Eradicating Ecocide website: http://eradicatingecocide.com/overview/rome-statute/

13. TEEB (2010) The Economics of Ecosystems and Biodiversity: Mainstreaming the Economics of Nature: A synthesis of the approach, conclusions and recommendations of TEEB.

14. Korten, D.C. (2010), Agenda for a New Economy: From Phantom Wealth to Real Wealth, San Francisco: Berrett-Koehler (2nd Edition).

15. Hewitt, A. (2014), GameChangers: The World's Top Purpose-Driven Organizations, Forbes: 4th November.

16. The focus on shareholder primacy has been driven by reference to Milton Friedman's view of business and responsibility, in his 1970 essay, where he concluded: 'There is one and only one social responsibility of business – to use its resources and engage in activities designed to increase its profits so long as it stays within the rules of the game, which is to say, engages in open and free competition without deception or fraud.'

17. Sjfjell, B. (2014), Shareholder Primacy: the Main Barrier to Sustainable Companies, Sustainable Economy Project site: http://www.the-sustainable-economy.org/beatesjfjell/shareholder_primacy_the_main_barrier_to_sustainable_companies

18. The Sustainable Economy Project: http://www.the-sustainable-economy.org/about

EVOLVE

In this section there are clear statements of what we have to achieve in order to halt and reverse environmental damage. We have to evolve better ways of caring for the earth.

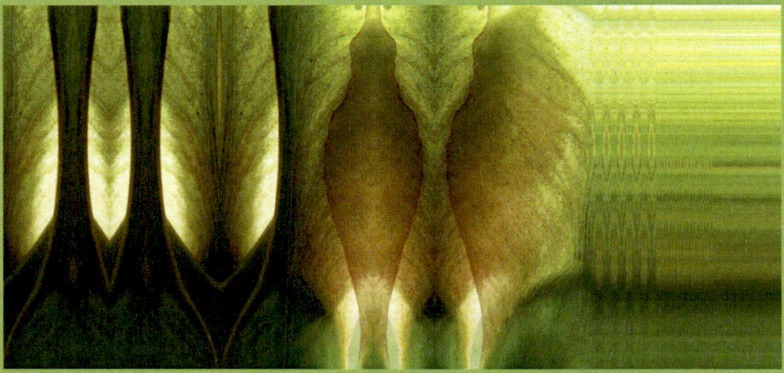

Seed Landscape: © ANNABEL WARD

Blow that horn – it is being heard. Our vision shifts when we can name the harm and when we can envision a better world. By making visible that which must be seen and heard, we can turn and move from Ecocide to Ecolibrium.

Vandana Shiva is creating a new space – a space based on greater freedom; seed freedom. Ecocide law protects that space and supports those who sound the horn. It closes the door to the destruction of our seeds and also the destruction of our soils and our society. The sacredness of life permeates every aspect of our being and to destroy it is a crime.

How we make visible our support for something new to emerge takes imagination – our capacity to envision what that world could be.

Polly Higgins

ECOLIBRIUM NOW

“The world produces enough food to provide 2,800 calories for every man, woman, and child each day. However roughly one-third of all food – the equivalent of one kilogram per person per day – ends up rotting in the fields or thrown away in the trash. But this news is both disheartening and uplifting. While it means that food waste needs to be severely curbed, it also means that current global food production is sufficient to feed the planet. Hunger is not the result of the scarcity of food but the scarcity of democracy.”

Danielle Nierenberg, President, Food Tank

“The most remarkable feature of this historical moment on Earth is not that we are on the way to destroying the world – we’ve actually been on the way for quite a while. It is that we are beginning to wake up, as from a millennia-long sleep, to a whole new relationship to our world, to ourselves and each other.”

Joanna Macy, author, Buddhist scholar and environmental activist

---

“Making ecocide a recognised law will place a cap on the irresponsible actions of fat cats who hide behind corporate shields to destroy lives and harm the planet. Polluting nations and corporations are engaging in acts of aggression against nature and against humanity. These are extreme acts of mass destruction that may affect the planet in cataclysmic ways. These acts must be recognised for what they are and duly punished.”

Nnimmo Bassey, Chair of Friends of the Earth International (2008-2012)

Creating a Legal Duty of Care

Lawyers use the term 'duty of care' when there is a fiduciary duty owed, often a duty owed by a trustee or a board member to an identified beneficiary or group of beneficiaries. There is a whole body of law known as Trust law. The trustee is given legal title to the trust property, but is obligated to act on behalf of the beneficiaries, to ensure their greater well-being comes first.

So, instead of ownership, trusteeship creates a duty of care. This is something we understand well; look at the duties of a parent to their children. This is another area of law that applies trusteeship to childcare provisions. It makes sense – we cede our overriding right to service our needs and instead put the interests of the child first. What we have is a relationship with our child; we do not view them as tradable commodities (property law) there in service of our needs.

As such, where children are traded or harmed we view that as a crime. The purpose of creating laws that put the well-being of the child first is to govern our relationship between ourselves as primary carers and the child. Whereas if we treat our child as a piece of property, in the legal sense, our rights over the object (the child) would be absolute. As you can see, the word 'care' brings with it duties and responsibilities. In fact a 'duty of care' refers to the sanctity of the relationship between the trustee (the parent) and the beneficiary (the child).

So how does this square with the Earth? Two choices; treat the Earth as a commodity and you can put a price on ecosystems services, to own, buy and sell. Or, treat the Earth as a living being. Just like a child, our Earth surely has the right to life as much as we do – the right to exist without threat of significant harm.

Very few benefit from ecocide. The land and air that is being traded certainly does not, nor do the communities that have

been injured. Carbon trading and levying fines do nothing to abate the harm. It's akin to putting a price on harming a child – which of course does not make sense. But more than that, it allows the cycle of harm to perpetuate. Because we have no legal duty of care to put the well-being of the Earth first, the cycle of harm spirals out of control. It is not enough to do a calculation: raze our forests, desecrate our ancient arboreal wetlands and despoil our land for future generations – none of this can be replaced simply by paying up a fine.

Caring for life comes from the nurturing of a relationship, not the placing of a price-tag. The right to life is priceless – what we are talking about is the very sacredness of life itself. No amount of money will bring back the land, the community, nor the sense that this was once a home for all who had previously lived in harmony with their land.

Leadership crime

Everything we choose to do in life has consequences. The consequences may be successfully hidden (such as child abuse or mining) for a time, but the problem is that the harm it causes remains at large. Just because it is not out in the open does not mean it is for the best. A severe violation has occurred, even when no one else knows. At some point we have to face the pain and acknowledge the role we have played in causing it.

So how does this play out at a corporate leadership or governmental level? At the moment we have an absence of law to govern decisions made at the very top level; decisions that can have significant adverse consequences for many, both directly and indirectly. Yet, although we are held to account for causing harm to a human, causing significant harm to the Earth (or the inverse: failing to take action to prevent the harm) is not illegal. A legal duty of care for those whose territories have been or are at risk of being destroyed simply does not exist.

Yes, we have a whole spectrum of approaches – from voluntary measures, treaties, conventions and protocols – but when any of these are breached (and many of them are) there is very little a territory that has been harmed or community that is at risk of being destroyed, can do. What is missing is a legal duty of care. A law of Ecocide creates a legal duty of care to prohibit decision-making that a) causes, or b) does not prevent, significant harm. Existing laws do not stop persons in positions of superior responsibility from making harmful decisions again and again. Quite simply, it is not – yet – a crime to cause mass damage to the Earth.

The absence of leadership crime – how the conduct of those in positions of superior responsibility and the decisions made on behalf of society is governed – disempowers. The very absence of an overriding duty of care serves to re-enforce the acceptance of harm as a norm, which in turn re-enforces a flawed belief that such a norm is a given that we must accept. But this is not the case; just because something is a norm does not mean that it is right. Especially when the norm causes significant harm.

Under a law of Ecocide, any territory at risk of or suffering significant harm shall be assisted first and foremost from a place of trusteeship. The primary determinant in sentencing terms is what assistance is required, not how much it will cost. Restorative justice is the truly innovative facet; the draft law of Ecocide includes far-reaching provisions. Incarceration is an option, but there are other routes available too, most importantly court powers to put in place a range of restorative -based procedures.

Criminal law has a number of defences, but profit is not one of them. This is because criminal law is a moral code made explicit. An ancient tenet of criminal law tells us that 'when something is so wrong in and of itself, it is prohibited'. Society's mores are shaped by our criminal law – we got to a point when we said 'enough, no more' to slavery, and it was banned; we outlawed genocide and apartheid. Now too the same can be said for ecocide – 'enough, no more'.

In so doing, our values become aligned with our belief in the most sacred duty of all – our duty of care for the well-being of Earth itself. Not just the land, but all beings – human and non-human. A law of Ecocide is holistic law; it recognises the interconnectedness of all life, past present and future. That is why I say it's a law for humanity, nature and future generations – but most of all it is a missing law for peace.

Language of war

Language acts as the carrier of our ideas, so how we give voice matters. The very terms, phrases and words we choose to use carry forward our intent – whether explicit or not. Thus, how we choose to frame our language, whether that be language of peace or war, makes all the difference.

A language based on the language of war where we talk of 'fighting against' means we step into the drama of conflict. Control of nature at its extreme leads to ecological ecocide as well as cultural ecocide. Take war out of our language however, and we open up a space for a different kind of conversation to emerge – one that aligns itself with laws of nature. Instead of harm, we are naturally drawn towards a state of harmony. By aligning our human-made laws with natural law, we find the path to life lived in greater freedom. The laws of nature are first and foremost life-affirming, as is a law of Ecocide. The very essence of life is such a powerful force in and of itself, it becomes untenable to destroy the Earth. To cause ecocide is to fight against the laws of nature; to embrace ecolibrium is to bring our state of being back into balance.

How we engage with the world is a mirror of how we conduct our lives and make decisions on a micro level. Are we at war with others? Do we view the world as a thing, to commoditise, buy and sell to the highest bidder – or, do we view the world as a living being, a world where we collectively owe a duty of care both here and now and for future generations? Do we choose to step back and observe or do we choose to step up and speak out and act from a place of deep connect, care and love?

Winning a war comes at a price – but even war cannot be justified in financial terms; the true cost is in loss of lives, human and non-human. Our conquering of our land, sea and air has already cost us the loss of lives, species extinction, biodiversity loss and so much more. Yet it is possible that instead of being at war, peace can be found in its place. That for me, means ending the era of Ecocide – but not through the use of war. What we choose to do next is up to us. We can collectively create the new story of our times; align our written laws with natural law, choose to be trustees, guardians and stewards of our Earth, and give expression to our heart-felt desire to end the conflict once and for all. For me, governance that comes from the heart can but only take us to a place of peace.

Polly Higgins is a legal expert on the law of Ecocide and author of award-winning 'Eradicating Ecocide' and 'Earth is Our Business'. She speaks about the law of Ecocide all over the world.

JANE DAVIDSON

How Can We Encourage People to Live More Sustainably?

I live in a refurbished barn where we grow most of our own food, run our well insulated house on our own wood, recycle, compost, and use renewable energy. I try to bring down my carbon footprint every year – yet nothing I do at home will change the systemic problems that face our generation. Although I firmly believe the personal and the political should go hand in hand and that we should lead by example, my individual actions, even if multiplied a thousand or million times over, would not secure a better life for future generations.

So how do we make beneficial changes for people and the planet? Ultimately it comes from action, either by governments or people and preferably both. The politics of nudge – small incremental improvements year on year – are utterly insufficient for the challenges ahead. The earth is a single complex system; the global challenge is to maintain the optimal conditions for life. John Rawls, the American philosopher, talks about inter-generational justice, where each generation should do unto future generations what they would have wanted past generations to do unto them.

We've tried the collective government route. Thousands of politician hours across the world have been spent in making global 'commitments' to tackle climate change and repair our damaged ecosystems, and still no one country has set or met the world's climate or biodiversity conservation challenges. Instead of world leaders responding by strengthening commitments, the opposite has happened; in each area, previously binding commitments have been replaced by non-binding 'strategic' targets. The global conferences carry on, yet so also do atmospheric emissions. Yet there has been no public outcry about the failure of government leaders to secure a safer longer term future for humanity. Business as usual and the systems that underpin it continue.

With every climatic and biodiversity indicator pointing in the wrong direction, the world stands as if paralysed. Nobody seriously believes that voluntary agreements will deliver, and yet that is the current trend. Collective action of the scale and pace needed requires legal underpinning. In 2012, the Earth Summit in Rio should have given the world a legal institutional framework for sustainable development and the green economy including appropriate monitoring and accountability in our common interest, and an international environmental court, but it failed to do either. Without legislation, there will be no action.

Polly Higgins' campaign to establish 'Ecocide' as the fifth crime against humanity focuses on the need for enforceable, legally binding mechanisms in national and international law to hold to account perpetrators of long-term severe damage to the environment. As a barrister who fully understands the importance of systems, Polly is a powerful proponent of changing the territory: establishing the fifth crime against humanity will inextricably link our futures to the health of the planet.

When the newly devolved Welsh Assembly came into being in 1999 it had a new and unique duty to promote sustainable development in the exercise of its functions. This was seen as an extremely innovative and exciting duty, representing a new kind of democracy. But there was no legal definition of sustainable development. Although the government has generally used the 'Brundtland' definition, '… development that meets the needs of the present without compromising the ability of future generations to meet their own needs', how do you interpret this to influence all government decisions in Wales?

By 2009, with the publication of 'One Wales One Planet', the Government in Wales was clearer about the 'the Wales we want' which would have certain characteristics. It would:

- live within its environmental limits
- have healthy, biologically diverse and productive ecosystems
- have a resilient and sustainable economy
- have communities which are safe, sustainable, and attractive
- be a fair, just and bilingual nation

To achieve these outcomes, there was a collective commitment from all ministers to use sustainable development as the central organising principle of government which included an explicit commitment to bring down the ecological footprint of Wales to its fair share within the lifetime of a generation.

For the first time, key policy decisions taken in Wales on waste, on carrier bags, on climate change, on retrofitting housing, on sustainability requirements in planning, on introducing Education for Sustainable Development and Global Citizenship into the Welsh curriculum were directly linked to sustainable development and were inherently different from decisions being taken elsewhere in the UK.

My last political act prior to leaving Government in 2011 was to propose that the commitment to put sustainable development at the heart of government should be a key manifesto commitment. I'm delighted that this was accepted and in its manifesto for the last election, the Government party outlined its vision for:

'a sustainable Wales to become a "one planet" nation by putting sustainable development at the heart of government; creating a resilient and sustainable economy that lives within its environmental limits and only using our fair share of the earth's resources to sustain our lifestyles.'

That commitment is now being taken forward. The First

Minister of Wales announced in 2011 that the Government of Wales would:

'legislate to embed sustainable development as the central organising principle in all our actions across government and all public bodies, and to monitor that externally.'

This will be undertaken by a new independent sustainable development body for Wales following the demise of the UK-wide Sustainable Development Commission. 'The Wellbeing of Future Generations Bill' was published in July 2014 and as I write has just commenced its committee cycle.

Like Polly Higgins, I believe that the interrelationship between people and planet is so important, it needs protecting in law. Prior to my introducing the legislation on recycling which has seen Wales come from behind to outperform the rest of the UK, we had voluntary agreements and targets with the local authorities; prior to my introduction of our carrier bag charge, the retailers' voluntary agreements couldn't reduce bag use by 50%; the charge reduced it immediately by 90% and has brought much needed income to the voluntary sector. Some things need legislation, because they are of wide public benefit but will not be achieved by individual action without a legal basis – smoking and seatbelt legislation come to mind.

If sustainability is our best defence, it needs to be championed by politicians and supported and protected by the law. When times are fiscally tough, public services retreat to the delivery of their statutory responsibilities. Making the future more resilient for people and planet seems to me to be at the heart of responsible government at all levels. The Wellbeing of Future Generations Bill must have teeth if it is to enable Wales to develop socially, economically and environmentally just policies for future generations. The Bill will need to create meaningful legal obligations, supported by monitoring and review mechanisms which impose significant consequences for failure. The Bill needs to be at the heart of the democratic process in Wales; the big vision of a sustainable future that helps the Government take decisions that are consistent with its principles.

We won't know what the Bill will look like until it has been through its democratic processes, but assuming its core principles remain unchanged when it becomes an Act in spring 2015, I would expect future governments to be having some very serious discussions about what it means to live within environmental limits – and who knows – perhaps in the future, Wales could use its legal commitment to future generations to be at the forefront of eradicating ecocide.

Jane Davidson is Associate Pro Vice Chancellor for External Engagement and Sustainability and Director of INSPIRE, (Institute for Sustainability Practice, Innovation and Resource Effectiveness) at the University of Wales. INSPIRE won the Guardian award for the best Higher Education sustainability initiative in the UK in 2013. Prior to her role at INSPIRE, Jane was Minister for Environment and Sustainability in Wales from 2007–2011.

"Trees are poems that the Earth writes upon the sky. We fell them down and turn them into paper that we may record our emptiness."

Khalil Gibran (1883-1931) artist, poet and writer

RICHARD OLIVIER

Evolving the New Story: From Cult to Culture

Those alive today have the truly sacred task of evolving the story of who we are, how we live and what we are for – as conscious beings on our planet. For around 6,000 years we have lived in what Riane Eisler calls a dominator culture (from warrior tribes to empire-building nation-states to global corporations), where the contrary human impulse towards partnership has been repressed or assimilated by powerful elites whenever it has re-emerged.

This time it needs to be different. The transition from competition to cooperation is, as evolutionary biologist Elisabet Sahtouris points out, 'a maturation rite of passage process that every organism on the planet learns at some point, if it is to survive and thrive'.

Just as a caterpillar eats the first imaginal cells that signify the prebirth of the butterfly, regarding them as an enemy, many early New Story Tellers over the past 50 years have experienced Old Story Dwellers negating and digesting their best efforts. But as the imaginal cells grow in number, they learn to resonate together, enabling more to survive and cohere to give shape and then life to the emerging new. With the unique combination of awareness and tools we have today, from morphic fields and consciousness-raising to the internet, social media and the Occupy movement, the potential to change a culture – without violent revolution – has never been greater.

Whether, as James Lovelock and others hold, we are doomed to catastrophic climate change, or whether we avoid it is no longer the key question. 'Evolve or die' or 'evolve and die' – either way those of us reading this will not be around to see the result. The questions I hear now are more, 'What is trying to be born through us?' 'How can we live together in a more interconnected way – whatever happens?' Others focus effort on the practical: 'If we have to wait until the old system implodes before "they" will listen, we need alternative ideas and structures in place to turn to, post-collapse.'

In 1978, Thomas Berry wrote his prescient warning: 'We are in trouble just now because we are in between stories. The Old Story… is no longer functioning properly, and we have not yet learned the New Story.'

Actually, today, we do have a new story – if we can connect the dots and facilitate the many individual threads to resonate with greater coherence. When we listen to people from the Global Ecovillage Network, Transition Towns, Forum for the Future, the Centre for Alternative Technology, Schumacher College, the World Future Council, the New Economics Foundation, Rights of Nature, and to other visionaries, project holders, facilitators, ritual guides and Indigenous elders, it is clear that there is an increasing number of exciting, hopeful and practical paths out there. Many combine ancient Earth wisdom with postmodern emergence, some are already proven, and many more are in experimental learning stages.

Yet the vast majority of these are still seen by the mainstream as 'alternative', some version of 'utopian, new age, hippie, green, tree-hugging, anti-nuke, anti-globalisation, ultra-liberal opt-outs and dropouts', and therefore dismissible. Along with the hope, I also hear a deep underlying frustration in many of those involved in what (for the sake of brevity) I will call the New Story Movement (NSM): 'Why is it taking so long?' 'Why isn't what is so obvious to "us" obvious to everyone?' The challenge may have subtly shifted from initial inquiry (sourcing the new) to gaining agency: from the 'what' to the 'how' – which requires the NSM to evolve from 'alternative cult' into essential cultural norm.

Having worked with story for 30 years, I know the energising effect that changing our story can have. But in itself it does not change our world. Separation from an old story is only the first step in a real rite-of-passage transition, which then requires effective initiation, followed by a final stage of cultural integration. The initiatory process gives a felt (and often sacred) experience of the new story – something the initiate can never forget – and the integration provides a culturally accepted role and place in which they can live into the new for real.

Machiavelli warned long ago of the difficulty of initiating a 'new order of things': 'For the reformer has enemies in all those who profit by the old order, and only lukewarm defenders in all those who would profit by the new order. This lukewarmness arises... from the incredulity of mankind, who do not truly believe in anything new until they have had actual experience of it.' Effective transformation moves from story to felt experience and into lived reality. From imaginal cell to chrysalis to butterfly.

While we can certainly use greater coherence and effective simplicity in the emerging story, there is even more crucial work required. We urgently need more experiential delivery systems to give an unforgettable taste of the new to, well, everyone really! But how do these delivery systems operate, and how can they be 'storied' so they do not intimidate those who most need them?

And how can we create enough roles and places so initiates can grow down into the new as a lived reality? Sustainable communities and projects create a landing place for the few, but not (yet) for the many. Eco-entrepreneurs can create new story jobs from the outside AND we need clusters of transformation inside the 'belly of the beast'. I know of global insurers considering making polluting companies uninsurable, lawyers preparing to take class action against corporate environmental damage, and Fortune 100 CEOs convinced the future requires organisational purpose that completely transcends shareholder value. These potential 'stealth agents for change' need help and support too, to land new story innovation within old story structure.

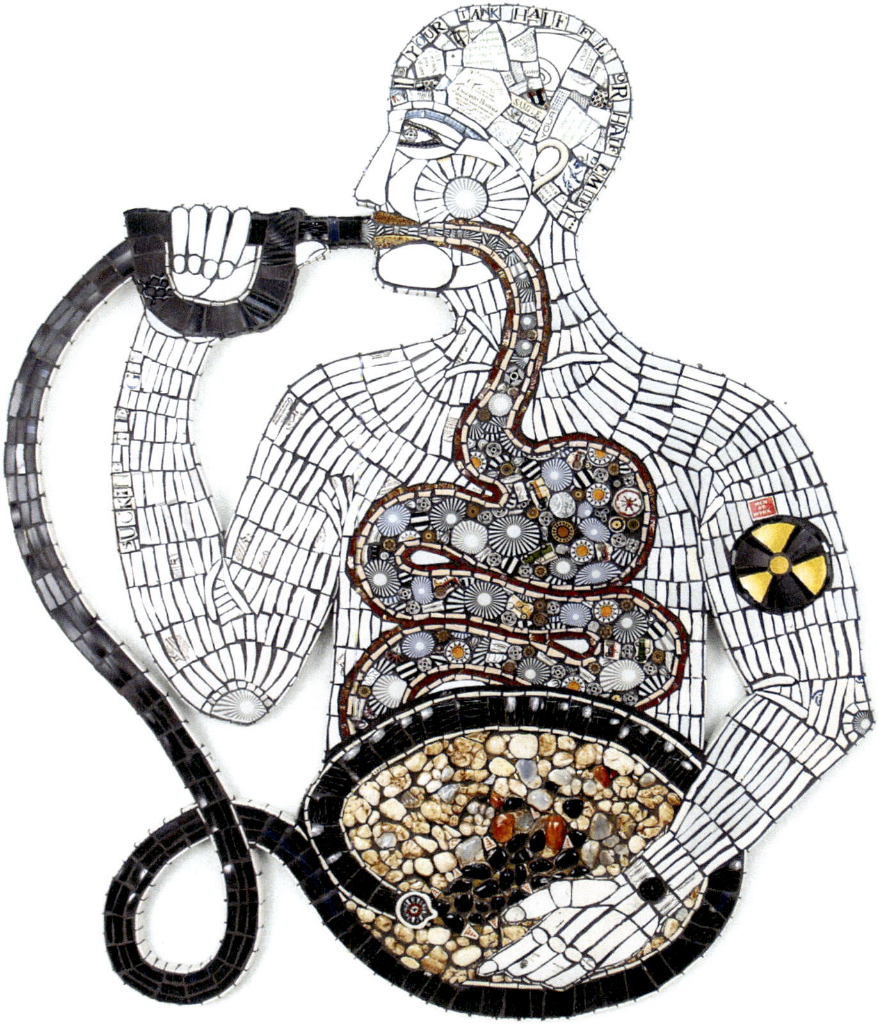

© CLEO MUSSI

Sucking the Gut *reclaimed ceramic mosaic*

Thirty-six years after Thomas Berry published his 'New Story' chapter, where we need to go is clear (enough); how we get there and how we mobilise others before it is too late require serious collaborative inquiry and co-creative practice. Can you help?

Richard Olivier is a leadership development consultant, Artistic Director of Olivier Mythodrama, and an Associate Fellow of Saïd Business School, Oxford, (www.findhorn.org/newstory). This article was first published by Resurgence & Ecologist in 2014.

NICOLA GRAYDON

The White Rhino and the Last of the Wild Places

When last I saw Dr Ian Player speaking in London he brought us all to rapt attention by perfectly imitating the shrill call of the fish eagle. When I interviewed him soon after that at his home on the outskirts of Durban in South Africa two zebra stood between me and his front door – a fitting obstacle for a man who has done so much for wild nature. It was 2006 and his legacy seemed assured.

While Ian Player has achieved many victories for the environment – among them rescuing the spectacular St Lucia wetlands from a mining consortium – his name will always be synonymous for saving the critically endangered white rhino from extinction in the 1960s.

'Operation Rhino' was one of the most successful conservation operations in modern history: the ground-breaking capture and translocation program took a tiny and critically endangered population of just 600 white rhino from a game reserve in Kwa-Zulu Natal and expanded it throughout Africa and the rest of the world. By the time I met him, there were over 17,000 white rhino in nine African countries and nearly 800 in zoos and safari parks around the world. 'We can honestly say that as far as the Southern White Rhino is concerned it is as safe a species as it is possible to be,' he told me at the time.

Then, in 2008, a new slaughter began. After a decade of quiet – with just a dozen or so rhino being taken a year – poaching suddenly started rising again. In 2008, numbers killed leapt to 83; then to 122 in 2009, finally soaring more recently to about 1000 annually. And dozens of game rangers have been shot trying to protect them.

For Ian Player it's a recurring nightmare. A life's work saving a species and, just at the moment when you think you can put your feet up and die happy, the slaughter starts to happen all over again. Only this time it's happening with helicopters, sophisticated tracking devices and semi-automatic weapons.

His distress at this drastic turn of events is palpable. 'The white rhino is a really decent wild animal that has suffered greatly at the hands of man,' he says on the phone from South Africa. 'It is such a docile, innocent creature that even in death has been instrumental in securing wild land. We have to stop the killing. As human beings we have a duty to protect the natural world and the white rhino is an iconic symbol. It's one of the oldest species on our earth. The world has to wake up. We're losing our heritage.'

At 87, Ian Player's mind is sharp as a tack but his body is broken from his days of rhino capture. Darting them with aneasthetic was one thing. It was administering the antidote that was the dangerous part. 'You had to climb onto their head in order to grab an ear to raise a vein and get the needle in. Because it had such a rapid effect one couldn't get off in time so one was flicked off like a fly,' he chuckles. 'I can hardly walk now but it was an honour to have been able to serve the rhino.'

Back in 2008 when the poaching began again, Player was tempted to leave his crusade to younger men but one night he had a dream that a baby rhino came into his room, climbed up onto his bed and laid its head on his shoulder. 'So there it was. The rhino had come to ask for my help so I am quite literally involved up to my neck.'

While Player's name will always be synonymous with this one species, his mission is far broader. He is passionate about the very existence of wilderness. His concern is that once we lose the iconic creatures of the wild – the elephant, the rhino, the lion, the tiger – we will lose the wild itself. He has lived much of his life in wild places and can perfectly imitate dozens of birdcalls and other animal sounds. The wild lives in his blood and he believes that it can be our salvation as a species; that our lives quite literally depend on it.

His relationship with the wild began when he fulfilled a promise he had made to himself as a young soldier on the eve of the final push into the Po Valley in Italy in 1944: if he survived he would canoe from Pietermaritzburg to Durban. When he came back broken by war and without prospects, he endured the mines and other odd jobs until he remembered his pledge. And, in 1950, he embarked on this challenging 120-kilometre journey along the Msundusi and Umgeni Rivers, travelling alone, sleeping on the ground at night and experiencing nature in its most primal form. It would change his life.

'The land of the thousand hills was sparsely populated then so day after day I paddled alone in those deep gorges, sometimes caught in thunder and lightning storms that swept the rivers. I had entered a new world. Like the Zulu warriors who cleanse themselves of the killing they had to perform in battle, I found my healing there in wild nature. Africa had awakened in my soul and set me on a new path.' And so he became a game ranger for the Natal Parks Board and thereafter devoted his life to wilderness.

A couple of years later, in the dark heart of an apartheid South Africa, he found his mentor, Magqubu Ntombela, a black elder ranger who captured his young mind and led him into a profound – and deeply African – relationship with the environment that also came to include an understanding of its role in the psyche of humanity. Ntombela was his 'midwife', Player is fond of saying, who birthed him into Africa after six generations of ancestral presence on the continent.

Ntombela, a descendent of the great Zulu chiefs, Shaka and Dingaan, was illiterate but understood nature in a way that it is difficult for a compartmentalized Western mind to grasp. He read nature like we read books. He sensed the presence of animals and birds in the bush; sniffed the change of weather on the wind. Animals were his 'brothers' and 'sisters' and the natural world was a sacred being that demanded respect and reverence. He died in 1993 but Ian Player never fails to greet the bronze bust of his friend that sits in his hall.

Together they set up wilderness trails around South Africa taking anyone from CEOs to township kids into the veldt. And it was on Ntombela's suggestion that Player set up the first Wilderness Congress sparking a global wilderness consciousness movement. 'Everyone who comes to the wilderness is changed by it,' says Player. 'No one who sleeps on the ground underneath the blaze of southern stars and hears the roar of the lion, the coughing of the leopard, the howl of the hyena, the scream of the elephant and smells the smoke of wild wood burning is ever the same again.'

In some ways, Ian Player is classic 'old school' white African – all discipline and starched khaki trousers – but he also walks to a different drum. He's a longtime Jungian and listens to the messages he receives in his dreams. And, amidst scientists and politicians, hard-bitten activists and safari elites, he's unafraid to talk about the 'spirituality' inherent in the natural world; of how the human 'soul' can be restored by the experience of wilderness and why Africa itself has a unique ability to heal the ills of modern humanity. He has seen too many people transformed on his wilderness trails.

'We don't do anything; the landscape does it for us. We are walking in an ancient landscape where early man walked so it is deeply imprinted on our soul. We evolved here alongside the mega fauna. This is a connection with a very, very ancient, primeval part of ourselves: the interior landscape meets the exterior,' he claps his hands, 'and the two click. I've watched it happen and it is a transformational experience – and a uniquely African one. I've had spiritual experiences in the Sierras in America or the Cairngorms or the Algonquians and the Himalayas but this is a different story. This is why people come to Africa.'

Player does not mean a safari experience with fancy cutlery although he thinks this is a good entry point. He means the wild where you walk, use canoes and animal transport; where you camp around fires and listen to the stories of local people and the sounds of the night. 'Just five days will take you back 50,000 years,' he says, 'and in those few days you can grasp the primary tenet of ecology – that everything is connected to everything else.'

The surge in poaching coincided with a crushing global recession, a rising demand for rhino horn from a burgeoning middle class in the Far East and a proliferation of splinter terror groups in Africa raising funds through the black market trade in ivory and rhino horn. At this rate, the southern white rhino could be extinct by 2022. Its cousins, the northern white and western Black Rhino have both been declared extinct in the last decade.

Ian Player is working on various fronts to ensure their survival: he is involved in plans to establish a population in Australia which has ideal conditions for rhino and he is lobbying various groups to encourage the trade in legal rhino horn. 'We are sitting on tons of rhino horn that have been accumulated through natural mortality which could be sold in a regulated and careful way. Why would one kill or risk being killed if one could buy it quite easily?' And, he argues, the funds raised could go into much needed conservation in game reserves around the country.

Scientists have also advocated farming rhino to harvest their horns – which grow about two pounds bigger per year – at minimal risk to the animals themselves. But experts at WWF and CITIES

(Convention on International Trade in Endangered Species) believe that legalising trade will result in more killing not less. Meanwhile, as the arguments go back and forth, the slaughter continues with two or three rhino killed every single day.

The rhino has always been an iconic animal. At the confluence of the Shashe and Limpopo rivers, a golden rhino was found buried in an 11th century tomb thought to belong to the king of an early Khoi San civilisation known as Mapungubwe. It's a poignant symbol of reverence when the survival of the species is threatened by the fact that its horn is now more expensive than gold.

However, the white rhino has shown enormous resilience and fortitude. It was thought to be extinct as early as 1895 when a hunter accidentally shot two white rhino. The furore of excitement led to the creation of the Umfolozi Game Reserve – the first of its kind in the world – to provide sanctuary where fate would bring Ian Player to ensure their resurgence in the 1960s. 'In protecting the rhino, we will be protecting their habitat,' Player reiterates, 'and in protecting their habitat we preserve the wild nature on which our humanity depends.'

Rhinoceros is derived from the Greek meaning 'nose of horn' and it has always been perceived as a thing of great value. In Europe rhino horn was once sold as unicorn horn and soon, if we are not vigilant and proactive, these gentle horned giants will enter our own mythology along with the wide-open savannahs in which they roamed.

Nicola Graydon is a writer, editor, journalist, and broadcaster who has written for national newspapers, and extensively on environmental issues for The Ecologist Magazine.

MARC BEKOFF

Compassionate Conservation and Rewilding Our Hearts

It's common knowledge that we're losing species and habitats at an unprecedented rate in a geological epoch known as the 'Anthropocene' – the age of humanity. While the term has not been formally recognized as official nomenclature, we know we're deep into a time when humans are devastating numerous species and their homes and we are behaving in the most inhumane and selfish ways.

Simply put, we humans are the cause of such massive and egregious ecocide because as big-brained, big-footed, overproducing, overconsuming, arrogant, and selfish mammals we freely move all over the place recklessly, wantonly, and mindlessly trumping the interests of countless nonhuman animals (animals). Every second of every day we decide who lives and who dies; we are that powerful. Of course, we also do many wonderful things for our magnificent planet and its fascinating inhabitants, but right now, rather than pat ourselves on the back for all the good things we do, we need to take action to right the many wrongs before it's too late for other animals and ourselves.

I see at least two ways out of the environmental and moral muck in which we're mired. The first centres on paying careful attention to the rapidly growing international and interdisciplinary field called 'compassionate conservation', and the second is our choosing to go through a personally transformative process that I call 'rewilding our hearts'. Rewilding our hearts calls for a global paradigm shift, a social revolution, in how we interact with other animals and with other humans.

The goals of compassionate conservation are clearly stated in the mission statement for a recently established Centre for Compassionate Conservation at the University of Technology,

JUDY BARBER

Sydney, and in a book I edited called *Ignoring Nature No More: The Case for Compassionate Conservation* (2013, University of Chicago Press). The mission statement promotes the protection of captive and wild animals as individuals within conservation practice and policy. Finding ways to compassionately and practically share space (coexistence), via trade-offs among different values, is vital if we are to reduce harm to animals.

A simple and morally acceptable approach is to utilize the universal ethic of compassion (and empathy) to alleviate suffering in humans and other animals to resolve issues of land sharing. A compassionate and practical ethic for conservation that focuses on individual well-being, in combination with other values, provides a novel framework of transparency and robust decision-making for conservation that will benefit all stakeholders.

Compassionate conservation stipulates that we need a conservation ethic that prioritises the protection of other animals as individuals: not just as members of populations of species, but valued in their own right. This is important because of what we now know about their cognitive and emotional lives (consciousness and sentience). Because compassionate conservation requires that we must protect animals as individuals, they are not merely objects or metrics who can be traded off for the good of populations, species or biodiversity.

A paradigm shift in our approach to other animals is vital because of what we now know about the cognitive and emotional capacities of other animals and their ability to suffer (sentience). With a guiding principle of 'first do no harm', compassionate conservation offers a bold, virtuous, inclusive, and forward-looking framework that provides a meeting place for different perspectives and agendas to discuss and solve issues of human-animal conflict when sharing space. Peaceful coexistence with other animals and their homes is needed in an increasingly human-dominated world if we are to conserve nature the best we can.

Surely, adhering to the principles of compassionate conservation will go a long way toward reducing the ecocide in which we are now engaged, and for which we all are responsible. My book *Rewilding Our Hearts: Building Pathways of Compassion and Coexistence* (2014, New World Library) lays out the details for a much-needed social movement and change to the pattern of doing things that also can help extricate us from our ecocidal ways and help to maintain our hopes and dreams for a more peaceful world for all beings in very trying times. We live in a world in which 'unwilding' is the norm rather than the exception. If we didn't unwild we wouldn't have to rewild. The concept of rewilding is grounded in the premise that caring is okay. In fact, it is more than okay; it is essential.

Rewilding our hearts is about becoming re-enchanted with nature. It is about nurturing our sense of wonder, being nice, kind, compassionate, empathic, and harnessing our inborn goodness and optimism. In the most basic sense, 'rewilding' means 'to make wilder' or 'to make wild once again.' This means many things, but primarily it means opening our hearts and minds to others. It means thinking of others and allowing their needs and perspectives to influence our own.

The word 'rewilding' became an essential part of talk among conservationists in the late 1990s when two well-known conservation biologists, Michael Soulé and Reed Noss, wrote a now classic paper called 'Rewilding and biodiversity: Complementary goals for continental conservation'. Dave Foreman, director of the Rewilding Institute in Albuquerque, New Mexico, a true visionary, sees rewilding as a conservation strategy based on the three premises of 'healthy ecosystems need large carnivores', 'large carnivores need big, wild roadless areas', and 'most roadless areas are small and thus need to be linked'.

Conservation biologists and others who write about rewilding or work on rewilding projects see it as a large-scale process involving projects of different sizes that go beyond carnivores, such as the ambitious, courageous, and forward-looking Yellowstone to Yukon Conservation Initiative, well known as the Y2Y project. Of course, rewilding goes beyond carnivores, as it must.

The core words associated with large-scale rewilding projects are connection and connectivity, the establishment of links among geographical areas so that animals can roam as freely as possible with few if any disruptions to their movements. For this to happen ecosystems must be connected so that their integrity and wholeness are maintained or re-established. Regardless of scale, ranging from huge areas encompassing a wide variety of habitats that need to be reconnected or that need to be protected to personal interactions with animals and habitats, the need to rewild and reconnect centres on the fact that there has been extensive isolation and fragmentation 'out there' in nature, between ourselves and (M)other nature, and within ourselves.

Many, perhaps most, human animals, are isolated and internally fragmented in their relationships with non-human animals so much that we're alienated from them. We don't connect with other animals, including other humans, because we can't or don't empathise with them. The same goes for our lack of connection with various landscapes. We don't understand they're alive, vibrant, dynamic, magical, and magnificent. Alienation often results in different forms of domination and destruction, but domination is not what it means 'to be human'. Power does not mean license to do whatever we want to do because we can.

Rewilding projects often involve building wildlife bridges and underpasses so that animals can freely move about. These corridors, as they're called, can also be more personalised. I see rewilding our heart as a dynamic process that will not only foster the development of corridors of co-existence and compassion for wild animals but also facilitate the formation of corridors within our bodies that connect our heart and brain.

In turn, these connections, or reconnections, will result in positive feelings that will facilitate heartfelt actions to make the lives of animals better. These are the sorts of processes that will help the new field of compassionate conservation further develop. When I think about what can be done to help others a warm feeling engulfs me and I'm sure it's part of that feeling of being rewilded. To want to help others in need is natural so that glow is to be expected.

Rewilding is an attitude. It's also a guide for action. As a social movement, it needs to be proactive, positive, persistent, patient, peaceful, practical, powerful, and passionate – which I call the eight Ps of rewilding.

Compassion begets compassion and there's actually a synergistic relationship, not a trade-off, when we show compassion for animals and their homes. There are indeed many reasons for hope. There's also compelling evidence that we are born to be good and that we're natural-born optimists. Therein lie many reasons for hope that in the future we will harness our basic goodness and optimism and all work together as a united community. We can look to the animals for inspiration. So, we need to tap into our empathic, compassionate and moral inclinations to make the world a better place for all beings. We need to add a healthy dose of social justice to our world right now.

We can all make more humane and compassionate choices to expand our compassion footprint, and we can all do better. We must all try as hard as we can to keep thinking positively and proactively. Never say never, ever. We can and must keep our hopes and dreams alive.

For some they're already there or nearly so, whereas for others it will take some work to have this happen. Nonetheless, it's inarguable that if we're going to make the world a better place now and for future generations, personal rewilding is central to the process and will entail a major alteration in how we view and live in the world, and how we behave. It's not that hard to expand our compassion footprint and if each of us does something the movement will grow rapidly.

The time is right, the time is now, for an inspirational, revolutionary, and personal social movement that can save us from doom and keep us positive while we pursue our hopes and dreams. Our planet is tired and dying and not as resilient as some claim it to be. When all is said and done, and more is usually said than done, we need a heartfelt revolution in how we think, what we do with what we know, and how we act. We can no longer act as 'Homo denialius', as if nothing is really happening. Rewilding can be a very good guide. The revolution has to come from deep within us and begin at home, in our heart and wherever we live. I want to make the process of rewilding a more personal journey and exploration that centres on bringing other animals and their homes, ecosystems of many different types, back into our heart.

Rewild now – take the leap – it'll feel good to rewild because compassion and empathy are very contagious. Ecocide is suicide. Let's make personal rewilding all the rage. When 'they' (other animals) lose, we all lose. We suffer the indignities to which we subject other animals. We can feel their pain and suffering if we allow ourselves to do so. Compassion begets compassion and violence begets violence. There really is hope if we change our ways. We owe it to ourselves and to future generations who will inherit the world we leave them long after we're gone.

Marc Bekoff is an ecologist, evolutionary biologist, and Professor Emeritus of Ecology and Evolutionary Biology at the University of Colorado, Boulder.

Fighting Ecocide in Nigeria

Environmental negligence must be punished. I firmly believe that businesses need to be held accountable wherever damage to the environment happens because of their negligent practices. As I have seen in Nigeria, oil spills cause major environmental damage and often there is very little compensation or accountability for them. In Nigeria, I chair the Senate Committee on the Environment and Ecology, and I see at first hand how oil spills and pollution damage the environment and those whose lives and livelihoods depend on it.

I have put forward a bill that will impose financial levies on the companies who through negligence or irresponsible business practices cause damage to the environment in Nigeria. The bill is focused on oil spills and associated damage as this is causing the most severe problems for the communities of the Niger Delta. It has not been an easy process to have the bill read before the Nigerian Senate, and as yet, it still has not passed into law. However, by addressing the issue of ecocide in my country, there has been a wider debate among environmentalists about the responsibilities of large corporations for paying compensation to assist in clearing up the damage caused.

Let's look at this from a financial point of view. A stated aim of the Ecocide Campaign is to stop businesses using environmental damage risk in their business models and impose real fines or actual prison terms for executives responsible. In 2010 BP accrued costs in excess of $7.8 billion for its Deepwater Horizon spill of 200 million gallons of oil into the Gulf of Mexico. In the last 50 years, there has been over 500 million gallons of oil spilt in the Niger Delta. Very little has come forward for these ongoing spills, definitely nothing near what BP paid. This can be put down to the lack of global attention and laws to impose fines.

If the proposed bill becomes legislation in Nigeria, then the financial compensation that the big businesses will have to pay will make it uneconomical to merely put the environment into risk categories in business plans. Responsible business practices that have the environment as a key factor will become a business norm.

Aside from the work with the Senate Committee, I am part of the Global Legislators Organization (GLOBE International) and World Summit of Legislators. As a group of environmentally minded legislators, our aim is to promote laws that work towards protecting our environment. Through the work with GLOBE, it has been found that ecocide is also a consequence of the unsustainable use of natural resources. Although exploiting natural resources can result in a country's short-term increase in GDP, in the long term it actually becomes poorer. GLOBE and other legislators worldwide can play a central role in preventing ecocide by making sure the value of natural resources is incorporated into national accounts, making it harder for countries to make short-term economic gains at the cost to the environment.

Making governments see how longer-term budgets will benefit from taking stock of natural resources may be a wiser way of getting these countries to take greater responsibility for protecting against ecocide. I am not alone in pushing forward these bills, and Nigeria is not the only country affected. For example, the EU has many countries that could benefit from the attention paid by this high profile campaign.

GLOBE is doing what it can to shape the international laws and eventually these will change. But we first need to make each country see that there needs to be change, which must start one country at a time. Nigeria, with its long history of ecocide in the Niger Delta at the hands of an unaccountable oil industry, is just the country to make that first move.

Dr Bukola Saraki is a member of the Nigerian Senate, the Global Legislators Organization (GLOBE International), and World Summit of Legislators.

ANDREW SIMMS

Cancel the Apocalypse

We are hypnotised by the possibility of life on other planets yet seemingly oblivious to its destruction on our own. If they found on Mars a single blade of grass there would be ecstasy at mission control. Visions of humanity spreading out across the cosmos would fill the news. And every time the discovery of yet another Earth-like planet is reported, it fuels fantasies of relocation. Paradoxically, the obsession with finding life on other, potentially habitable planets somehow excuses or blinds us to the trashing of this one.

From the space tourism entrepreneur Richard Branson to physicist Stephen Hawking there's a fascination with the possibility of escape that seems to relieve the pressure to look after our own, extraordinary planetary home, as if we can readily relocate if we scorch it.

Trembling with anticipation at the prospect of finding a single microbe in outer space, under our feet we're wilfully executing a mass extinction event. For example, once a fashionable cause, threats to our forests, cradles to the diversity of life, have been largely forgotten. But this century we've been losing them at the astonishing rate of 50 football pitches per minute. That's an area the size of Greenland since the turn of the Millennium.

All attempts to reconcile the industrial scale exploitation of the biosphere with staying the right side of key environmental thresholds are failing. Forest certification schemes, for example, have done nothing to slow their degradation. Why do we treat the abundance of life on our doorstep with such disrespect, when it throws up glories like the Namibian fog basking beetle, which taught us how to build greenhouses in the desert? Or the bark beetle, which can detect a forest fire more than 10km away and is showing how to make better fire alarms.

When we lose forests we lose a lot more than that. We also say goodbye to the rich cultural diversity which is intrinsically linked to them. Languages, for example, are being lost in lock-step with disappearing species. Declines in both of 30% since 1970 have been recorded. Around half of all languages are thought to be under threat. It is worth spelling out that 'ecocide' inevitably means the death of cultures as well as life-supporting ecosystems within the biosphere.

River otters, lichen on trees and coral in oceans are not just beautiful to look at, they tell us something important about the environment around them. The return of otters to a river can point to water becoming cleaner, lichens typically appear when the air is clear and free of pollution, while corals – the large animal group known gloriously as cnidarians – bleaching and dying can be a sign of oceans warming. Collectively such organisms are known as 'indicator species' because they tell us when an equilibrium shifts or a natural threshold is crossed.

Limits govern everything – from the speed of light, to our ability to absorb oxygen or withstand heat. The art of operating within the tolerance thresholds of the material world is what keeps roofs above our heads and bridges standing. Yet, we blithely disregard this at the level of the whole economy. When Daedalus, the Athenian master craftsman flew, it was a triumph of intelligently crafted ambition. The fall of Icarus, his son, however, when he failed to respect the heat tolerances of the wax and feathers keeping him aloft, is a lasting monument to fatal disregard of material boundaries.

The economy is in the grip of an Icarus complex. It touches everything from, appropriately, the debate on aviation expansion, to our increasing dependence on fossil fuels and the historically unprecedented scale and speed of tropical deforestation driven by over-consumption.

At the micro-scale, engineers learn to work within the thresholds of the material world, but at the macro-scale economists do not. Their models allow them to externalise the cost of failure. However, as with pyramid-selling schemes, this only delays and makes larger a later, system-wide collapse. The macro-economics practised by government remains clueless with regard to any theory of optimal scale. Yet, as finance and the sub-prime mortgage market discovered, bigger often doesn't equal better.

A straightforward proposal logically follows: the economy should operate within the biosphere's thresholds, its ability to absorb our waste and replenish its productivity. Good estimates are available for what this means in terms of most of our planetary boundaries from the climate to forests, farming and fisheries.

Once this simple principle is adopted it introduces an urgent and immediate decision tree. If something like a new airport runway, or expansion of fossil fuel extraction is going to take you closer to, or further beyond one of the biosphere's tolerance thresholds – such as potentially runaway climate change, you branch-off and do something else.

You might not think of humanity itself as an indicator species. We have an extraordinary ability to inhabit everywhere from the most polluted inner cities, choking mines and factory sites, to the sweetest meadow and untouched island paradise. We can make camp in harsh sub-zero Arctic conditions and live as nomads in the sweltering desert.

But, look more closely at the fate of particular groups of people, and you can tell an awful lot about what is happening to certain key environments and the planet more generally. From endangered tropical forests in Brazil and Liberia, to contested tracts of fertile land under threat of being 'grabbed' across Asia, people defending the environment and land rights are increasingly under attack and being killed.

Thinking of such environmental defenders as an 'indicator species' would be too technical and reductive. But as people under ever more violent threat, who find themselves on the front line of humanity's transgression of planetary boundaries, they have become bellwethers, those who reveal the existence of a trend.

In the grip of the Icarus complex, competition for access to natural resources is intensifying. Logging and mining concessions and land grabs for industrial scale palm oil plantations pitch powerful vested interests against the livelihoods of communities and the environment. This plays out against a backdrop of the still unquestioned pursuit of economic growth and rising consumption in rich countries, together with extreme global inequality.

Humanity in the meantime is crossing the threshold of several vital ecological life-support functions. As a result, more and more people find themselves like border guards at our planetary boundaries, defending their environment from corporate or state abuse and unsustainable exploitation.

In the decade between 2002 and 2013 there were 908 known killings of people across 35 countries resulting from their work on environmental and land issues. The worst year on record was 2012, but numbers for 2013 are expected to rise due to a time lag in data. These figures, though, are just the visible tip of a larger veiled mountain of harassment and intimidation. Because of the failure of the international system to properly recognise, record and report on the plight of environmental defenders, these known deaths – on a par with the number of journalists killed over the same period as a result of their work – are almost certainly a significant underestimate.

So, all around the world, as well as the other species that move or die in response to a shifting climate or destroyed habitat, an increasing number of individuals and communities operate like guardians, look-outs, watchers, pioneers, messengers on the edge of our planetary boundaries – feeling the brunt of resource competition and providing the human face of the consequences of global overreach. Their example challenges us to accept ecological limits and devise a new economic compact for how we can all survive and prosper by sharing a finite world.

Yet, the killers of environmental defenders enjoy almost complete impunity. Only 10 perpetrators – around one per cent of the overall incidence of known killings – are known to have been tried, convicted and punished between 2002 and 2013. When government officials from around the world gather for climate change talks and struggle toward a paper agreement on progress, the murder and intimidation of ordinary people actually defending the environment and land continues outside the conference halls largely ignored.

With crushing irony, environmental defenders who find themselves in conflict with powerful vested interests get depicted as enemies of development. Yet a model of economic development that undermines planetary life-support systems and kills and intimidates those who would protect them, cannot really be called 'development' at all. As long as human progress in lower income nations is premised on the exploitation of their natural resources to feed relentless over-consumption elsewhere, this problem will remain and worsen. New approaches to development must begin with communities first and foremost being able to manage and benefit, securely and in environmentally resilient ways, from their own natural resources.

In finding the frontline of the struggles of environmental defenders globally, we will be drawing a map of planetary boundaries and, most likely, the scenes of the crime of ecocide. For the sake of our own collective survival, we must then work out how to stay the right side of the lines and protect their defenders.

I was an infant while the Apollo programme was happening and understand the obsession with exploring outer space. But, even sending a single person to the hostile, arid environment of a planet just next door like Mars, would require years of training for a fabulously expensive one-way trip. The question of whether or not there is life 'out there' is often asked. But, from a different view of the cosmos, aren't we ourselves also and already 'out there'? And, we happened to luck-out, evolving on what we would view now, if seeing it for the first time, in comparison to any other known planet, as a breathlessly beautiful, paradise-like Eden.

Perhaps the greatest gift of space exploration is that it enabled us to see ourselves as an island planet, where the greatest wonder is to be found in the world around us, the relationships between living things, and even within ourselves. A single tablespoon of Earth's soil can contain more microorganisms than there are people on the planet.

In Milan Kundera's *The Book of Laughter and Forgetting* there is a scene involving Kundera and his father who, a stroke victim, has difficulty speaking. The father had studied Beethoven's sonatas and their magical variations for years. His barely coherent remarks trigger in Kundera an understanding that the greatest journey is not into the infinity of the external universe, but to 'that other infinity, into the infinite diversity of the interior world lying hidden in all things'. To explore that is more than a lifetime's rich work. Right now, the greater challenge is to offer an irresistible invitation to look differently and afresh at our world, and imagine how we can allow life here to flourish.

PATRICIA OLIVIER

We sense we're living through hard times, and that makes the idea of fleeing to other worlds attractive and, perhaps, leaves us prone to disregard our own. But times have been harder. On a cold dark night when in prison during the apocalyptic upheaval in Europe of 1917, the writer and radical Rosa Luxemburg found her spirits lifted, despite her perilous situation, by an awareness of the strangeness and beauty of the force of life. Her heart, 'beats with an inconceivable, unknown inner joy'. The secret', she decides, is 'nothing but life itself', and even in the sound of sentries' heels grinding in gravel outside, 'there is the small, lovely song of life – if one knows how to hear it'.

A couple of years ago I saw for the first time at dusk a field of fireflies. They were all around me, pulsing, drifting, lighting-up the darkening landscape. I thought of Luxemburg's song of life, and of the millions of people around the world who, rather than dreaming of escape, don't accept the world as it is, but use their life's pulsing energy to protect and improve it.

Andrew Simms is the author of several books including 'Cancel the Apocalypse', 'Ecological Debt', 'The New Economics', and 'Tescopoly'. He works for Global Witness, is a Fellow and former policy director of nef (the new economics foundation) and is a co-founder of The Green New Deal Group, and the New Weather Institute.

JULIAN JONES

The Water Proxy: An Empirical Approach to Eradicating Ecocide

The human footprint on our planet has been catastrophic – more like the carnage caused by a vast beast rampaging blindly across our landscapes. However, by looking at the effects of this monster on the water cycle, we may identify some empirical means to resolve this destruction.

'Climate change' represents a more recent recognition of this damage – but the wider social and ecological costs are evident through the thousands of years of human intervention on the biosphere, long pre-dating the use of fossil fuels and agrochemicals. Our basic needs – energy, food and water (all exploited unsustainably) – are now seen only by their scarcity across vast areas of the globe; the accumulated result of human excesses over the generations.

Consequently, 60% of the land surface of our normally beautiful blue green planet is now scarred and desertified; much still being so by ongoing human activity. It need not be like this. It could be made verdant and sustainably productive once again; if only we better manage land and water to tackle ecocide and reverse wider economic and ecological damage.

Of all components of global ecosystems, the water cycle has arguably suffered the most severe degradation. And, as with all ecocide, much of this degradation is caused by exploitative actions for short-term gains, with the long-term costs ignored, externalised, suppressed or otherwise unaccounted for. Just some of the earliest examples are deforestation, eradication of keystone species that maintain ecosystems, and slash and burn agriculture. It's to our greater cost and detriment that our species' awareness extends no further than the collective 'ends of our noses'. Yet these costs can be quantified empirically.

Exploitation of the planet's resources has had some great benefits for a few, but we have now reached an economic tipping point.

Now, the living standards of the majority in the prosperous Western nations seem to have peaked and are wilting – owing largely to the competitive pressures of globalisation, plus the cumulative effects of these externalised environmental costs.

'Think global, act local' runs the well-known ecological saying; but as EU and US living standards peak, an unpleasant side of local self-interest is now arising, currently focused on immigration pressure. Yet this new politics fails to properly consider that the immigration burdens at home are mainly driven by corporate lobbying and the cumulative consequences of our exploitive actions overseas. These break down the indigenous economies and cultures of the immigrating peoples – just another example of our externalised ecocide returning to us as socio-economic 'blowback'.

A completely free market is simply no longer sustainable, nor ever really should have been, but the planning required here should be based upon ecological determinants. Our planet with its growing population has a limited carrying capacity with restricting ecological factors that require restraint and responsibility. Yet there is little proper corporate or even governmental recognition that we all must live within such finite natural constrictions; which, furthermore, can and should be defined empirically in a wholly non-partisan manner.

This is well evidenced in the UK, where half a century of largely unregulated agrochemical farming practice has so degraded soil carbon (humus), and thus also contaminated water aquifers, that the public now have to bear significantly increased costs for flood insurance and water charges. These are both very specific proxy measures that combine economic factors with ecological ones, brought into focus by soil and water cycle mismanagement. Use of agrochemicals destroys soil water retaining and infiltrating properties; chemicals become concentrated in ground water, while rain water runs off much more quickly.

In both cases of mismanagement, the less well-off suffer. Those forced to live in low cost flood-blighted properties are so often also those unable to afford the inflation-busting charges from water companies, arising from the ever escalating costs of removing agrochemicals from the water supply; yet society as a whole has also to pay to subsidize all this in many different ways. Just one insight into the true non-wealth producing nature of our way of life; unnecessary social and economic complexity without logical rationale.

In less well-off countries, similar effects of ecocide are often terminally catastrophic for those affected. And often just described as the effects of climate change; which grossly over-simplifies the problem, and actually obscures effective action to resolve the direct causes here, or even also the dire issue of atmospheric greenhouse gases.

Myopic governmental policies are often based on flawed and incomplete science, or even just wishful thinking. After more than a decade of Nitrate Vulnerable Zones (NVZs) in the UK, 69% have shown no improvement in groundwater nitrate levels, with 31% getting worse – and apparently the government ministry involved has no idea why.

Loss of soil carbon has only recently been recognised as a key issue in 'developed' nations – but has long been an implicit consideration in traditional agriculture, from the indigenous Terra Preta of pre-Columbian Amazonia to the traditional European methods still maintained by Biodynamic practices. Such 'Carbon Farming' is now growing in popularity with fresh thinking contributed by a range of other techniques

(Permaculture, Mob Grazing, Nature Farming/Effective Microorganisms etc).

Holistic farming attempts to consider the whole ecological cycle in its practices, protecting the soil and thus also protecting the water cycle. The holistic consideration also extends to within these practices and their implementation – so different from the prescriptive agrochemical methods that can only maintain an illusion of greater productivity either by way of hefty subsidies, or by implicitly hidden subsidising of the presently unaccounted for ecological consequences.

By maintaining or increasing soil carbon, not only the causes but also effects of climate change are moderated. The major processes that enable this are microbial and very sensitive. A combination of management techniques are required to achieve this – the right microbes must be present and encouraged to sequestrate atmospheric CO_2, producing humus and water via the Calvin Cycle.

A variety of criteria are involved – the correct nutrients (compost or other biological fertilisers); the correct plant cultivars that can host the appropriate microbial activity; the correct cultivation or grazing practices. All are only possible by largely avoiding agrochemicals; and therein is the obstacle – the vast inertia of corporate lobbying which prevents governmental support of such non-ecocidal agriculture, or even sound empirical science.

Avoidance by governmental regulation of even such simple metrics as building soil carbon in our farmland is a shocking deficiency in our struggle with climate change, quite apart from protecting the public interest and spending but it is for obvious reasons of vested interests and corruption.

Most people are uninterested in and disengaged with these issues, yet often still complain about the circumstances they find themselves in. Inept politicians, either ignorant or corrupted, are not just allowing but often actually promoting all this; yet they are now suffering at the ballot box. The wider public are still mostly unaware of the phony science (and worse) that underpins their lifestyle, yet voters are now suspicious that things are not as they should be. Correctly so, as the now degraded economic and ecological systems in total only create wealth for a few, while impoverishing the majority.

The principle of reciprocity is quite central here; in terms of how we view others – who very often might be suffering the consequences of our demands; this might be in terms of the effects of our purchasing decisions; for apparently cheap food or energy, or any other goods. And also quite literally (certainly in terms of water availability and links with soil carbon), 'reaping the effects of what we have sown'. Ethics and science should be considered together here in resolving ecocide.

Fracking and nuclear power are simply the latest racketeering projects of this continually degrading system of collective irresponsibility; both promoted and implemented on the basis of flawed and incomplete accounting of their true costs, that extend into future generations, and are clearly identifiable by their huge effects on water.

Nuclear power is wholly spurious in its claimed benefits for tackling global warming; just another concentrated thermal energy source that warms vast quantities of water around its environs, and uranium mining causing a huge legacy of acidic and radioactive water contamination in many areas. It's much the same for other hydrocarbon energy sources – coal, gas and oil.

Similarly, fracking is another demand on limited water availability, also then dosed with toxic chemicals. The huge intelligence and defence-industry costs of meeting our demands for these energy supplies, petrochemicals and minerals are never accounted for in the true comparative costs against renewable energy sources; quite apart from additional costs in human lives, liberties, and well-being.

The social, economic and ecological Beast that we have created can only be tamed by a global agreement and legislation to end all this ecocide. Defining what is – or is not, ecocidal is an important part of this process. The measures to control ecocide might best be determined by the effects of any activity or undertaking on the water cycle. These can all be clearly and empirically defined in terms of eco-toxicity, soil carbon and water availability benefits, thermal effects, biodiversity, and wider social gains. This would set a new course for humanity, of abundance and harmony with each other and our environment.

Julian Jones is a water expert providing technical support for Water21. www.Water21.org.uk

KATE DAVIES

People and Pollution: The Consequences of Ecocide on Human Health and Well-being

Cultural historian and eco-theologian Thomas Berry once remarked that you can't have healthy human beings on a sick planet. Today, there is mounting evidence he was right. Ecocide, pollution and other environmental damage have now been linked with more than two hundred health problems and nearly one-quarter of all human disease, including almost half of all asthma, about one-fifth of all cancers, about one-sixth of all cardiovascular disease and one-twentieth of all birth defects. Tragically, the proportion is even higher for children – about one-third.

Environmental hazards and toxic chemicals are responsible for more than eight per cent of the total number of deaths worldwide – about five million people a year. More than the combined deaths from HIV/AIDS, tuberculosis and road traffic accidents, this heavy burden represents an enormous loss of human potential and productivity, as well as untold pain and suffering. What's even worse is that much of it could be prevented.

Environmentally related diseases and disabilities are also a huge drain on the economy. Whether it's the costs of medical and nursing care, lost productivity, premature deaths, or additional health and social services, the bill quickly adds up. For example, in the US, the health costs of air pollution are estimated to be about $53 billion a year and the costs of children's environmental health problems are at least $76.6 billion a year.

The high rates of environmentally related diseases and disabilities and their economic costs should not be surprising because we are all exposed to dangerous pollutants every day of our lives. We cannot escape the toxic environment in which we live. There are about 80,000 chemicals in use and about 1,000 new ones are added each year. Many end up in the environment as polluters dump millions of pounds there 24/7. Environmental

FRANCES MARSH

contaminants are present in the air we breathe, the water we drink and the food we eat.

Virtually everyone alive has residues in their bodies – you, me, our children and grandchildren, our neighbours and friends, and people who live on the other side of the planet who we will never know. Present in our hair, blood, fat, bones, teeth and other tissues, they provide incontrovertible evidence of involuntary human exposure. Unbelievably, only a few have been adequately tested for safety. Whether we like it or not, we are all part of a massive, unprecedented and uncontrolled scientific experiment, and the early results are extremely troubling.

But it isn't only our health that's affected. The damage we do to the environment comes back to haunt us in other ways too.

In 1992, I was living in Canada when overfishing wiped out the North Atlantic cod fishery. The industry that had sustained the island of Newfoundland and many mainland communities for five hundred years disappeared virtually overnight. The socio-economic consequences were enormous. Over 35,000 fishermen and plant workers from over four hundred coastal communities suddenly lost their jobs and a $500 million a year industry vanished. Many people became dependent on hastily assembled government welfare programmes, as they lost the only source of income they had known for generations. The demise of the North Atlantic cod fishery destroyed a way of life and led to a mass emigration of young people and families from Newfoundland that devastated many towns and villages. Sadly, the fishery has never recovered and remains closed to this day.

This example and many others like it, including the US Dust Bowl in the 1930s, the destruction of the Amazon rainforest, and the virtual disappearance of the Aral Sea in central Asia, reveal that environmental damage is never just environmental damage. It always affects communities and their health, economies and often, entire societies. The truth is that when we harm the environment, we harm ourselves. Even scientists who usually focus on only a small piece of the puzzle are realizing this basic truth and warning that the emerging environmental crisis will have cataclysmic impacts on humankind.

It is true that some societies have endured horrendous environmental catastrophes and survived. For instance, in the mid-1300s, the Plague wiped out somewhere between 30 and 50 per cent of Europe's population but, despite this appalling loss of life, the Renaissance took root and blossomed. On the other hand, many societies have completely collapsed. Examples in this category include the people of Easter Island and the Mayan culture, who over-exploited their natural resources, and the Norse of Greenland, who failed to adapt to an increasingly harsh climate and destroyed their surroundings.

But what's happening now is different. This isn't about a single society or culture. It's about a global crisis that affects every man, woman and child, as well as countless other living beings and future generations. Moreover, we know that this one is caused by humans. We know we are to blame. Unlike earlier disasters, this one can't be blamed on vengeful gods, natural forces or ignorance.

The spectre of human-caused, global ecocide first emerged in the mid-twentieth century with the development of nuclear weapons – weapons so powerful they could easily destroy the entire human race and most other species. The prospect of a terminal disaster has hung over us ever since. Like the sword of Damocles, it is an ever-present reminder of the human ability to annihilate life. As a child growing up in the 1960s, I was terrified of nuclear war. It seemed inevitable that I would die, or even worse that I would survive and that everyone and everything I loved would be destroyed.

Then as a teenager, I read Rachel Carson's book *Silent Spring* and my terror was compounded by fears about pollution and toxic chemicals. I was not alone. Many shared my concerns and gave voice to them in the environmental movement of the time. But more than forty years later, little has changed. Humankind still faces the threat of global ecocide. In fact, the vast majority of people alive – everyone under about seventy years of age – has lived with this terrifying possibility all their lives.

Joanna Macy calls this realisation 'the pivotal psychological reality of our time'. She says 'every generation throughout history lived with the tacit certainty that there would be generations to follow. Each assumed, without questioning, that its children and children's children would walk the same Earth, under the same sky. Hardships, failures, and personal death were encompassed in that vaster assurance of continuity. That certainty is now lost to us, whatever our politics. That loss, unmeasured and immeasurable, is the pivotal psychological reality of our time.'

The psychological reality of global ecocide is huge, not only because it is so scary but also because everyone can experience fearful feelings about it. In fact, surveys and studies confirm that most people are alarmed about what's happening to the environment. Internationally, public opinion polls consistently show that between half and three-quarters of the respondents are very worried about issues such as air and water pollution.

In China, about eighty per cent are deeply concerned about the country's environmental problems. In Australia, a survey of children reported that over half are nervous about not having enough water, almost half are anxious about climate change and just under half are troubled about air and water pollution. In the US, a 2012 study forecast that two hundred million Americans will experience serious psychological impacts from climate disruption and that in many instances this distress will be severe.

So what's to be done? It's clear that ecocide is already harming our physical and psychological health, our communities and the economy. And predictions for the future are grim. Given this reality, how can we avert catastrophe? Traditional approaches to problem solving don't appear to be up to the job. Although scientific, technological and policy solutions have been extraordinarily effective in the past, they now seem puny in comparison with the magnitude of the problems we face. Although these types of solutions are necessary, they aren't sufficient because they don't deal with the roots of the crisis.

Together with a growing number of environmentalists, anthropologists and sociologists, I believe that the fundamental cause of the global ecocidal crisis is the anthropocentric belief that human beings are separate from and superior to all other forms of life. Originating in ancient Greece, spread by Judeo-Christian religions and fostered by the Scientific and Industrial Revolutions, this belief has been used to justify the exploitation of the Earth's resources and the pollution of its air, water and land.

But this belief is a fallacy and the consequences of ecocide on human health and well-being prove it. In fact, the damage to human health and well-being reveal the opposite is true – that we are completely dependent on other species and the Earth itself. As Chief Seattle allegedly said 'All things are connected. Whatever befalls the Earth befalls the sons of the Earth. Man did not weave the web of life; he is merely a strand in it. Whatever he does to the web, he does to himself.' Only when we understand this truth and act accordingly will we be able to stop ecocide.

This may sound like a tall order, and it is. But the emerging environmental health movement is helping to remind us about this basic fact of life. This movement was born in 1978 when a young, stay-at-home mom called Lois Gibbs first raised the alarm about the health effects of toxic chemicals leaking from an abandoned waste site in Love Canal, New York. Since then, it has spread across the US and around the world. By drawing attention to the effects of pollution on human health and well-being, the environmental health movement has achieved many victories.

In the late 1990s and early 2000s, European environmental health groups successfully advocated stronger regulations for toxic substances, resulting in the 2007 adoption of REACH (the

Registration, Evaluation, Authorisation and Restriction of Chemicals) throughout the European Union. In 1999, Canadian activists secured passage of the landmark Canadian Environmental Protection Act that called for the virtual elimination of persistent bio-accumulative toxic chemicals. In the US, environmental health groups succeeded in passing 71 chemical safety laws in 18 states between 2003 and 2011, many on a bipartisan basis. In 2014, 33 states are considering about 170 bills and several have already passed.

But this vibrant social movement is doing more than passing legislation. It is also disrupting the anthropocentric belief that human beings are separate from and superior to the Earth and all other species. In fact, the more the environmental health movement highlights environmental health problems, the more it calls attention to the fallacy of anthropocentrism and to the awareness that our health and well-being are completely dependent on the health of the planet. And the movement's ability to do this offers us hope.

This brings me to my final point – there is hope for the future, despite the mounting toll of disease, disability, death and destruction. Maybe we won't stop ecocide in our lifetimes, but that doesn't mean we shouldn't try. Indeed, the future of life on Earth depends on us trying. But our hope should not depend on the expectation that we will succeed. It should not be contingent on achieving any particular goal or outcome because hope based on the anticipation of success is always accompanied by the fear of failure.

And if we do fail, we'll end up disappointed, frustrated, resentful and angry. Rather, our hope for the future should rely on a deep inner conviction that we must take action because we care and because it is the appropriate thing to do. As Vaclav Havel said,

'Hope is… an orientation of the spirit… an ability to work for something because it is good, not just because it stands a chance to succeed.'

This type of hope is not based on the anticipated consequences of our actions or on changes in the external world. It is innate and intrinsic to humankind and to life itself. It is trees scattering millions of seeds even though none may germinate, and it is salmon returning to their natal rivers and streams to spawn even though they will die. It is the mother who cares for her child, even if he has a potentially fatal disease, and it is the environmental activist who works on behalf of the Earth, even as it is being destroyed.

Indeed, the more dire the situation, the more we are called to live from this type of inner hope because it holds fast to goodness and is motivated by love and a sense of responsibility towards each other, the Earth, other species, and future generations. It is life's longing for itself. If you ask environmental activists what motivates them, they will almost invariably say things like 'I care too much to stand by and do nothing' and 'I have no choice, what else would I do?' This is intrinsic hope and it is my hope for the future. As poet Adrienne Rich wrote:

'My heart is moved by all I cannot save:
So much has been destroyed
I have to cast my lot with those
who age after age, perversely,
with no extraordinary power,
reconstitute the world.'

Kate Davies is a writer and lecturer.

Waste Migrations

India has its rag-pickers; Bangladesh its ship-breakers. In Niger's dusty mining towns, slum dwellers recover radioactive scrap metals from uranium mines to build homes and fashion cooking utensils. Around the world, the poor are combing landfills in search of precious materials that escape official waste management circuits. Unable to participate themselves in the consumer economy where the interval from shop to trash is ever diminishing, they nonetheless peck away at the toxic legacy it leaves behind.

But one needn't cross the globe to see these human scavengers in action. Thousands of Roma live in shantytowns of Paris, tucked away in dark corners of the City of Light – beneath motorways and in vacant lots. In scrap yard settings and under threat of police raids and expulsion, they burn electric wires and take apart white goods. Some say it's the quality of the trash that lures them here and keeps them coming back.

The Roma are the most disliked immigrants in France, according to a recent study by the French Commission on Human Rights. Nearly four French out of five see them as beggars and thieves. Some Roma undeniably resort to this. But dare penetrate into one of dozens of encampments scattered around the periphery of the French capital and a different kind of story emerges. In makeshift enclaves, shacks of discarded planks and plastic tarps stand teetering along muddy alleys, strewn with litter.

Without running water, sanitation or electricity, it requires a certain kind of bustle to get through the day and the camps are a clamour of activity. Women with colourful headscarves cook giant stews outdoors from open stoves carved out of metal drums. Old men in dishevelled suits and battered hats wander off with shopping trolleys presumably in search of discarded treasures. All around, gutted machinery, rotting mattresses, empty water bottles and great nests of tangled cables pile up, providing habitat for sizable rats.

Over time, the trash spreads into the surrounding fields creating wastelands that delineate the perimeter of the settlements. Thick clouds of black smoke rise from giant bonfires in the distance, where electric cables and car batteries are being burned down to their elements. On a grim winter's day, these scenes resemble what science fiction might portray as the end of the world. A place where a handful of survivors survey the remains of a civilisation recently vanished – sifting through the rubble to salvage what's needed to get through the day.

But look beyond the misery, and there's a faint scent of disorderly industry here too – in a very literal sense, of resourcefulness. Many Roma get by scouring the streets of the capital for anything useful that might be used in the camps, or otherwise reduced to their constituent elements for resale. With the most basic of tools – hammers, chisels, fire – they participate in a vital transformation process from which precious resources are reclaimed and flushed back into the economy.

On my visits to the Roma camps, during a particularly harsh crackdown by the French government, I saw gorgeous, dark-eyed babies learning to crawl in the mud. One girl told me she was home from school looking after her little brother while her mother was at the factory. In a different world, she might have been someone I too would have entrusted with my own child. Bright, poised, self-reliant – she looked barely eight years old – but had cultivated the authority of a matriarch.

The sights of children living in squalor were heartbreaking. But what struck me most was not the display of poverty. It was the legacy of spoiled abundance. Despite a relatively efficient municipal waste management program, a city like Paris generates enough residual trash for an entire community to subsist on, and the sight of people rooting through supermarket and municipal waste bins has become commonplace in the capital.

Unlike the traditional market forces – labour, resources – that long stimulated the migration of people in search for a better life, the more recent presence of Roma gypsies in many of Europe's wealthy capitals can perhaps be said to have been spurred by an excess of trash. Of course, this is an oversimplification, and the question of Roma integration within Europe is far more complex. But the message is this. The destitute near and far need never starve for the magnitude of waste generated by modern consumer societies.

In some cases – such as that of the Roma – the remains of our throw-away economy attract a category of informal 'eco-workers' much disdained by average citizens. Put otherwise, there is an import of 'human resources' to affluent regions. In other cases, our e-waste is exported – often illegally – to vast dump yards in the developing world, to countries like China, India and Ghana. Greenpeace estimates that in Delhi alone, about 25,000 people toil in scrap yard settings, handling tens of thousands tonnes of defunct electronic goods each year.

According to the Basel Action Network, about 80% of e-waste collected for recycling in the USA is exported in this way, while more than half of the electronic waste stream in Europe simply goes unaccounted for. The volumes of waste generated by our de-facto industrial model is thus spurring the movement of people and obsolete goods around the globe on a massive scale.

These movements represent the tail end of material flows through the global economy – materials whose inherent value do not cease to exist simply because they're embedded in products that we no longer want, or that no longer work – often by design. The average mobile phone has a lifespan of less than 2 years in developed countries and contains some 40 elements from the periodic table – including indium, one of several rare metals believed to be quickly running out.

Trapped in billions of discarded mobile phones and electronic devices, copper is another metal whose known reserves at the source pose concern. Estimates of exploitable copper reserves differ significantly, but the differences appear negligible when one considers how dependent we've become on this malleable element for everything from power cables to water pipes. At current production levels and conservative growth rates in demand, new copper production is expected to fizz out over the next 20 to 60 years.

This doesn't mean that, over the next few decades, all copper will have been extracted from the Earth's crust. It means instead that additional copper exists only in theory. It either hasn't been found yet, or when it has, it may be present in such diluted form that it just won't be worth the effort and cost to dig it up. For mining is itself a resource-intensive industry that leaves its own trail of waste and pollutants, often damaging local ecologies and contaminating water supplies. Final consumer products contain only a minute fraction of the resources that went into producing them. Look for the rest, upstream – in mines, factories and waterways.

Many of our planet's finite resources are experiencing a similar fate to copper and indium as they're sifted through our economy at an incredible rate. They're bottoming out. Colossal efforts are put into locating and extracting them, only to find them – a few years later – abandoned in landfills, reduced to ashes in incinerators, sequestered in the most improbable of places

– from the peaks of Everest to the bottom of the Arctic Ocean where bottles, plastic bags and other litter were recently discovered by scientists.

Only in the best of cases are they recycled into hybrid materials of lesser quality in official recycling centres that can more aptly – than the Roma – deal with the toxic elements often contained therein. Of the 50 million metric tonnes of e-waste generated each year around the world however, only about a fifth is recycled.

Great advances have been made over the past century, bringing material comfort, longer life expectancies and simply incredible technologies and devices. With more that 80% of products consumed by only 20% of the world's population however, many people around the globe will only ever collide with our modern riches along assembly lines, in mine shafts or dump sites.

Even if we are of the mind that our planet and the majority of its inhabitants exist only in service of our supply chain, that nature has little intrinsic value over and above the raw materials it delivers, there is reason for concern. In simple accounting terms, the books show that production inputs have been vastly depleted, calling into question the entire business model. How will we keep feeding the factories? If the global economy had but one CEO, surely he'd be investigating this question.

He'd no doubt find inspiration in the 'Cradle to Cradle' doctrine – a closed-loop approach to design that would see finite resources shape-shifted as needed in perpetuity. He'd perhaps consider that as we enter an age of resource scarcity, any form of planned obsolescence as an impetus for continued economic growth is no longer tenable: we were once cunning enough to create products that could reliably stop working on schedule; we must now be wise enough to build for longevity.

Finally, he might see that any virgin mineral extracted from the earth's crust today is far too precious to ever be let out of one's sight. This might give rise to innovative new business models that simply reshuffle organisational functions along new lines: parts of the budget dedicated to sourcing and procurement might go into recycling. Parts of marketing would go into after-sales service; lobbying into R&D.

We already have plenty to work with – it's a matter of doing things radically differently. In the meantime, the Roma may be onto something. The semi-organised wastelands in which they attempt to eke out a living may one day become the kinds of places where industry must look to, to sustain production – the mines of tomorrow.

Carolyn Lebel is a journalist and consultant specialising in food, water, and the environment.

It's the Ecology, Stupid

To some eyes the high mountain shrub-lands that cover the Andean slopes above the Colombian capital Bogotá look like an unproductive wasteland, and indeed that is the meaning of the word *páramo* first used by Spanish Conquisadors to describe this wild and remote place. For any naturalist, however, this high land, with its amazing wildlife that includes Spectacled Bears and Andean Condors, is anything but a wasteland. It's a treasure trove.

As I squelch through the wet grasses, breathless with altitude, I'm told by Colombian conservationists just how valuable this landscape actually is. For not only does it harbour endangered wildlife, it helps reduce flooding and purifies the water used by the people and industry in Bogotá, and it does these jobs much cheaper than concrete engineered solutions would cost.

The fact that wild areas like this are being appreciated for the economically valuable services they provide marks an important new departure. How best to keep those services going is a question that is rising in prominence, and fast.

For example, as countries and companies invest billions in the renewable energy technologies needed to cut carbon dioxide emissions from fossil fuels, one study estimates that the value of the carbon capture services that could be maintained through halving the deforestation rate by 2030 are in the order of US $3.7 trillion. And the wildlife in the same forests has huge value as well, seen for instance in the way about 50 per cent of the United States' annual US $640 billion pharmaceutical market is based on the genetic diversity of wild species, many of which were first found in forests. Seeing the value of the trees in the wood and fibre they supply is evidently just one small part of a far bigger picture.

The vast genetic powerhouse found in the forests and other natural systems not only brings economic benefits in carbon

capture and new drugs, it is also the basis of all of our agriculture (and therefore food security) and a source of inspiration for solutions to challenges faced in (among other fields) engineering, construction and energy.

Termites have mastered low energy ventilation systems that maintain near constant temperatures in their mounds without, of course, power-hungry air-conditioning or heating. The boxfish has inspired a car body design that is stronger but which uses less steel than conventional design. A species of snake that lives in South Australia is being studied because it has found a method to very effectively collect solar heat in a cool climate. The means by which geckos walk on vertical walls has been copied in new adhesives. This application of survival solutions that have evolved among wild species to improve conditions in the human world is called bio-mimicry, and it holds multi-trillion dollar potential – if only the species upon which it is based continue to exist.

The value of wildlife is not only seen in how genetic diversity can be harnessed in ways that present economic opportunities, the relationships that have evolved between different species also provide essential and highly valuable benefits.

For example, and perhaps surprisingly, wildlife helps limit the spread of disease. The cost associated with the loss of India's vultures presents a case in point. These birds were inadvertently wiped out by residues of a veterinary drug left in the dead bodies of cattle and buffalo. The drug, which was administered to sick cattle by vets, proved lethal to the birds, even at very low doses. During the early 1990s the vulture population plummeted from about 40 million birds to just a few tens of thousands – in other words they went virtually extinct. When the birds were gone, the 12 million tonnes or so of rotting meat that they were hitherto between them eating each year became food for something else.

The main beneficiaries of this nutritional windfall were wild dogs. Their number rocketed by about 7 million animals. More dogs meant more dog bites, and that in turn led to more rabies infections, and about 50,000 more dead people than would otherwise have been the case had the vultures still been there. It is estimated that between 1993 and 2006 the costs arising from public health and other consequences arising from the loss of vultures were in the order of US $34 billion.

Wildlife also helps to control pests. One study estimated that the annual pest-control value provided by insectivorous birds in a Jamaican coffee plantation was US $310 per hectare, while the annual per hectare value added from birds controlling pests in timber-producing forests has been put at US $1500. Great tits predating caterpillars in a Dutch orchard were found to improve the apple harvest by 50 per cent.

The services provided by animals, such as bees, doing the pollination work that underpins about one trillion dollars-worth of agricultural sales annually has been valued at US $190 billion per year. The annual spring scene in parts of south-western China of fruit farmers climbing trees with feather dusters to move pollen between blossoms says a great deal about the consequences of over-using pesticides, to the point where even the beneficial and economically essential insects are killed.

Healthy marine ecosystems are generating massive economic benefit too. The GDP value derived from marine fish stocks and the industries associated with them are about US $274 billion per year – and this could be worth another US $50 billion if the fish were managed more intelligently. And the same photosynthetic plankton that comprise the solar-powered base of marine food webs are also replenishing oxygen in the atmosphere.

At least half of the life-sustaining gas you just sucked in with your last breath was put there by plankton drifting in the sunlit layer at the surface of the seas. Those same numberless trillions of photosynthetic micro-organisms also help to seed rain clouds and each year capture about a third of the carbon dioxide released from the combustion of fossil fuels. The value of these and other ocean-based services have been estimated as worth about US $21 trillion per year (and that is at 1998 values).

Set against this multi-trillion annual economic contribution by Nature (in one famous study from Robert Costanza and his colleagues the services provided by Nature each year were estimated to be worth about double global GDP) is a mounting body of evidence as to the scale of degradation being caused to it.

The loss of natural habitats, over-exploitation of valuable resources, such as fish and timber trees, pollution, acidification of the oceans (caused by rising atmospheric carbon dioxide) and climate change are all taking a toll on the ability of natural systems to function properly, and are leading to a mass extinction of animals and plants at a scale and pace not seen on Earth for tens of millions of years.

When it comes to how much this degradation of Nature is costing, a 2008 study by Trucost estimated that it was then about US $6.6 trillion per year (11 per cent of world GDP) and on present trends will reach US $28 trillion by 2050. By contrast, a study from a group of leading conservationists published in 2012 suggested that to meet global goals that would avert a mass extinction of species would cost around US $76 billion per year – or 0.12 per cent of annual world GDP.

Fortunately, however, some of the fundamental errors that societies have made in their valuation of Nature can be corrected. It is still early days, but progress can be seen in initiatives being taken forward by a growing number of countries, cities and companies, demonstrating through practical action how the economic value of Nature can not only be quantified, but also translated into steps that capture those values in tangible economic benefits.

In those mountains above Bogotá I saw how local and national authorities, The Nature Conservancy and Bavaria (a major beer producer) are cooperating in a project that one day might lead to the protection and restoration of the upland woodlands and shrubby grasslands that help to capture and store water. These vast natural sponges have become highly degraded, mainly by farming. If they could be restored, then considerable economic value might be gained in the fast growing built-up areas below.

This will be seen in reduced flood risk and in enhanced water storage and purification. These benefits can not only be secured with less cost than engineering but also with valuable co-benefits – including the conservation of wild species and the capture of carbon dioxide from the atmosphere in trees and soils.

And at sea effective steps are being taken to rebuild Nature's value. One example is the halibut fishery in the US North Pacific, where a reform programme that cost the equivalent of about 3 per cent of the annual revenue earned by the industry was spent in ways that increased its productivity. Income from catching this valuable species increased from around US $50 million a year to $245 million – an improvement of 390 per cent!

In New Zealand some US $25 million was spent on better fisheries management and the national value of fisheries increased from $1.57 to $2.3 billion – an increase of 46 per cent. Norway spent about $90 million in reforming its fisheries, including putting in place a ban on discarding any fish that had been caught. This helped change fishing practices, stocks recovered, and the value of the annual catch went from $347 to $546 million. The benefits are also reflected in businesses and jobs based on fishing, including boat building and fish processing, being more secure.

These and other examples demonstrate how it is rational (and indeed essential) to see Nature as a supplier of vital services, including as insurance provider, disease controller, waste recycler, water utility, controller of pests, massive carbon capture and storage system and as the ultimate converter of solar energy into food, including fish.

Political leaders, economists, investors and planners have become used to seeing Nature as supplier of resources and dump for waste. We have reached the point now, however, where it is clear that Nature is also a supplier of vital services and our greatest ally in securing human needs indefinitely into the future, and that conclusion is based not only on a great deal of ecological science, but also economics.

Some ecologists see the economic valuation of ecological services as riven with dangers, however, not least through the commodification of the natural world and 'putting a price on Nature'. Far better, some say, to advocate the protection of nature for its own sake and the irreplaceable intrinsic values it has.

I see their point, but disagree. This is not least because the reasons for the continuing decline of Nature are not down to people not seeing its intrinsic values, but more to do with how economic valuations nearly always trump the feelings many of us have toward the natural world. The sad truth is that beauty and irreplaceability rarely beat dollars.

And this is not to say that economic values must replace intrinsic ones. It is for me more a matter of seeing Nature's multiple values – aesthetic, spiritual, intrinsic, scientific and economic all at once. If we can succeed with that then the last barrier to the rational coexistence of people and the rest of the natural world might be achieved. Perpetuating the worldview whereby most of us regard Nature and economy as in inevitable conflict will most likely lead to much of what is left going the same way as the Dodos.

If we are to avoid the impending ecocide that present trends are taking us toward, then one powerful approach must surely be based on showing how the 'growth at any cost' policies being pursued by companies and countries worldwide are in the end self-defeating. Nature is not our enemy but our ultimate ally in achieving human well-being. The sooner that we realize that, the sooner the revolution we need will begin.

Tony Juniper is an environmentalist and author, whose book 'What Has Nature Ever Done For Us?' charts the practical value provided by natural systems in sustaining human welfare. www.tonyjuniper.com

Who Speaks for the Earth?

The earth is dying – being killed by those with large boots and loud voices who stomp across her face pillaging and destroying. As we watch the death of species and inexorably rising temperatures it is easy to slip into the despair which prompted Caroline Lucas to suggest that we may be the first species able to scientifically monitor its own extinction.

We are unique in being a self-conscious animal. When other animals receive indications that they are reaching the limits of their evolutionary niche they respond to these by finding a new niche, or by failing to reproduce, or otherwise by ensuring that their numbers decline. As humans we are too clever for that. We can use our clever technology to keep pushing the boundary outwards, ignoring and filtering out the clear evidence that the ecological safety-limits have been exceeded.

Yet we can also use this self-consciousness and the ingenuity that accompanies it within the human psyche to think our way out of the mess we are in. Taking Gramsci's advice we must find a way to match our pessimism of the intellect with an optimism of the will. We suggest a novel approach to our system of political representation that is an example of the sort of utopian optimism we believe is essential in these dark and threatening times.

We begin with a question: In the age of information and media, where rights are established and defended by advocacy, and where the competent adult individual is the paradigm of a rights-bearer, who speaks on behalf of the earth? The idea that ecocide should become a crime suggests a legalistic approach to advocacy against those who would destroy the natural world. We can see the strong attractions of such an approach, in a world where legalism can appear the only force able to stop the machine. However, we wish to sketch a more 'direct' form of democratic representation for the Earth.

We should not be considered critics of the idea of 'ecocide', as we are impressed by the idea of designating 'ecocide' as an international crime, and are similarly impressed with the new South American constitutions that seek to attribute 'rights' to the Earth. Both moves are forceful and potentially successful modes of defending the Earth.

But in our view it is also necessary to make more radical moves that step outside the prevailing juridico-rational framework – we need ideas that challenge legalism and rights as central to an ecocentric philosophy of life. We want to move further from the liberal individualism model, to suggest the importance of listening to and embracing the Earth's voice. Only by doing so can we produce a true philosophy of life.

We need to listen to the Earth's voice, or rather we need to listen to the voice(s) of her denizens, and think that the way to understand what it means to speak for or listen to the earth is to speak for or listen to life on earth. We are not interested in the earth as a rock, but as a – as the – home for life. So the questions 'Who speaks for the Earth?' or 'How can we actually listen to the Earth?', which seem more extravagant than that asked in the course of Polly Higgins' proposal, are rendered modest by being turned into the question: 'Who speaks for the living beings of the Earth?' What we are suggesting is that someone must, and they must do so by 'listening' to what those beings need and want.

How is such listening possible? It may help us reach our conclusion if we travel by way of the somewhat more established idea that future generations should be represented in our democratic processes. Rupert Read has developed this idea at some length in his proposal for 'guardians for future generations', the merits of which were discussed with Polly

Higgins alongside her law-of-ecocide proposal at an event arranged in 2013 by the Guardian newspaper.

Such 'guardians' should be envisaged as caring for and, indeed, seeking to represent future people. They should sit as an additional House of Parliament above the upper house, (or above the existing EU institutions, in the case of the European legislative process). They would future-proof legislation. Read suggests that the only sound way to pick these special legislators, the guardians, would be by lot – just as juries are picked; and juries, of course, are a vital pillar of democracy.

The details of the proposal are less important than the principle, which is that future generations should also be included in present decision-making. Such a principle was exercised for an experimental period in the Hungarian constitution, through their 'Ombudsman for future generations', but subsequently weakened by the change in Hungary to a less sympathetic government.

Just as we need to include consideration of future generations when making policy we also need to proof our legislative processes against prejudice towards non-human life. We need some kind of 'super-jury' or novel parliamentary institution that is going to be designed explicitly to achieve this requirement. There are a couple of slightly different ways in which this idea could be implemented.

One would be by creating a body of 'guardians for non-human beings', analogous to 'guardians for future people/generations'. It would be a chamber of citizens selected by lot specifically to represent non-human life. They would be expected to operate as a 'jury', removing themselves from their personal and egocentric interests to always prioritise non-human nature's interests.

Another, slightly more evocative way of doing much the same thing would be to create a Parliament of all Beings, an idea with origins in the essay 'Thinking like a Mountain' by Seed and Macy. This would be a chamber where the voices of non-human species with which we share this planet would be heard alongside our own voices. Such a proposal is instantiated in a colourful and imaginative way in Marge Piercy's novel *Woman on the Edge of Time* (1983).

Such an idea is also hinted at by philosopher Mary Midgley who, in her short essay 'Granting Citizenship to Wildernesses', comments on the poor levels of protection that species and habitats have been afforded by the existing system of contract-based economics: 'Even over animals, the legalistic notion of contractual rights works badly. And when we come to such chronic non-litigants as the rain forest and the Antarctic it fails us completely. If duties are essentially contractual, how can we possibly have duties to such entities?' Rather than protection in contract we suggest that such 'chronic non-litigants' are given real human advocates to speak on their behalf.

By creating two new legislative chambers – for future generations, and for non-human animals – we would introduce checks on the rapacious expansionism of human interests at the cost of the ecosystem as a whole. We could give voice to the richness of nature and give all the planets' creatures, and generations as yet unborn, a chance to speak on their own behalf.

This vision of an extended polity could inspire (as well as already being part of) a new democratic revolution. It could be more robust in the tools it offers to counter growthism, materialism, anthropocentrism, and commodification than a law of ecocide or than new 'Earth-centred' constitutional settlements because it brings alive the life that animates our world. We could see and hear it being represented, in all its manifold beauty and diversity, in the present and in the future. In seeking to speak for the Earth, living and breathing human people would have to speak for the future people of the Earth and for the many non-human creatures that share the Earth as home.

The proposal itself, even as a thought-experiment, moves us into a domain more alive and exciting than any law or constitution could ever be – into a space of debate, a space of imagination, a space of representation; a vital space; a space of voice and listening, not of short-circuiting. Entrenched laws short-circuit democracy and the processes of acknowledgement, acceptance and internalisation of values. A politics of resistance to ecocide requires such an inclusive and open-ended democratic impulse in order to be fully alive and fully effective.

Dr Rupert Read is vice-chair of Green House, and author of 'A Political Philosophy for All Beings', and Prof. Molly Scott Cato is Green Party MEP for SouthWest England, whose ideas for an economy based on 'common wealth' can be found in 'The Bioregional Economy' (Routledge, 2012).

References

Midgley, M. (2001), Science and Poetry (London: Routledge).

Piercy, M. (1983), Woman on the Edge of Time, 2010 edn. (Random House).

Read, R. (2012), Guardians for Future Generations (Green House) http://www.greenhousethinktank.org/files/greenhouse/home/Guardians_inside_final.pdf

CHARLES EISENSTEIN

Climate Change: The Bigger Picture

I've noticed some parallels among three defining institutions of our civilisation: money, war, and mainstream religion. All three demand, in one way or another, the sacrifice of the immediate, the human, or the personal in service to an overarching ulterior goal that trumps all. Disciplined by economic exigency, millions of people sacrifice time, energy, family, and what they really care about in pursuit of money. Disciplined by an existential threat, a nation at war turns away from culture, leisure, civil liberties, and everything of no utility to the war effort. Disciplined by the promise of heavenly rewards or hellish punishments, the believer distances themself from unimportant worldly things.

Anyone who is wary of these institutions might also be wary of the standard climate change narrative, which lends itself to the same mentality of sacrifice to an all-important end. If we agree that the survival of humanity is at stake, then any means is justified, and any other cause – say reforming the prisons, housing the homeless, caring for the autistic, rescuing abused animals, or visiting your grandmother – becomes an unjustifiable distraction from the only important thing. Taken to its extreme, it requires

cgi of design IMAGE: © ADJAYE ASSOCIATES

MEMO Project

Mass Extinction Monitoring Observatory, Dorset, UK
Spiralling out of ancient cliffs, an unfolding memorial to all species made extinct in modern times. *www.memoproject.org*

that we harden our hearts to the needs in front of our faces. There is no time to waste! Everything is at stake! It's do or die! How similar to the logic of money and the logic of war.

That climate-change alarm sits so comfortably within our culture's familiar way of thinking, should give us pause. It doesn't mean that climate change isn't dangerous or that humans aren't causing it, but it does suggest that our approach to the problem could be strengthening the psychic and ideological substructure of the system that is devouring the planet. This is especially relevant given the near-universal agreement among activists that efforts to limit carbon emissions have failed miserably.

This failure comes not because the movement is too radical and needs to 'work more closely with business' or embrace the oxymoron of 'sustainable growth'. It is rather that it is not radical enough – not yet willing to challenge key invisible narratives that drive our civilisation. On the contrary, the movement itself embodies them.

One thing that war, money, and religion all offer is the simplification of complex problems. In the case of war, there is an identifiable enemy – the source of all evil – and the solution is simple: to overcome that enemy by any means necessary. In the case of money, it invites the subsumption of a multitude of values into a single standard of value; money becomes the universal means to all good things, and therefore the pursuit of it becomes a universal end in itself – if only we had enough money, all our problems would be solved. In religion too, one thing becomes the key to everything.

Following this template, greenhouse gases are the enemy, and the solution, the way to 'fight climate change' or 'combat global warming' (common phrases both), is to reduce emissions (or increase sequestration). Or to use the money metaphor, CO_2 emissions become the standard of value, a number to minimise, a metric upon which to base policy. This approach also sits comfortably in our culture: it is the epitome of rationality to make decisions by the numbers. To decide something scientifically, you gather data, make projections, and evaluate the likely results according to some metric value. Doing that creates three problems: (1) the unmeasurable and the qualitative is necessarily devalued; (2) the metric applied encodes and perpetuates existing biases and power relationships, which themselves implicate ecocide, and (3) it fosters an illusion of predictability and control that obscures the likelihood of perverse unintended consequences.

To see the problem, consider the Tehri Dam project on India's Bhilangana River, which submerged pristine ecosystems, ancient farms and displaced a hundred thousand villagers. It was touted for its contribution to greenhouse-gas reduction and has been one of many dams to generate carbon trading credits. On a superficial level at least, it attained its measurable objective. But what about the displaced villagers? In the particulars that are measured, their lives improved: each was rehabilitated in housing superior to their ancestral homes in terms of square metres, plumbing, and electrification. However, in terms of the lost traditions, severed social ties, lost memories, lost knowledge, and the uniqueness of each submerged place – in short, in terms of all that could not be measured (problem 1) and all that was considered not worth measuring (problem 2) – human beings and Nature suffered a grievous loss.

As for problem 3, in the long run it is doubtful whether the dam even reduced CO_2 levels: consider that traditional agricultural practices can sequester carbon in the ground, and that the newly urbanised villagers probably soon adopted more carbon-intensive consumer lifestyles. Further, the hydroelectric dam contributes to a trend of industrialisation. Each power plant adds to an infrastructure that is always hungry for more. It doesn't come in place of coal-fired plants; it comes in addition to them.

Similar perverse results have plagued biofuels and other CO_2 reduction strategies. It is tempting to conclude that we are simply using the wrong approach to fight carbon emissions: perhaps instead of financial incentives we should rely on regulation. But their failure might exemplify something more general. The problem is not that we have chosen the wrong method to minimise a number; it is in trying to minimise a number to begin with.

Please, my argument here is NOT 'Various greenhouse-gas curtailment schemes have failed, so we shouldn't even try'. I am, rather, proposing that these failures have something in common

– they emphasise the global over the local, the distant over the immediate, the measurable over the qualitative – and that this very oversight is part of the same mentality that is at the root of the crisis to begin with.

It is the mentality that sacrifices what is precious, sacred, and immediate for a distant end; it is the mentality of instrumentalism that values other beings and the Earth itself in terms of their utility for us; it is the hubris of believing we can predict and control the consequences of our actions; it is the trust in mathematical modelling that allows us to make decisions according to the numbers; it is the belief that we can identify a 'cause' – a cause that is something and not everything – and that we can understand reality by dissecting it and isolating variables. Usually, of course, making decisions 'by the numbers' means making them according to financial considerations. Is it really a very deep change to take the same methods and mentality and apply it instead to some other number?

We are in familiar territory in addressing problems by attacking their isolable, direct causes. That again is the mentality of war – end crime by deterring the perpetrators, end evil by dominating the evil-doers. End drug abuse by banning drugs. Stop terrorism by killing the terrorists. But the world is more complicated than that. As the war on crime, the war on drugs, the war on weeds, the war on terrorism, and the war on germs show us, causation is usually not linear. Crime, drugs, weeds, terrorism, and germs might be symptoms of a deeper, systemic disharmony. Poor soil invites weeds. A run-down body offers a salubrious environment for germs. Poverty breeds crime. Imperialism breeds violent resistance. Alienation, hopelessness, loss of meaning, and disintegration of community foster drug addiction.

Climate change is like these.

Earth is a complex living system whose homeostatic maintenance depends on the robust interaction of every living and non-living subsystem. I suspect that the biggest threat is not greenhouse gases, but the loss of forests, wetlands, and marine ecosystems. Life maintains life. When these homeostatic relationships break down, the results are unpredictable: global warming, perhaps, or global cooling, or the increasingly unstable gyrations of a system spinning out of control. This is the threat we face, and because it is multifactorial and nonlinear, it cannot be addressed by linear strategies for reducing CO_2 emissions. Yes, we should reduce direct CO_2 emissions – the loss of homeostatic equilibrium is worsened by increasing the energy throughput in a dissipative system – but primary emphasis must go to the health of human and natural systems on every level, down to the local and the personal.

As with terrorism, drugs, or germs, if we crack down on the proximate cause without addressing the underlying condition, the symptoms will return in a new and more virulent form. Similarly, when we make decisions by the numbers, then that which is not measured, the excluded other, will come back to haunt us.

What would happen if we revalued the local, the immediate, the qualitative, the living, and the beautiful? We would still oppose most of what climate change activists oppose, but for different reasons: tar sands oil extraction because it kills the forests and mars the landscape; mountaintop removal because it obliterates sacred mountains; fracking because it insults and degrades the water; offshore oil drilling because oil spills poison wildlife; road building because it carves up the land, creates roadkill, contributes to suburbanisation and habitat destruction, and accelerates the loss of community.

On the other hand, many of the technologies I find beautiful might also be justified on climate change grounds: agricultural practices that regenerate the soil; restoration of forests and wetlands; smaller homes in higher density communities; economies of reuse, upcycling, and gift; bicycle culture; home gardening. As such, I am wont to tolerate climate change arguments as a useful ally, a legitimiser of things that I wish people would embrace on their own merits. However, as the Tehri Dam example illustrates, it is a double-edged sword. There are many reasons to be wary of it:

1 By resorting to climate change arguments to oppose fracking, mountaintop removal, and tar sands excavation, we put ourselves in a vulnerable position should global warming come into doubt. This could happen due to a change in scientific opinion, or the hijacking of science by vested interests. More likely, we might face not monotonic warming but increasingly unstable gyrations that are impossible to attribute convincingly to a single cause.

2 If advocates of fracking or nuclear power can argue plausibly that their technology will reduce greenhouse emissions, then by our own logic we must support those too. This is already happening: witness the 'Think about it' campaign touting the climate change benefits of natural gas. I don't believe that the arguments of the gas industry can withstand careful scrutiny; nonetheless, they seem plausible enough to bestow a pro-environmental gloss onto natural gas. 'It's cheaper. It's more patriotic. It is even better for the climate than existing energy sources.' Notice the natural alignment of these instrumental arguments, one based on money, one on competition among nations, and one on carbon emissions.

3 By focusing on CO_2, we encourage potentially disastrous geoengineering schemes like dumping iron oxide into the oceans or sulphuric acid into the atmosphere. We imply that a technological tweak to CO_2 levels will solve the problem without a fundamental change in our relationship to the planet, and promote the idea that we can endlessly engineer our way out of the consequences of our actions. It is in the same vein as using force to stop 'terrorists', and then protecting ourselves against the resulting hostility with even more force. Here again then, is a parallel with the mentality of war.

4 The common argument that climate change is bad because it threatens our future strengthens the mentality of instrumental utilitarianism: Nature is valuable for its usefulness to us. Doesn't the planet and all its beings have a value in their own right? Or is the world, in the end, just a pile of instrumental stuff? Sure, it is in our self-interest to limit CO_2, but it is also usually in one country's, company's or individual's self-interest to limit it less than its competitors. By appealing to self-interest and fear we strengthen the habits of self-interest and fear, which, let's face it, usually conspire to destroy the planet not save it. We will never increase the amount of care in the world by appealing to self-interest. We have to appeal to care, to respect, and to love.

5 Invoking climate apocalypse devalues work that has little foreseeable relevance to climate change. Causes like reforming the criminal punishment system (I cannot bring myself to use the word 'justice'), housing the homeless, ending human trafficking, ending coercive schooling, and legitimising holistic medicine have at best a tenuous, indirect relationship to atmospheric health. Indeed, a cynic, channelling Ebeneezer Scrooge, might argue that rehabilitating homeless people worsens climate change by transforming them into consuming members of society. Perhaps we should put all these causes on hold – after all, what will they matter if the planet becomes unlivable – until we've solved the climate change problem? Here again we see the mentality of money and war. Don't live life now but wait until you've achieved financial security. Sacrifice everything to the war effort.

This mentality is mistaken. The issues listed above have everything to do with climate, because the cause of climate instability is everything: every dimension of our separation from Earth, Nature, heart, truth, love, community, and compassion. We are moving into a deepening understanding of our interdependency with Nature, and beyond that, our 'inter-beingness'. If indeed self and world, humanity and Nature, mirror each other and are part of each other, then it should stand to reason that climate instability will accompany any instability in the social and political climate and that imbalances in the natural realm will mirror imbalances in the human. Greenhouse gases are but a medium – probably one of many that we aren't even aware of – by which this principle operates.

If we ignore this principle then the symptomatic fever of climate change will only worsen, whatever macroscopic measures we take to address its proximate causes. These measures will be impotent, or even backfire as they have already, unless we operate from a narrative that values each species, each person, each forest, each river in its own right and not for its instrumental utility. Let us abandon the war on climate change, and revalue the things that the mentality of war excludes. Paradoxically, then and only then will the fever abate and CO_2 levels fall.

Charles Eisenstein is author of 'The More Beautiful World Our Hearts Know is Possible' (North Atlantic Books). www.charleseisenstein.net. This article was first published by Resurgence & Ecologist in 2014.

RASHID MAXWELL

Ecocide Is Suicide – We Need to Change Our Mind

The night wood is a cavity, looming in the darkness before dawn. Winter's rain and wrath are past – the turned page of a book – yet spring is not entirely settled on the waiting land. Sky glows faintly through the dense black tracery of trees, a beckoning of brightness. Time has almost no existence here.

The rooks begin their hoarse and clattering exchanges. A grey green paleness spreads across the east. A robin sings a tentative few notes and some slight fragrance draws notice to the primroses, glowing in their scattered clumps like markers for a landing site.

Now the fields across the valley are aglow. The sun lights up a tasseling of hazel catkins. Chaffinch, wren and blackbird sing the day into existence. With the day come time and space. I have articles to write, many spring-time jobs to do. My mind begins its usual agitated dialogues.

These trees are for the most part native sessile oaks. That's changing. More frequently now, young sapling beeches sow themselves on their northward march – attributed to global warming. Beech seedlings can outgrow and over-shade the slow maturing seedlings of the oak. As steward of this piece of land, I wonder how, or if, to intervene.

It appears to me that humanity is in that awkward stage between the states of childhood and maturity. We are a population of teenagers who start to see the limitations of our way of life; our institutions and authorities, our infantile gods and our monstrous, vertically integrated corporations. And, like teenagers, we see the illness and don't want the medicine. Shouldn't we grow up?

It's just a phase, says one voice in my head.

Just a phase? replies another. Killing off the earth that gives us life is just a passing phase?

We're all going to die! cries a third.

Yes and take the planet with us into nonexistence.

We are drowning in a slough of problems and you call it just a stage?

The mess of problems are perhaps one problem.

What? Global warming and vanishing resources, one problem? Water, land and air polluted, deforestation, widespread desertification – one problem? What about economic meltdown and mass migrations, the chronic worldwide interlock of starvation and obesity, rising nationalism, incurable viral epidemics, holes in the ozone layer, the die-off of species, the risks of thermo-nuclear disaster, global food insecurity – just one problem? Add to the above – extreme weather events becoming the new normal and you call it just one problem?

Aren't you wasting the magic of a morning in the ordered chaos of these woods to tangle with a set of profoundly useless questions?

What don't you understand? The rape and plunder of our planet has to stop. Or we won't have any woods. We are killing off the planet. Including ourselves.

Yes, ecocide is suicide.

So what's your useful question?

Have you noticed that we who look for solutions to the problem are just as much the problem as the ones who don't? In solving one problem we create another set of problems?

That's offensive! Please tell us, Mr. Know-it-all, what then?

Isn't the problem the modern mind? Primitive man has lived a million years in harmony with Mother Nature. Sometimes there were struggles; sometimes there were die-offs and migrations: always we accepted we were part of nature's breathing in and breathing out. With modern mind we have transcended nature – so we think.

The grumbling conversation of the rooks has risen to excited chatter. I watch a score of birds rise in the air calling their alarm. I hear the danger; a throaty croaking draws me to a pair of ravens spiralling above the woods. Unfazed by the rising cloud of rooks, they circle lower, calling to each other. Kraaak. Kraaak. The rooks rise high above the pair and dive-bomb them so diligently that, very soon, they drift towards the east.

The human mind is a brilliant tool. It has taken us from the primeval forests into every corner of the earth and beyond. As an instrument of imagination and creation the power of the human mind is seemingly unbounded. And here lies the problem, the single existential problem of today. Modern mind is a good servant but a poor master. Mind as conceptual thought has become the high chamberlain who displaces his king, the footman who supplants his master, the tool that controls the hand that wields it. Our mind does not dwell in the here and now but seems constantly preoccupied with past or future.

There are exceptions to this state of mind. Sports players talk of being 'In the Zone' when they experience peak moments of clarity and calmness, of invincibility, of a super-consciousness. These arise because sport demands its players to be totally in the present moment. Sportsmen are competing and yet they must cooperate with flowing, unfolding events. They have all submitted to the disciplines of their training and, at a certain point, fresh energy arises, another layer of consciousness emerges.

Sportsmen aren't the only ones who have such vivid moments of course. Dancers, poets, artists of all types are having them, expressing them, searching for them – and kids are mostly dwelling in them. All of us have had these peak moments at one time or another; in nature, during sex, listening to music; unexpected moments of utter calm and unity.

Is not this what the wise men down the ages have been trying to show us? We are the peace we seek. We are not separate from the whole. This state of heightened awareness is ours for the asking. It is our birthright. We don't have to be kids or artists or sportsmen or religious to arrive at this awareness; these fleeting moments can become our permanent state of being.

This awareness demonstrates to us our absolute connectedness with nature – with all that is. This awareness does away with greed and fear, anger and desire. Rules and principles and codes of conduct are very useful handrails when we cannot see what's needful or is right. Many countries have passed laws to make the wearing of a seat belt mandatory in cars and later laws to ban tobacco smoking in a public place. This saved the lives and health of many of those who did not know or did not want to know that cars and tobacco can be dangerous. Laws are important but the real thing is a change of mind; to live with more awareness. That cannot be legislated for, that comes with growing up, meditation and education. Then there is no need for any commandments. Then it is seen that killing your neighbour or your habitat is indeed killing yourself. Respect spontaneously arises.

The Western conceptual mind promotes the science of outer reality to create this iPad that can tell me, in the middle of a sun-bright, song-filled, Devon wood, how Mr Einstein's theory of relativity is reconciled with quantum mechanics by shadow images created as the Big Bang banged; how maths and intuition dance together. Western mind knows the objective truth and has forgotten subjective wisdom; denies inner reality, our consciousness.

Conversely the Eastern wisdom has explored the subjective reality and largely ignored matter as revealed by Western science. It has developed the science of the inner to create unbroken lines of enlightened beings; those who live in the world but are not tainted by it; who live in awareness, love, compassion and an existential harmony.

One of the great contemporary mystics, Osho has created dozens of meditation techniques for the modern man who is largely unable to live at peace with himself or to understand his integral place in nature. To meditation he has brought humour, psychological insight and a practical understanding of the needs of humanity at this time.

Through meditation – a state of being, not a state of mind – the chatter and the contradicting and confusing inner voices become still and we bring ourselves again into this sun-warmed, patch of woodland, the clustered blades of bluebells rising through dead leaves, the hum of honeybees amongst the dandelions and the ever-constant cadence of the song thrush calling from a cherry tree trembling into blossom.

We are part of nature. Ecocide is suicide. We need to change our mind.

Rashid Maxwell is an artist-painter who also designs buildings and landscapes for sacred use, keeps bees, writes poetry and meditates.

FRITJOF CAPRA + PIER LUIGI LUISI

The Systems View of Life

The great challenge of our time is to build and nurture sustainable communities, designed in such a way that their ways of life, businesses, economy, physical structures, and technologies respect, honour, and cooperate with Nature's inherent ability to sustain life. The first step in this endeavour, naturally, must be to understand how Nature sustains life. It turns out that this involves a whole new conception of life. Indeed, such a new conception has emerged over the last 30 years. In our new book, *The Systems View of Life*, we integrate the ideas, models, and theories underlying this new understanding of life into a single coherent framework. We call it 'the systems view of life' because it involves a new kind of thinking – thinking in terms of relationships, patterns, and context – which is known as 'systems thinking', or 'systemic thinking'. We offer a multidisciplinary textbook that integrates four dimensions of life: the biological, cognitive, social, and ecological dimensions; and we discuss the philosophical, social, and political implications of this unifying vision.

Taking a broad sweep through history and across scientific disciplines, beginning with the Renaissance and the Scientific Revolution, we chronicle the evolution of Cartesian mechanism from the 17th to the 20th centuries, the rise of systems thinking in the 1930s and 1940s, the revolutionary paradigm shift in 20th-century physics, and the development of complexity theory (technically known as nonlinear dynamics), which raised systems thinking to an entirely new level.

During the past 30 years, the strong interest in complex, nonlinear phenomena has generated a whole series of new and powerful theories that have dramatically increased our understanding of many key characteristics of life. Our synthesis of these theories, which takes up the central part of our book, is what we refer to as the systems view of life. In this article, we can present only a few highlights. One of the most important insights of the systemic understanding of life is the recognition that networks are the basic pattern of organisation of all living systems. Wherever we see life, we see networks. Indeed, at the very heart of the change of paradigms from the mechanistic to the systemic view of life we find a fundamental change of metaphors: from seeing the world as a machine to understanding it as a network.

Closer examination of these living networks has shown that their key characteristic is that they are self-generating. Technically, this is known as the theory of autopoiesis, developed in the 1970s and 1980s by Humberto Maturana and Francisco Varela. Autopoiesis means 'self-making'. Living networks continually create, or recreate themselves by transforming or replacing their components. In this way they undergo continual structural changes while preserving their web-like patterns of organisation. This coexistence of stability and change is indeed one of the key characteristics of life.

In our synthesis, we extend the conception of living networks from biological to social networks, which are networks of communications; and we discuss the implications of the paradigm shift from the machine to the network for two specific fields: management and health care.

One of the most rewarding features of the systems view of life is the new understanding of evolution it implies. Rather than seeing evolution as the result of only random mutations and natural selection, we are beginning to recognise the creative unfolding of life in forms of ever-increasing diversity and complexity as an inherent characteristic of all living systems. We are also realising that the roots of biological life reach deep into the non-living world, into the physics and chemistry of membrane-bounded bubbles – proto cells that were involved in a process of 'prebiotic' evolution until the first living cells emerged from them.

One of the most important philosophical implications of the

new systemic understanding of life is a novel conception of mind and consciousness, which finally overcomes the Cartesian division between mind and matter. Following Descartes, scientists and philosophers for more than 300 years continued to think of the mind as an intangible entity (res cogitans) and were unable to imagine how this 'thinking thing' is related to the body. The decisive advance of the systems view of life has been to abandon the Cartesian view of mind as a thing, and to realise that mind and consciousness are not things but processes.

This novel concept of mind is known today as the Santiago theory of cognition, also developed by Maturana and Varela at the University of Chile in Santiago. The central insight of the Santiago theory is the identification of cognition, the process of knowing, with the process of life. Cognition is the activity involved in the self-generation and self-perpetuation of living networks. Thus life and cognition are inseparably connected. Cognition is immanent in matter at all levels of life.

The Santiago theory of cognition is the first scientific theory that overcomes the Cartesian division of mind and matter. Mind and matter no longer appear to belong to two separate categories, but can be seen as representing two complementary aspects of the phenomenon of life: process and structure. At all levels of life, mind and matter, process and structure, are inseparably connected.

Cognition, as understood in the Santiago theory, is associated with all levels of life and is thus a much broader phenomenon than consciousness. Consciousness – that is, conscious, lived experience – is a special kind of cognitive process that unfolds at certain levels of cognitive complexity that require a brain and a higher nervous system. The central characteristic of this special cognitive process is self-awareness. In our book, we review several recent systemic theories of consciousness in some detail.

Our discussion also includes the spiritual dimension of consciousness. We find that the essence of spiritual experience is fully consistent with the systems view of life. When we look at the world around us, whether within the context of science or of spiritual practice, we find that we are not thrown into chaos and randomness but are part of a great order, a grand symphony of life. We share not only life's molecules, but also its basic principles of organisation with the rest of the living world. Indeed, we belong to the universe, and this experience of belonging makes our lives profoundly meaningful.

In the last part of our book, titled Sustaining the Web of Life, we discuss the critical importance of the systems view of life for dealing with the problems of our multi-faceted global crisis. It is now becoming more and more evident that the major problems of our time – energy, environment, climate change, poverty – cannot be understood in isolation. They are systemic problems, which means that they are all interconnected and interdependent, and require corresponding systemic solutions. We review a variety of already existing solutions, based on systems thinking and the principles of ecodesign. These solutions would solve not only the urgent problem of climate change, but also many of our other global problems – degradation of the environment, food insecurity, poverty, unemployment, and others. Together, these solutions present compelling evidence that the systemic understanding of life has already given us the knowledge and the technologies to build a sustainable future.

Fritjof Capra, physicist and systems theorist, has been engaged in a systematic examination of the philosophical and social implications of contemporary science for the past 35 years. Pier Luigi Luisi is Professor of Biochemistry at the University of Rome. His main research focuses on the experimental, theoretical, and philosophical aspects of the origins of life. This article was first published by Resurgence & Ecologist in 2014.

ANNE B RYAN

Enough: Foundation for a Moral and Ecological Economics

How can we live in harmony with nature? How can we eliminate poverty, provide security and create sufficiency for all the people of the earth? How do we restore an ethic of care for people and for the earth? In short, how can we put human and planetary well-being at the centre of all our decision-making?

The philosophy of enough provides a sane basis for moving into the future. The absolute reality is that we need to contain the economy and the kinds of work we do within the limits of the planet. Rich countries are the worst offenders in all of these matters, since ecological footprint grows with income.

Thus I am primarily addressing all inhabitants of wealthy countries and wealthy inhabitants of poor countries. Economy must fit the planet via societies of sufficiency. The big overall thrust must be to stop indeterminate and exponential growth and direct economic activity towards human well-being within planetary limits, and restore the health of our planet's natural systems.

Sufficiency, sustainability and security are key needs of people and living systems all over the world, as we move into the rest of this century. We also need maximum citizen participation, diversity, resilience and whole-system health. This adds up to a different paradigm of progress and economic development. Legislation, attitude and lifestyle will have to go hand in hand and will need to be centred on a moral and ecological principle that enough is plenty.

Enough has important philosophical and reflective aspects, but it is also at the heart of many concrete proposals and frameworks for making the changes we need, in order to live well in the future.

One of the most important frameworks concerns a universal basic income, which provides sufficient cash for all people to have the basics for a decent life, regardless of whether they work for pay or not. This proposal provides security for all in ways that means-tested social welfare cannot do. Personal security is a prerequisite for reducing economic demands to sustainable levels, and for creating a social and cultural climate where everybody is free to act on their moral and ecological concerns. It also has the potential to contribute to general security and a global reappraisal of growth.

A basic income means that individuals are no longer dependent on jobs for their daily needs and are free to choose how they work. At this time, our large, globalised, market-oriented societies structure our paid work towards environmental ruin, because work is how most people get money, no matter how soul-destroying or destructive that work is. In work, we expend our time and energy and it has the potential to be hugely enjoyable and satisfying. We all deserve and need the opportunity to structure our work – paid or unpaid – to be a force for good in the world.

Basic income would allow people to work shorter hours on the job, or in many cases to leave unsatisfactory or harmful jobs, and to be productive in society, in, for example, sustainable food-production, other community-economy activities, personal development, caring work and household production. It would also support the individual members of the many activist and pioneering groups already engaged in practices and projects designed to transform economy and society. Their work is often without pay, or, if paid, it is low-paid and precarious.

One source of finance for a basic income is income tax and most rich countries could finance it from this source already. But there are much more creative and sustainable possibilities for financing it, such as the sharing of dividends from earth resources, in other words, capturing economic rents. One of the most effective forms of collecting economic rent is through land- or site-value taxes (LVTs or SVTs). Such taxes are paid on all land, even if it is idle, and this makes it less attractive for someone to buy and retain land in the hope that its sale-price will increase. An incentive thus exists for an owner to use a land or site, to rent it or to sell it on to someone who can develop it. In addition, because owners of land cannot make huge profits on it, they may use their capital for more economically healthy enterprises than land speculation and these enterprises will most likely need employees.

Where LVTs are in place, banks are no longer prepared to lend to landowners using the future value of their land as security. This prevents bubbles and keeps stable the prices of homes, freeing people from slavery to exorbitant mortgage repayments. In turn, this eases stress and pressures on personal and family budgets.

The function of government, in the philosophy of enough, is to regulate at the broad parameters, in order to create basic securities such as energy, water, climate, food, medicine and transport, and to facilitate unlimited creativity and diversity within those parameters. In an ideal world, governments introduce frameworks such as a universal basic income and economic rents.

They would also sign up to the Global Climate Commons Trust and adopt a Cap and Share framework, which allocates tradeable carbon-emission quotas to all citizens of the globe, within safe, scientifically agreed limits. The state can also introduce legislation to support cooperatives, non-profit organisations, local and regional currencies and other commoning activities, which make it possible for people to do work of benefit to society. Currently, such projects are often disadvantaged by legislation and taxation.

States and currency unions could also bring money under democratic management. The privatised issue of money, where banks issue money as debt and demand interest on it, has become the norm over the last forty years or so. This system drives indeterminate and exponential economic growth. It forces people to generate money through growth, to pay the interest on the loans they have assumed, and, in the case of businesses, to turn a profit.

This system is undemocratic and has fuelled vast social and environmental damage. Democratic monetary reform, in order to provide a public money supply, would require the state, local authority or currency union to issue debt-free money, control the interest-bearing issue of money by banks and end fractional-reserve banking.

With key structures for security in place, citizens would see an improvement in the quality of life. In turn, this would give a new culture of enough a chance to flourish; its potential could emerge, co-created by government and citizens. It is important, therefore, that activists push for such structures and initiatives to be formally introduced.

Of course, to support such reforms, the state (and the politicians who form government and make its laws) has to align itself with the planet and the people, instead of with markets, as most states currently do. Big money has to be taken out of politics and important ingredients such as a society's values and moral orientation constantly debated and acted upon. Somehow, the things that people value need to be reflected in the type of government elected to run the state.

Few states at this time, however, are providing structures and policies that foster virtuous action. Constrained by harmful legislation and lack of appropriate legislation and structures, ordinary people in civil society stand in the gap between what is and what might be. All of us have the capacity to be citizen-leaders while we stand in that gap, acting together in pioneering initiatives for local food, currencies, transport and energy, as well as working in national and international campaigns for structural and policy changes. We dig where we stand and strive to educate elected and aspiring leaders and lawmakers.

As individuals, we need to develop the resources and capacities for enough that exist within all of us. An appreciation of enough can help us to challenge the dominant media and government obsession with getting back to 'business as usual'. Imagination is crucial in this project. We cannot all be official, designated leaders, but if leadership is about taking risks and bringing other people along in a new vision, then we can all do it.

Enough has a good history; it is rooted in past generations and has been valued and practised by several great wisdom traditions. The current movement towards enough is founded on a belief that humans have the inherent capacity to be cooperative and participative, to share resources and to devise an inclusive social economy and forms of work that foster these capacities and care for the planet.

An attitude and practice that 'enough is plenty' draws on human capacities for cooperation and sharing and at the same time it develops them in action. Enough is a key concept for the future because it is living, adaptive and dynamic; it encourages creativity and diversity for groups and individuals around the world, who can forge connections and discover common ground, centred on Enough.

Anne B Ryan, author of 'Enough is Plenty', is an adult educator, a member of Basic Income Ireland, a trustee of Feasta, the Foundation for the Economics of Sustainability and a member of Cultivate Celbridge, a resilience and mutual help network.

The Invisible Nature of Ecocide

A few years ago, I threw an empty toothpaste tube and its cap into the trash, and as they made their way to the refuse transfer station in my city, a gust of wind blew the cap off the garbage truck. It rolled into a gutter, and from there rain washed it into the storm water system, where it floated down to San Francisco Bay. For three years, this durable little product of petrochemicals drifted out to sea to join quadrillions of other bits making up the Great Pacific Garbage Patch. It decayed a bit from sunlight, and since plastic is good at absorbing toxic chemicals, it soaked up PCBs and DDT from seawater along the way.

A mother albatross spotted the cap while soaring over the Pacific with its hyper-advanced flying technique and dove to get it. She carried it a hundred miles back to Midway Island where, thinking it's food, she's feeding it to her chick even as I write this sentence. Born on a degraded planet, the magnificent animal will die either from a clogged digestive system or poisoning or both.

Further West, in Guiyu, China, a father is dying of lung cancer. Five years ago, he was recycling parts of my old printer by burning the plastic shielding off the wires to get the copper. That released carcinogenic dioxins into the air he breathed. Just a few molecules of the poisons were enough to make some of his cells go into reproductive chaos.

In East Kalimantan, Indonesia a young female orangutan (a name that means 'forest people') is writhing in pain at this very moment. She ruptured her spleen and punctured a lung when she fell from a tree in the midst of five hundred hectares of rainforest being cleared for a palm oil plantation. One day in May 2012, I bought margarine containing palm oil, and my purchase was the tipping point that made the company decide to build this plantation.

I'm killing off whole ecosystems. I used to travel often, flying around the world and releasing tons of carbon dioxide into the atmosphere from jet engines (I still do sometimes). That exhaust is making the ocean water off the coast of Australia acidic, which is bleaching the corals of the Great Barrier Reef. They and the rich ecological communities they support ('the rainforests of the sea') are collapsing because of all the flights I took.

These vignettes reside in a strange grey area between truth and fiction. Although they're made up, they could be literally true. But I don't know if they are because the ties between these ills and my everyday life, as real as they are, are nearly impossible to trace. So I'm haunted by the real possibility that albatrosses have died eating my plastic waste.

Ecocide is happening behind our backs, in a nether region beyond our personal experience. We watch the horrors in the news: The Deepwater Horizon oil leak pumping five million barrels of crude into the Gulf of Mexico over many months in 2010. The ongoing radioactive contamination of a large swath of land and sea around the Fukushima Daiichi nuclear power plant since 2011 (engineers still struggle to contain the mess). The clear-cutting and fragmentation of the Amazon and other tropical rainforests that produce the oxygen we breathe. Violent conflicts in Africa around coltan, an ingredient of the electronics in our lives.

But all that happens out there somewhere, in a world remote from the everyday experiences of most of us living in industrialized places (though many others do live directly among the degradations). The world right here, the one most of us smell, feel, see, and touch, is another place altogether, consisting of cars, airplanes, cellphones, flat-panel televisions, office paper, restaurants, getting online, and parks. As the context in which we live, it's the place where we form our opinions, make our

choices, and take action. These two worlds rarely intersect, so efficient is modern technology at separating the two.

But the two realms are inextricably linked. Our actions percolate through layers of industry and governance and end up out there, where orangutans die, glaciers melt, and seas rise. And our lives are nourished and sustained by the distant seascapes and landscapes where our oxygen, food, and belongings originate.

Some of the consequences of our actions do touch us directly. But modern markets manage it so that those are mostly the positive ones such as the shiny new smartphone we wield. The harms from producing that smartphone – the toxins released into the environment and into workers' bodies and the soil, the climate change contribution of its production – linger out there in the great beyond. They may trickle back to us, say in the form of a 'toxic body burden', the accumulated collection of poisons that each of us carries. Yet the gap between these two worlds, the one of experience and the one of consequence, obscures the connections between actions and outcomes. So how can we know – and more importantly feel – what the right choices might be? What can provoke us to change?

We can of course act on abstractions such as global climate change and the suffering of animals in factory farms, and many of us do. Knowledge of these harms, however ethereal, is an essential part of any effort to navigate toward a more sustainable world. But knowledge is not enough. Experience is necessary –

experience of our own impacts out there and wild nature in need of protection. We have to see the pain in the orangutan's eyes. We must witness intense drought and crop losses from climate change. The ecopsychologist Laura Sewall argues that without such sensory experiences, the perceptual apparatuses in our brains atrophy, making it harder to sense nature and its needs.

Direct experience of consequences does not guarantee choices that are healthy and positive for communities and the natural world, but its absence pretty much guarantees the opposite. The modern era stands apart from hundreds of thousands of years of human history not just in the technologies and materially rich lives it affords (though not to all people, to be sure), but also in the degree to which those same technologies insulate us from the brunt of our own actions and thus lead us to make choices that undermine our very sustenance. And as the environmental historian John R. McNeill points out, modernity also stands apart in that so many of its outcomes – particularly the ones constituting the global environmental crisis – are unintended.

This modern divorce of act from consequence has an even darker side: it thwarts our desires to be ethical actors. Without the knowledge and experience of our own consequences, we can no longer choose the course that best agrees with our values. It becomes hard to know what to do. Will the father in Guiyu still get cancer if I choose not to buy another computer? Modern life shifts our ethical agency onto corporations and government agencies, so we're forced to have confidence that they'll do the right thing on our behalf. Meanwhile, they claim to take the lead from us, acting on consumer 'demand' for gas guzzling cars, for instance. Ethics falls through the cracks.

All is not lost. We can begin straight away to work toward a healthier, more just planet by making it a lifelong project to learn how our individual choices play out in the world (goodguide.com is a good starting point that reveals a lot about consumption choices). We can grow a portion of our own food to become more involved in the earthly processes that sustain us. We can demand that our governments better connect choices with consequences by adopting policies that incorporate more of the environmental and human rights costs of things into their prices.

Participating in field trips to learn about local nature or ecological restoration projects such as 'daylighting' streams in urban habitats can remind people of what's at stake and teach ecological connections. Promoting neighbourhood organizations and participatory government, working against the intrusion of corporations between people and their elected representatives, beginning the long shift toward more local-scale economies – all these efforts will move us toward a world in which we more directly learn about or experience our consequences. Then we'll better align our actions with our values.

The good news is that these less global, less technologically slick lives will be richer in community and nature. Meanwhile, remember: the wolf still howls, the stream meanders, the worm nourishes the soil, the tree sprouts from the damp rainforest floor, the whale swims and breaches, the grass covers the plains, the albatross plies the oceans, and the rainbow paints the sky. We need experiences of these things, too, to remind ourselves that there is still much to save.

Kenneth Worthy PhD is author of 'Invisible Nature: Healing the Destructive Divide between People and the Environment', and a research associate at the University of California, Santa Cruz. He teaches at St. Mary's College of California and UC Berkeley and blogs at PsychologyToday.com

ROMAN KRZNARIC

An Invitation to the Climate Futures Museum

Just as Holocaust Museums can now be found in the world's major cities, calling on us to empathise with those who have suffered in the past, I hope to see Climate Futures Museums appearing in those same cities, to inspire an empathic revolution for the future of our planet. Walk into one of these new museums and you will not be confronted by dusty exhibits behind glass cases or touch-screen computers with clever graphics. Instead you will be immersed in an experiential adventure that will expand your empathic imagination.

What is empathy, and why does it matter? Empathy is the art of stepping into the shoes of others and seeing the world through their eyes, and sharing in their emotional lives. In the last two decades evolutionary biologists and neuroscientists have firmly established it as a natural human trait which is one of the most effective ways we have of bonding with one another and creating social cooperation. Once you make that empathic connection with somebody and understand their fears, hopes and attitudes towards life, you see them as an individual who has value, and are more likely to treat them with respect and take action on their behalf. 98% of us have the ability to empathise. It is wired into our brains: we are homo empathicus. Our selfish inner drives exist alongside a more cooperative, empathic self that seeks out human connection.

At the same time, we are facing a growing global empathy deficit. In the United States, for instance, empathy levels have dropped nearly 50% over the past 40 years, with the steepest drop occurring in the last decade. We urgently need to harness the power of empathy as an antidote to the culture of hyper-individualism that has come to dominate modern society, and to create social change for both people and planet.

Tackling the twin crises of climate change and biodiversity loss

PETER MAYNARD

requires developing our empathy in three directions: across space, across time, and across species. Climate Futures Museums will be dedicated to this task, with the aim of spurring us to take practical and radical steps to confront the crises. So what would it be like to visit one of these museums?

Empathy across space concerns stepping into the shoes of those who are being hit by the impacts of climate change and biodiversity loss today, right now, especially in the developing world. That means drought-struck farmers in Kenya, rice growers in Bangladesh facing flash floods, and indigenous peoples in the Amazon whose food sources have been depleted as their forests are decimated. Individuals, governments and businesses in the rich nations might have knowledge of their plight, but so far they have failed to take substantive action on their behalves.

This gap between knowledge and action is largely due to a failure of empathy. We simply have not made enough effort to imagine ourselves into their daily lives. Climate Futures Museums will be designed to close the gap. Walk into one in New York, Paris or Tokyo, and you might find a Climate Refugees Hotel within the Empathy Across Space section. Staying there will be Kenyan farmers and others hit by changing weather patterns or the erosion of species diversity. You will be able to speak to them, hear their stories first hand, look them in the eye and make a human connection.

Continue your journey through the museum and you will enter the wing for Empathy Across Time. It's needed because we are failing to empathise across time with people from future generations who will bear the consequences of our carbon-intensive lifestyles and the destruction of the delicate ecological webs that sustain our livelihoods. We need to catapult ourselves forward, and try to imagine what it might be like to be a teenager living in Shanghai, Dublin or Rio in 2100.

How will they be living and adapting to a climate-changed world? What will they think of us, and our inability to take action when we could all see the coming dangers? Your task visiting this part of the museum is to create a Climate Capsule, which will be sealed and preserved for the future to discover. You will make an artwork showing your vision of what life on our planet might look like a hundred years from now, and also send a video message to the teenagers of 2100, describing what the ecological crisis means to you and what actions you are taking – or failing to take – to tackle it.

Now you are ready to enter the most avant-garde wing of the museum: Empathy Across Species. We normally think of empathy as something that happens between human beings. Yet we know that animals – particularly mammals like chimpanzees and elephants – can not only empathise with one another, but also with humans. A gorilla named Binti once rescued a three-year-old boy who fell into her cage at a Chicago zoo, picking him up, comforting him, and carrying him to a door where a keeper could remove him.

So it makes perfect sense that we too may be able to empathise with some animals. And we do. Although we may not comprehend exactly what happens in the mind of a gorilla, we can identify with core emotions such as fear, and their desire and struggle to stay alive. That's why we wince when we see an animal being beaten. Only a generation ago it seemed eccentric to attribute rights to animals, but this is now commonplace. We need a similar attitudinal shift to recognise the possibility of empathising with other species.

Doing all we can to empathically understand other species helps us value them more and want to protect them. This is essential for generating the momentum we need to rebalance the teetering ecosystems on which we all depend. We should also consider whether we can empathise with living organisms such as trees or the earth itself. The idea of making an empathic connection with an oak tree is currently beyond my own thinking (I'm not sure how to step into the mind of an organism that does not have one, that lacks a central nervous system) but human beings have been so busy destroying nature that we have made little effort to attempt empathising with its myriad forms. Are you ready to take this next step in the journey of developing your empathic consciousness and nurturing your instinctive biophilia?

You might be wondering what will be in this final area of the Climate Futures Museum. I would like to invite you to join me in the imaginative endeavour of inventing this new arena for creating empathic bonds beyond humankind. We must find a way of making every visitor feel that the fate of the Earth, and all its life-forms, is bound up with their own existence. Gaia is, therefore I am.

Now is the moment in history to found the first Climate Futures Museum. Let empathy become the guide to a different climate future for all of us.

Roman Krznaric, a cultural thinker and founding faculty member of The School of Life in London.

Mushrooms Love Coffee

A group of earthworms are working their way through a pile of organic waste.

'I need a rest,' screams the old earthworm, 'but I still feel so energized, so hyper!'

'I feel the same,' cry his 1,000 babies together, who were all born last month.

'How can we ever tell these people not to throw coffee or tea on the compost heaps?' asked the father earthworm.

'Exactly, they do not like to drink coffee before they go to bed, so why do they throw all this caffeine into our food? I am stressed out!' says the youngest of the colony.

'Well, what do I hear,' wonders the shiitake mushroom, 'you are all suffering from too much caffeine?'

'You see people have learned they cannot feed cattle with coffee waste, because although it is rich in nutrients, the cows get too stressed from caffeine, and give less milk!' says a worm.

'And since you do not give milk, people do not care?' enquires the shiitake mushroom.

'Well they do not know what we are going through, but having to eat and digest your own weight every day, is quite a job.'

'I can help,' says the shiitake. 'I can grow here happily with my friends because I get my energy from the caffeine!'

'What? You get energy from caffeine without getting stressed?'

'No, actually the more caffeine there is, the better for me. I like to grow, converting the coffee with caffeine into food for others!'

'Wow, that would be great. But how does this work?'

'You are an animal, and coffee is a plant. I am a fungus, and we each belong to three different kingdoms.'

'I know that even though we do not have legs, and we are blind, we belong to the Animal Kingdom,' says the earthworm proudly.

'So, animals suffer from caffeine, but some fungi can live off any fiber which includes caffeine. Then we produce waste, which is rich in protein, without much caffeine.'

'That is so clever! Fungi make food; earthworms prepare food for plants… and the cattle eat the plants. Everyone does their bit, and together we suffer from no stress!'

… and it only has just begun.

Prof. Gunter Pauli is an author, teacher, activist, and entrepreneur.

When Zarathustra Spoke

Zarathustra, also known as Zoroaster, was the founder of Zoroastrianism, in what today is eastern Iran; (he is conventionally thought to have lived around 600 BCE). To exuberantly celebrate the sanctity of The Good Creation is a distinctly Zoroastrian trait. Feasting, music, merrymaking, and joyfulness have traditionally characterised the chain of festivals held throughout the year in honor of the Amesha Spentas, divine entities that are believed to dwell in each earthly creation.

The vitality of painted pottery from 7,000 to 6,000 BCE suggests that a similar exuberance may have prevailed in the farming villages of that epoch. Armaiti the earth spirit, one of the six Amesha Spentas, was perceived to watch over farmers and herdsmen, and life in these small agricultural communities would have been lived with a richness and depth of meaning that are, for us, unimaginable.

By contrast, the agribusinesses of today are particularly joyless industries. Their goal seems to be the replacement of the world's agricultural diversity with patented, bioengineered monocultures that profit only the corporations. But we find a countering force for renewal – the small-farm activist Michael Abelman has spoken of a new agricultural revolution in which workers on community-scale farms are blending the wisdom of traditional agriculture with today's innovative technologies.

He sees this new generation of farmers as artisans, creating a way of farming that restores its integrity as 'an honorable profession, an art, a craft', and regards a farm not as a factory but a living organism. The people on them work the land in a way that satisfies the needs of the earth as well as those of the market place. 'To farm well,' he tells us, 'you have to merge with the biological world, which has inherent spiritual value.'

The small farm activists are engaged in a struggle between two opposing ways of relating to the earth. And although we are separated by more than eight thousand years from the struggle of forces that characterised Zarathustra's time, the outcome now as then will be determined by individual human choices. Around 7,000 BCE, thousands of hunter-gatherers, joined perhaps by groups of nomadic herdsmen, chose to give up their mobile ways of life, form permanent settlements, and cultivate the earth. In our interpretation, these newly converted farmers were consciously following the way of asha (truth, right order), which placed humans in the role of steward, 'husband' of the earth.

It has fairly been said that those who made that choice shaped the future of civilisation. It seems no less fair to assume that the choices made by individuals living in the early 21st century will have an even greater impact, not only on the course of civilisation but on the future life of the planet. To discover, or rediscover, the right relationship between man and the natural world, is perhaps the most critical challenge of our time, one that is fundamental to all possibilities of renewal.

From 'When Zarathustra Spoke' 2005, Mary Settegast, scholar and author specialising in the Neolithic Age.

"Fossil fuels are merely a part of the natural capital which we steadfastly insist on treating as expendable, as if it were income. If we squander our fossil fuels, we threaten civilisation; but if we squander the capital represented by living nature around us, we threaten life itself. An attitude to life which seeks fulfilment in the single-minded pursuit of wealth – in short, materialism – does not fit into this world, because it contains within itself no limiting principle, while the environment in which it is placed is strictly limited."
From 'Small is Beautiful' 1973, E F Schumacher (1911-1977), economist and statistician

Seed Freedom

The right of farmers to save their own seeds should be defended.

Seed is not just the source of life. It is the very foundation of our being. For millions of years, seed has evolved freely, to give us the diversity and richness of life on the planet. For thousands of years farmers, especially women, have evolved and bred seed freely in partnership with each other and with Nature to further increase the diversity of that which Nature gave us and adapt it to the needs of different cultures. Biodiversity and cultural diversity have shaped one another. Today the freedom of Nature and culture to evolve is under violent and direct threat. The threat to seed freedom impacts the very fabric of human life and the life of the planet.

Seed keepers, farmers and citizens around the world have joined together as a Global Citizens' Alliance for Seed Freedom to respond to this Seed Emergency and to strengthen the movement for the freedom of humanity.

Seeds are the first link in the food chain and the repository of life's future evolution. It is our inherent duty and responsibility to protect them and to pass them on to future generations. The growing of seed and the free exchange of seed among farmers has been the basis to maintaining biodiversity and our food security. But increasingly seed has become a commodity of private seed companies, traded on the open market.

Consider the following:

• The last 20 years have seen a very rapid erosion of seed diversity and seed sovereignty, and the rapid concentration of control over seed by a very small number of giant corporations.

• Acreage under GM corn, soya, canola and cotton has increased dramatically.

IMAGE: © ADRIAN ARBIB

This woman stands beneath a Neem tree, a tree that WR Grace & Co. attempted to patent.

• Besides displacing and destroying diversity, patented GMO seeds are also undermining seed sovereignty, the right of farmers to grow their own seeds and to save and exchange seed.

• In countries across the world new seed laws are being introduced that enforce compulsory registration of seed, thus making it impossible for small farmers to grow their own seeds, and forcing them into dependency on giant seed corporations.

• Genetic contamination is spreading – India has lost its cotton seeds because of contamination from Bt cotton, and Mexico, the historical cradle of corn, has lost 80% of its corn varieties, and these are but two instances of a significant loss of local and national seed heritage.

• After contamination, biotech seed corporations sue farmers with patent infringement cases. More than 80 groups came together recently in the US and filed a case to prevent Monsanto from suing farmers whose seed had been contaminated.

• As farmers' seed supply is eroded, and farmers become dependent on patented GMO seed, the result is indebtedness. Debt created by Bt cotton in India has pushed farmers to suicide.

These trends demonstrate total control over the seed supply and the destruction of the very foundation of agriculture. The disappearance of our biodiversity and of our seed sovereignty is creating a major crisis for agriculture and food security around the world.

A reductionist, mechanistic science and a legal framework for privatising seed and knowledge of the seed reinforce each other to destroy diversity, deny farmers innovation and breeding, enclose the biological and intellectual commons, and create seed monopolies.

Farmers' varieties have been called land races, primitive cultivars. They have been reduced to a 'genetic mine' to be stolen, extracted and patented. Not only is the negation of farmers' breeding unfair and unjust to farmers, it is unfair and unjust to society as a whole. Industrial breeding has been based on strategies to sell more chemicals, produce more commodities and make more profits.

The high-yielding varieties (HYV) of the Green Revolution were bred to respond to chemicals. Hybrids are designed to force the farmer to the market every season. Yield, focusing on the weight of a single commodity, is an inappropriate measure.
Commodities do not feed people – they go to producing biofuel and animal feed. Quantity empty of quality, and weight empty

of nutrition do not provide nourishment. Industrial corporate breeding gives us seeds and crops that are not only nutritionally empty, but also loaded with toxins.

Industrial breeding has used different technological tools to consolidate control over the seed – from so-called HYVs to hybrids, genetically engineered seeds, 'terminator seeds', and now synthetic biology. The tools might change, but the quest to control life and society does not.

What I have called the 'Monoculture of the Mind' cuts across all generations of technologies to control the seed.

• While farmers breed for diversity, corporations breed for uniformity.

• While farmers breed for resilience, corporations breed vulnerability.

• While farmers breed for taste, quality and nutrition, industry breeds for industrial processing and long-distance transport in a globalised food system.

Monoculture of industrial crops and monocultures of industrial junk food reinforce each other, wasting the land, wasting food, and wasting our health.

Every seed is an embodiment of millennia of Nature's evolution and centuries of farmers' breeding. It is the distilled expression of the intelligence of the Earth and intelligence of farming communities. Farmers have bred seeds for diversity, resilience, taste, nutrition, health, and adaptation to local agro-ecosystems. Industrial breeding treats Nature's contributions and farmers' contributions as nothing.

Just as the jurisprudence of terra nullius defined the land as empty and allowed the takeover of territories by the European colonies, the jurisprudence of intellectual property rights related to life forms is in fact a jurisprudence of bio nullius – life empty of intelligence. The Earth is defined as dead matter, so it cannot create. And farmers have empty heads, so they cannot breed.

We are all members of the Earth family, stewards in the web of life. Yet corporations are now claiming the role of creator. They have declared seed to be their 'invention', hence their patented property. A patent is an exclusive right granted for an 'invention', which allows the patent holder to exclude everyone else from making, selling, distributing and using the patented product. With patents on seed, this implies that the farmers' right to save and share seed is now in effect defined as 'theft', an 'intellectual property crime'.

In defining seed as their creation and invention, corporations like Monsanto shaped the global intellectual property and patent laws so that they can prevent farmers from saving and sharing seed.

Life forms, plants and seeds are all evolving, self-organised, sovereign beings. They have intrinsic worth, value and standing. Owning life by claiming it to be a corporate invention is ethically and legally wrong. Patents on seeds are legally wrong because seeds are not an invention. Patents on seeds are ethically wrong because seeds are life forms; they are our kin, members of our Earth family.

Biopiracy – the violence to the farmers is threefold.

Firstly, their contribution to breeding is erased and what farmers have co-evolved with Nature is patented as an innovation. We call this biopiracy. Patents on life are the hijacking of biodiversity and Indigenous knowledge; they are instruments of a monopoly control over life itself. Patents on living resources and Indigenous knowledge are an enclosure of the biological and intellectual commons. To end this new epidemic and to save the sovereignty and rights of our farmers it is required that our legal systems recognise the rights of communities, their collective and cumulative innovation in breeding diversity, and not merely the rights of corporations.

Secondly, patents lead to royalty collection, which is simply extortion in the name of technology and improvement. In Brazil, farmers have been fighting against seed giant Monsanto, most recently filing a lawsuit hoping to sue the company for over €6 million on the grounds that the company has been unfairly collecting royalties from the farmers. The seeds Monsanto has been collecting royalties on are from what are known as 'renewal' seed harvests, meaning that the seeds have been collected from the previous harvest, a practice used for centuries. But because these seeds are from Monsanto's genetically modified plants, Monsanto is demanding that farmers pay. Not only are these royalties unfairly enforced, but they are pushing farmers deeper into debt that they cannot pay back, leaving them floundering in their fields of failed genetically modified crops.

Thirdly, when the genetically engineered crops contaminate neighbouring farmers' fields, the 'polluter pay' principle is turned on its head and corporations use patents to establish the principle of 'polluter gets paid'. This is what happened in the case of Percy Schmeiser in Canada, and thousands of farmers in the US. Owning and controlling life through patents and intellectual property rights was always the primary objective. Genetic engineering was the gateway to patents. Now the corporations are taking out patents on conventionally bred and farm-saved seeds.

Patents on seed are unjust and unjustified. A patent or any intellectual property right is a monopoly granted by society in exchange for benefits. But society derives no benefit from toxic, non-renewable seeds. We are losing biodiversity and cultural diversity; we are losing nutrition, taste and quality in our food. Above all, we are losing our fundamental freedom to decide what seeds we will sow, how we will grow our food and what we will eat. Seed as a common good has become a commodity belonging to private seed companies. Unless protected and put back in the hands of our farmers, seed is at risk of being lost forever.

To break out of this viciousness of monocultures and monopolies, we need to create virtuous cycles of diversity and reclaim our biological and intellectual commons.

Participatory breeding of open-source seeds, and participatory framing of open-source rights are innovations that deepen seed freedom.

Seed freedom has become an ecological, political and cultural imperative. If we do not act, species will irreversibly disappear. Agriculture and the food and cultural spectrum dependent on biodiversity will disappear. Small farmers will disappear, healthy food diversity will disappear, seed sovereignty will disappear, and food sovereignty will disappear.

By speaking and acting strongly with one voice in defence of seed freedom as the Global Citizens' Alliance, we can put the obscenity, violence, injustice and immorality of patents on seeds and thus life itself behind us.

This is an edited extract from the introduction to 'Seed Freedom: A Global Citizens' Report', coordinated by Navdanya. www.navdanya.org. Vandana Shiva is a scientist, activist and founder of Navdanya. This article was first published by Resurgence & Ecologist in 2014.

MADDY HARLAND

Responding to Crisis: Regenerative Agriculture and Other Solutions

ROB MEHTA

In 2008, the celebrated scientist, James Lovelock, declared global warming is irreversible and said we should now focus on enjoying life because planting trees, recycling and other eco-activities are a 'waste of time'.

From December to February 2014, Britain and many parts of Europe experienced the wettest winter in over 100 years. The flooding focused the mainstream media and political attention on the financial and human cost of climate chaos for a short period of time. This serious inattention to one of the greatest challenges in human history causes many of us anguish. How do we cope with our own awareness of ecocide and climate change and what stories of our time do we need to hear to counter the balance?

When I look through a pessimistic lens to our future, I remind myself of the celebrated activist, Joanna Macy's counsel: 'We do not know whether we are nursing a terminal patient or birthing a new civilisation. We must not despair but integrate the practice of detachment into our work. We need to continue to do what is right simply because it is the right thing to do, not because we are seeking outcomes with specific deadlines.' This is a kind of Zen and the art of environmental activism.

Nature is a profoundly powerful force. Regenerative agriculture teaches us that small actions can have large effects. We can rebuild soil and regenerate landscapes at surprising rates and Nature, rather than being an inanimate collection of objects is, as Thomas Berry observed, a 'communion of subjects'. She responds to our ministrations.

You may remember two Devon farmers and film makers, Rebecca Hosking and Tim Green, who made 'Farm For The Future', a BBC documentary about peak oil, climate change, permaculture, agroforestry and the future of farming. Since then they have experimented with soil building, carbon sequestering and regenerative agriculture techniques on Rebecca's family farm. Last winter was a real test of their work.

She told me, 'People are finally realising that how we manage and farm the land affects not only how much carbon is released but also how much we can sequester. Similarly how much water, which once washed off our fields, is now being absorbed. In just 18 months of soil building we noticed the herb and grass regrowth dramatically speed up and increase in density; all the time acting as a large carbon sink.'

The real eye-opener for them was the clarity and low flow levels of water leaving their land compared to that of their neighbours. 'By implementing simple money-saving land management changes we have seen dramatic results which are now not just benefiting us but others around us. Imagine if many other farms were to do this, we'd see a high reduction in floods and all of us sequestering carbon to build fertility.'

Rebecca and Tim practise mob grazing with sheep, fertilise pasture with compost teas, lay old boundary hedges, repair dry stone walls and plant top fruit, nut trees and edible shrubs on the margins of grazing areas. Re-establishing a more mixed ecology and mimicking nature by mob grazing with animals has kick-started the farm into a regenerative state, building soil, improving the sward, augmenting animal health, creating greater biodiversity and, significantly, absorbing more rainwater on the land.

In 2014, they moved to a new farm of their own to test out their techniques on a larger scale. The land they now steward was overgrazed, compacted, with little topsoil and the hedges almost flailed to the point of extinction before they set to work. Again they are planting fruit and nut trees, repairing the ancient stone walls and planting up the banks at the edge of the fields. They are also seeding arable land, once used to grow animal fodder, with wildflowers.

Their hardy sheep, a Nordic Shetland cross, do not require additional winter fodder and this frees up the land for wildflower meadows that can be selectively grazed. Their sheep produce lambs with little difficulty, can survive on arable weeds and pasture, and are ideal to kick-start the ecology of the land. They have beautiful fleeces and produce tasty cuts of meat with no inputs. Rebecca and Tim graze the flock in small areas and move them daily, avoiding compaction or overgrazing ... and all without a sheep dog. Rebecca explained, 'If you are gentle and never shout at them, the flock will follow a bucket of sheep nuts.' One hundred and twenty biddable sheep is quite a sight!

Rebecca and Tim's farm is just one example that I have visited. There are many more all over the world using new techniques to repair ravaged land, even replanting areas of the rainforests in Guatamala and Indonesia, for example. We do not know what a global movement dedicated to reforestation and sequestering carbon through new regenerative agriculture practices and forest restoration could do to reverse climate change and preserve endangered species. The human race has yet to try to solve its problems on a cooperative global scale. Yet this doesn't mean that we cannot.

Nor do we have an understanding of what whole countries are capable of in terms of energy conservation. For example, after the tsunami and meltdown at Fukushima nuclear power plant, the Setsuden movement was formed to encourage energy conservation and attempt to avoid power blackouts. With a public education programme, energy saving innovations and some government restriction, Japan was able to save 20% of its total energy use in 2011/12.

We also know that Germany and Denmark are both capable of being net generators with their network of renewable energy solutions. Why then are our governments supporting disastrous energy practices like fracking and nuclear power in the UK and USA, for instance? Is it a total lack of imagination on the part of

HELEN TAYLOR

our politicians? Partly, but it is also because these dirty technologies make money for a very few. We cannot allow a tiny percentage of humanity who want to stay obscenely rich to dominate our energy choices at the expense of our planetary health.

Whatever we do now will not change the climate chaos that is coming to us in the next few decades. Lovelock was right in that one aspect: climate change is as implacable as a supertanker that has gained momentum and it takes a long time to reduce speed and turn the ship around. The carbon load is already doing its work in our planet's higher atmosphere. What we can do, however, is work towards stability for future generations.

It is vital that we build an effective, vocal global movement and tell stories of the power of regenerative agriculture, permaculture and all the other life enhancing practices that are being tested and developed. Whilst it is inevitable that things are going to get worse, there are still solutions to our global problems. We just need the collective will to initiate them and the courage to ride the storms. Never give up hope.

Maddy Harland is co-founder and editor of 'Permaculture – solutions for self-reliance', an international print and digital magazine. She also co-founded Permanent Publications, awardwinning book publishers, and The Sustainability Centre.

COLIN TUDGE

Agrarian Renaissance – The Great Fight Back: A People's Takeover of the World's Food Supply

IMAGE: © MERLYN CHESTERMAN

Our planet, its people, wildlife, and very fabric – are in a shocking mess. Ultimately that's because humanity does the wrong things for the wrong reasons, and the wrong people are in charge. We need to change radically – what we do, the thinking behind it, and those we have allowed into positions of power – and with all possible speed.

Reform – tweaking the status quo – has some part to play but reform takes too long and there is no plausible route by which we can shift, step by step, all the way from where we are to where we need to be. The only plausible way forward is through a Renaissance – building the world we want and need in situ. The powers-that-be will resist – are resisting – because they are

convinced that their ideas and modus operandi are right, and believe that they ought to be in charge. Thus if people want to bring about serious change, then we have to create the Renaissance for ourselves, despite the powers that be.

Most urgently, a renaissance is needed in food and agriculture – at the heart of world affairs, affecting everything and affected by everything. A billion people are chronically hungry – and the root cause is inappropriate agriculture. A billion now live in urban slums – almost a third of all city-dwellers – mainly because traditional agriculture has been replaced by plantations that don't need people to work them. At least a billion live on only a dollar a day – because agriculture worldwide is the main employer and if the work is done by machines and agro-chemistry then there are no jobs. Half our fellow species are in danger of extinction – their forests cleared to make way for plantations, the run-offs from which poison the reefs.

This global disaster is presided over by giant transnational corporations, which benefit from governmental backing. They are supported by armies of intellectuals, notably economists and scientists, with help from lawyers. This isn't a conspiracy – it's just that those who go along with the status quo are rewarded, materially and with positions of power; and those who protest – including many scientists, economists, and lawyers – generally find work hard to get.

Thus corporations, banks, and governments, plus increasing slices of academe form a self-reinforcing oligarchy, supporting each other in a positive feedback loop. The corporations finance scientific research – but only of a kind that will help them to expand; and governments use taxpayers' money to pump-prime – providing the fundamental science on which the technologists may build.

In turn, corporations support the government in many ways – not least with board placements. In this, science is both a beneficiary and a victim. It gains – or some scientists gain – from the shower of wealth bestowed upon it. But distressingly it has lost its integrity. Much of the best-endowed science can no longer be seen as a dispassionate search for truth, but as the means to provide high technologies of the kind that help corporations grow richer, and governments like Britain's to claim that they are forward-looking and are achieving 'economic growth'.

The present oligarchy truly got into its stride in the 1980s, when governments of the US, UK, and others adopted 'neoliberalism' – an extreme form of capitalism that effectively gives supreme power to the allegedly 'free' global market. In a neoliberal economy the government's role is primarily to smooth the market's path – to enable generation of as much wealth as possible, ostensibly in the belief that it 'trickles down'. Economic growth – measured as GDP – becomes the only acceptable goal of the entire economy. All attempts to control or direct the market are condemned, e.g. as 'interventionist'. Subsequent governments of all parties bought into the neoliberal idea.

The global market is supposed to be maximally competitive but in practice it, and therefore the world as a whole, is dominated by transnational corporations, structured expressly to compete for wealth. They in turn make the rules, so the 'free' market in reality is tipped very much in their favour. Everything is for sale to the highest bidder – including Britain's farmland. All human values – moral, aesthetic, spiritual – are trumped by money, and that too is called 'realism'.

The downside of market rule is starkly obvious in agriculture. Basic biology and several thousand years of experience tell us that productive and sustainable farming should be maximally diverse and low-input – which basically means mixed and as organic as possible. So above all it must be complex and skills-intensive. There is little or no advantage in scale-up; thus in general the kinds of farms we really need should be small to medium-sized.

They can demonstrably achieve what's required, in rich countries and poor: providing at least adequate amounts of excellent food in the places where it is needed; offering work that is often hard but also satisfying and, when well done, wonderfully wildlife-friendly. Such farms also help us realise the supreme goal of 'food sovereignty'; they give people everywhere control over their food supply, an arrangement termed 'Enlightened Agriculture' – or 'Real Farming'.

But as enlightened farms return neither maximum wealth, nor concentrate it, they are not oligarch-supported. Instead, we have high-tech, high-input, industrial agriculture, basically an exercise in industrial chemistry; high capital – plenty of interest for the banks; with minimum and preferably zero labour – practised on vast estates to achieve economies of scale, and all controlled from above. This kind of oligarch-promoted farming keeps them in power. It's the precise opposite of what we would be developing if we aimed to promote social justice and provide everyone in the world with good food, without wrecking the planet.

The role of ultra-high tech, like GMOs, is to tighten the corporate grip. Soon GMOs will become the norm, and they will be controlled solely by the few giant companies able to supply them. The whole GM bonanza is supported by untruths – notably being billed as the world-saver – appearing in the nick of time like the US cavalry in a B-movie western to rescue us all from starvation.

No GM food crop of unequivocal value to humans or wildlife has been produced in the past 30 years that could not have been produced by conventional plant breeding, and without any of the unforeseen or unforeseeable side effects of GM. Scientists perjure themselves horribly in defence of GMOs. The power-structure that presides over this disastrous position looks invulnerable. It has the money, commands the technologies, and largely controls the main conduits of public information, including government reports and large sections of academe.

Yet, bleak though things may appear, huge numbers of people worldwide are increasingly aware that all is not well – not just the starving millions in a state of desperation and with very little power, but increasing numbers of the Western middle classes, who collectively can still have influence, seeing all too clearly that the world is in a mess, we're poorly governed, and the neoliberal economy is unfit for purpose. Much of the global anger is rightly focused on food and farming. Out there are enough disillusioned and angry people to form a critical mass – all that's needed is a little coordination.

The Renaissance aim is not – as in revolution – to overthrow everything. We can and must build on the best of what exists already, which is a great deal. There are still many farmers worldwide, not least in hyper-industrialised Britain and the US, who know how to run complex, low-input but high-output, sustainable farms, and are keen to share their knowledge; and a lot of scientists who yearn for the opportunity to do world-benefiting research. More immediately, despite the big banks' dominance, there's a battery of financial and legal mechanisms making it possible to set up the kinds of business enterprises – small farms and corresponding markets – which the world really needs.

There's also a growing interest in community ownership and control – manifested not least in CSAs (community supported agriculture), in the broad notion of ethical investment, enabling people to invest small or large sums in enterprises of the kind that they think are really worthwhile, and in the concept of 'social enterprise' – businesses that are required to make some profit but are intended primarily to serve the community and the biosphere. There are also novel ways of raising instant sums via the internet, notably by crowd funding; and a range of legal structures suited to each enterprise, including Community Interest Companies and Community Benefit Societies.

Various groups worldwide are also beginning to re-acquire farmland – which at present in Britain remains largely owned by ancient families and, increasingly, by miscellaneous financial 'investors' with no interest in how the land is used; they want it simply as a hedge against inflation. In Britain, groups which seek to democratise land include the Biodynamic Land Trust and the Ecological Land Co-operative; France has produced the wondrous Terre de Liens; and worldwide there is Via Campesina, represented in Britain by the Land Workers' Alliance.

Since British farmland now costs around £25,000 a hectare, it seems that people who aren't rich can't acquire worthwhile areas – but that's not so. A three hectare community-owned market garden/smallholding can make a huge difference to a village; a thousand such holdings nationwide would significantly impact on the whole country. Three hectares would cost around £75K – a trivial sum for an entire village community. In fact, at £25K a hectare Britain's 60 million people could buy all its farmland – 20 million hectares – for about £8K each – the price of a modest car, and a tiny sum when spread over a lifetime. Public or community ownership of land could allow farmers to free themselves from oil-based agro-chemistry, and stabilise food prices forever.

The kind of change we need in the world is indeed radical – everything from the mode of governance to science to the general mindset – but the means to bring this about are not frightening. Indeed, the kind of economy that's needed, rooted in small businesses (but with strong moral and social consciences) has often been derided as 'petit-bourgeois', but which all governments once felt perfectly at home with – so let's go for it – starting now.

Colin Tudge is co-founder of The Campaign for Real Farming. He helped set up the annual Oxford Real Farming Conference and establish Funding Enlightened Agriculture. His latest books are 'Good Food for Everyone Forever', and 'Why Genes Are Not Selfish and People Are Nice'.

VICKI HIRD

Enough Food for Everyone

CLARE WIMPERIS

We are in danger of exhausting those key resources we think of as renewable – especially food and fresh water.

While many blame dwindling resources on the world's growing population, and struggle to find solutions, we at Friends of the Earth have a different perspective. Our focus is on finding ways to manage renewable resources so they aren't lost to us, or future generations. Key to this is what we do with land and in particular our global food systems.

If you were designing the global food system from scratch, you'd want to ensure that enough food was grown of the right variety in the right way to fulfil 7 billion – and even 9 billion – people's nutritional needs. By using the right techniques, you could protect the natural systems on which future production depends – soil, water and biodiversity – and you would store surplus food for lean times. You could safeguard good governance of this vital system so that producers, consumers and the planet were fairly treated and were protected from any harmful influence.

But our current system is dysfunctional. Globally around 50% of food grown is wasted in the field or along the food chain – not even composted or used as feed. A third of all the crops grown and two-thirds of fresh water available are used to grow feed for farm animals. These animals are poor feed converters and the meat is sold cheaply, creating even more demand. Millions of hectares are used to produce biofuels for cars, and a large proportion is used to produce sugary foods.

On top of that, vast quantities of energy-intensive fertilisers and pesticides are used to drive yield growth in monoculture systems. Natural methods of fertility and pest control are largely neglected or rejected and grain is used as a tool for global financial transactions, not food. Meanwhile, a billion are underfed, a billion suffer effects of over-nutrition, and many farmers and workers cannot gain a decent living.

The system is broken in many ways, and experts and politicians know it. Models of good practice do exist in how we grow, consume and govern what comes from the land. Many good ideas are being discussed and debated and even practised at the local community level and by governments, so we're not starting from scratch. It is possible to repair this system if we put our minds and political will into it. But change is not going far, or fast, or deep enough and politicians are running shy of the systemic and governance changes that are now required.

More than 100 UK NGOs and aid agencies recently launched the anti-hunger 'Enough Food For Everyone IF' campaign. Their demands are policy-focused – to address the causes of hunger, including land grabs, tax loopholes, and damaging investments in poor countries. What the campaign highlights is the sheer absurdity of the current food system, and why major system change is needed if we are to address poverty and the growing problem of obesity globally.

But where is the environment in the food security debate? What if, in our efforts to feed more people on a limited planet, we trash the soils, water and natural systems we depend on long-term to feed, fuel, clothe and house future inhabitants? This is a mammoth political issue that requires a long-term view, not short-term solutions. Focusing on measures to intensify crop and livestock yields, using techno-fixes such as genetic modification, more artificial fertilisers or mega livestock farms, is not the answer. Clearly technology has a role to play going forward but we'll need to look at the risks as well as the benefits.

We need to create resilient systems that provide the diverse foods we need in cities and rural areas whilst sustaining the soil and other systems for the future. This will also help resolve significant health issues associated with our broken food system – including hunger, obesity and communicable diseases.

There isn't a silver bullet, but there are key interventions that will set us on the critical pathway for change. Underlying any changes must be far better governance of the food system, putting the growing corporate control over land and water – to get ever-cheaper raw materials – under greater regulation through national and global policies and ensuring accountability.

We are pursuing key interventions needed on production, consumption and governance to feed ourselves within planetary and social boundaries. These are our top ten recommendations:

1 Keeping global temperature increases to less than 2°C. Greater temperature increases, which will lead to more extreme weather events, could devastate crop yields in many places.
2 Changing levels of consumption and promoting sustainable diets – critical and significant to reduce greenhouse gases and conserve natural systems.

3 Reducing food waste pre and post harvest, (e.g. through improved food storage and transport systems and better infrastructure) and post consumption.
4 Enhancing yields and increasing resilience to climate change impacts through protecting soils, crop diversification and biodiversity, plus a move towards agroecology.
5 Scrapping mandates for biofuel production from food crops and instead developing efficient vehicles, including electric cars, and enhancing public transport.
6 Increasing nutrient and water resource efficiency.
7 Ensuring low-income access to seeds, land and food, and stopping land grabbing.
8 Shifting trade and other global frameworks to enable and encourage countries to have greater focus on meeting local and regional food needs.
9 Providing agricultural extension services so farmers can access and implement knowledge to enable them to farm more sustainably.
10 Controlling financial speculation on food crops and controlling supermarket and retail buying power where it harms worker, farmer and other suppliers' abilities to farm sustainably.

Change won't be easy. Key interventions such as changing diets are poorly understood and perceived as unpopular. But political will is needed to get government, business and individual action on challenging issues such as changing our diets so we eat less meat and eat more of the good green stuff. We're keen to get your feedback on the challenges ahead and would welcome your thoughts, particularly on sustainable diets.

Vicki Hird is Senior Campaigner for the Land, Food and Water Programme at Friends of the Earth (Vicki.hird@foe.co.uk Twitter @vickihird).
This article was first published in Resurgence & Ecologist in 2014.

Carbon-conscious Farmers: Rebuilding Soil Carbon and Soil Health

In 1943, before the advent of agriculture based on fossil fuels, chemicals and big machinery, Eve Balfour wrote in *The Living Soil*: 'The health of soil, plant, animal and man is one and indivisible.' Since then, the soils of Britain have been severely depleted, especially where they have been cultivated for annual crops like cereals. Nearly all the organic matter stored in the soil – that precious resource upon which we all depend for food – has been 'mined' and converted into ever-increasing crop yields supported by artificial fertilisers. It took from the 1940s to the 1990s for the reasoning of organic pioneers like Balfour to be taken seriously.

But fast-forward to 2014, and carbon-conscious farmers are not just endorsing the same message as Balfour, but putting it into practice with enthusiasm. The principles of feeding the soil, not the plant, understanding and encouraging soil biology, and harvesting sunlight to maximum effect are all-embraced. These farmers understand that we must repair our damaged soils because fossil fuels (from which artificial fertilisers are produced) are a non-renewable resource, and equally importantly they reduce the health of soil systems. Carbon-conscious farmers aim to work with the grain of Nature in soil ecosystems, not against it.

Martin Howard farms 400 acres in the Tamar Valley and has seen life breathed back into his soils by a combination of minimising compaction (caused by overuse of agricultural machinery), increasing aeration of the soil, and introducing beneficial bacteria and fungi. He is passionate about improving soil biology, not least because this actively improves the water quality of the nearby river Tamar.

Rob Richmond is a dairy farmer on 500 acres in the Cotswolds who has increased soil organic matter at an extraordinary rate whilst maintaining high milk yields. He uses a complex mix of forage species (such as clover, vetch and alfalfa) that grow robustly as good companion plants and allow him to graze and rest the land for optimum efficiency. Furthermore, his soils retain more water and his cows are healthier.

Julian Gold is an arable farm manager on over 2,000 acres in Oxfordshire. He has been working hard to reduce chemical inputs and increase soil carbon, whilst maintaining profitability. Through carefully controlling compaction from machinery and minimising cultivation depth, he has seen a significant increase in earthworm populations and better soil quality.

All these farmers are serious about building carbon in their soils, realising that the crops are secondary to the health of the ecosystem. Their approach is backed up by hard scientific data from leading soil scientists such as Pete Smith and his colleagues at Aberdeen University, and world-renowned soil scientist Rattan Lal, who also advises the IPCC. Building soil carbon is not an approach of idealists. These are professional farmers who have to make their farms profitable, but who are also concerned about the health of their soils for future generations.

The amount of atmospheric carbon that can be absorbed in well-managed soils is extraordinary. Lal estimates the potential for soil carbon sequestration across the world as 'equivalent to a draw-down of about 50 parts per million of atmospheric CO_2 by 2100'. This amazing figure proves that carbon sequestration in soils is one of the few tools we have to actually reduce global atmospheric CO_2 levels. To build organic matter in the soil is a win-win situation for climate change as well as soil health and crop yields. Carbon farming needs to become the focus of farmers everywhere.

Jonathan Smith is pioneer of the Farm Carbon Cutting Toolkit (www.farmcarbontoolkit.org.uk). This article was first published by Resurgence & Ecologist in 2014.

True Cost Accounting

Not having experienced any other system, I guess I have always accepted implicitly that a market economy is the most practical means of regulating the exchange of goods and services. We put a price on 'stuff' based on what people will pay, and through doing so we create an environment, which enables us all to navigate through life in a reasonably fair and equitable fashion.

Furthermore, to be honest, until quite recently, I have not given any thought at all to the question of what would transpire if an unfair value, or even no value at all, was assigned to some critically important goods and services, so critical in fact that the future prosperity of the sustainable food supply of all civilisation depended on them. Yet these are exactly the 'Alice in Wonderland' economics that have applied for most of my adult life in relation to our food and farming systems.

Specifically, the financial environment in which all food producers operate has been distorted in such a way that the polluter, in this case the farmer, does not pay, with the result that those using intensive methods have not been financially accountable for any of the damaging environmental and social consequences of their practices.

I am referring here to the polluter not paying on a vast scale. The long list of uncosted damage includes greenhouse gas emissions (which cause climate change), environmental pollution by fertilisers and pesticides, depletion of natural capital such as biodiversity, mineral fertilisers, fossil fuel reserves, soil carbon and water, and a wide range of indirectly linked social costs such as reduced animal welfare, loss of jobs, and perhaps most costly of all, damage to public health. This might be from bacterial immunity to antibiotics caused by overuse in intensive livestock systems, diseases linked to endocrine disruption from pesticide residues and poor nutrition, or damage to public health from over-processed, nutritionally impoverished food. Virtually none of these costs has been factored into the economic equation of food production for the last century.

As a direct consequence, there has been and remains, a far better 'business case' for intensive than sustainable production for producers, and intensively produced food has been more affordable for consumers. Since most producers and consumers alike are constrained by economics, having to follow the most profitable or affordable option, the scale of production and consumption of food from intensive methods continues to totally eclipse the percentage of land producing and food sold from sustainable production, self-limiting the sector to affluent consumers and to producers who are classic 'early adopters' typically either selling into affluent middle class markets, or blessed with entrepreneurial skills, perhaps also having day jobs to supplement their income.

When I first went into farming in the early 1970s, as a naive and idealistic 'hippy' dairy and carrot farmer, with a total commitment to applying the principles of sustainable agriculture on my Welsh hill farm, it did not occur to me that in doing so, we would be having to survive economically in a totally un-level playing field, with dishonest food pricing. This was because we were having to compete with farmers using intensive methods who were not only subsidised for every tonne of grain and litre of milk they produced, but were also not having to pay for any of the damage arising from their production systems, as listed above.

Pretty soon, we found we were not getting a good enough return to make a living, so in addition to seeking outside employment, which by the way is still a familiar story in our food world, we had a bright idea – why not write down the 'story' of our sustainable production, take it to the consumer and by doing so, persuade them to pay a premium to support sustainable agriculture in the market place. This is actually the story, scaled up, of the development of the organic standards and market, in which I am proud to say I have played a modest part, for instance by writing the first draft of what became the organic dairy standards.

It seemed like a great idea at the time, and I have no doubt that the organic market will continue to play a vital part in enabling citizens to preferentially support sustainable production in the market place. After all, the principle of the market is tried and tested, and the resultant growth has been a great success story, with organic sales enjoying double digit annual growth for many years and still continuing to expand in many parts of the world, although sadly not in the UK in recent years. This is due to the recession and other negative factors, many of which deserve further examination, and some of which are outside the scope of this article.

But the factor I want to focus on here is not whether we should either rely on the organic market or True Cost Accounting, but rather on how and why the two approaches should work hand in hand. This is because I now see that it really was a somewhat critical oversight, all those years ago, to believe that we could overcome these massive distortions in the economics of food production and enable sustainable agriculture to thrive and become mainstream merely by putting a premium on organic and biodynamic food and lobbying for the introduction of EU organic subsidies. I say this because in so doing, we were treating the symptom rather than addressing the root cause of the problem.

To better understand this, let us ask a question – if one added up all the damaging costs arising from intensive dairy farming, for instance, the emissions, the pollution, the damage of soy production from cleared rainforest in South America etc, etc, then added all those costs to the price of a litre of intensive milk, how much would this narrow the price differential between conventional and organic milk in the shops?

You could even take things further, for instance by doing the same thing in reverse, rewarding organic farmers for the (at present uncosted) benefits they deliver, such as increased soil carbon, biodiversity and better public health outcomes. If we did all this (and that is now a long-term commitment for part of the future work plan of the SFT), then hopefully organic/biodynamic food might actually become as affordable as the so-called 'cheap' food that forms the basis of everyone's, or nearly everyone's, diet today.

Put simply, this is all about the need to 'engineer' more honest food pricing and hopefully, it goes some way to explain why I have become something of a passionate advocate for the introduction of True Cost Accounting in food and farming. But there is a long way to go to ensure that this actually happens! In order to unlock the mess, there will be a need for a series of organised collaborative initiatives, involving multiple institutional partners, the aim of which must be to identify, categorise and quantify the range of different externalities, both positive and negative, arising from different food systems, then develop a series of fiscal policy and economic instruments through which we ensure that the true cost of food will be reflected in the price we pay in the shops.

Taking an example, at present farmers pay around 1 Euro per kilo for nitrogen fertiliser, the application of which delivers benefits worth 3 Euros in extra income, thus justifying its use in economic terms. However, according to EU experts, if you put a conservative figure on the damage caused, from emissions, pollution and the impact on ecosystems and biodiversity (none of which are presently factored in), the cost of this indirect damage is likely to exceed the total commercial benefit of using nitrogen fertiliser in the first place.

Following the Sustainable Food Trust's very successful conference on True Cost Accounting held in London in December 2013, (view all the keynote speeches on our website) there are now plans to launch a 'Stern' scale study of agriculture and food system externalities led by Pavan Sukhdev, the result of which will be the assembly, for the first time, of such a body of robust data on the costs and benefits of different farming systems thus paving the way for the introduction of legislation, targeted taxes, redirected subsidies and other carrot and stick measures, which will hopefully collectively transform the future economic environment for sustainable food production.

To enable its introduction, it is also very important that we make these issues understandable to ordinary citizens, without falling into the trap of using jargon and other inaccessible language that only economists would understand! Because you can reasonably assume that politicians will be reluctant to introduce such measures unless they feel the heat from informed public opinion. That is why, even though they eat organic food at home, neither the Obamas nor the Camerons of this world mention this as they believe doing so would render them vulnerable to the charge of elitism. So how to make this a people's cause, that is the question!

In terms of action on climate change, the precedents are not good, but somehow I feel we have more chance with food. I feel this not least because food is very personal, because individual citizen action is possible and everyone is potentially concerned about the connection between food and what is probably the greatest, but as yet least quantified, of all food system impacts, health!

Patrick Holden CBE is Patron of the Biodynamic Association and Director of the Sustainable Food Trust (sustainablefoodtrust.org). This article first appeared in issue 121 of the Journal of the Biodynamic Association 'Star and Furrow', June 2014.

The Armchair Activist's Handbook

I always wanted to change the world, but I never knew where to start. I dreamed of doing more than signing online petitions but didn't want to camp out on a pavement to prove a point, turn my life upside down, or risk hurting myself or others in the name of action. And so I went in search of an alternative sort of activism, one that would enable me to be part of a wider movement that tackled environmental degradation and injustice without getting dirty, cold or arrested.

Along the way, I discovered something vital.

Although everyone was talking about the economy being in a mess, how supermarkets rule our food supply, fast fashion owns the high streets, energy prices are rising and space is a vanishing commodity, that was only half the truth. I saw there was another economy, another food network, another energy system and another, slower, type of fashion. You just didn't hear about them very often.

Here was a colourful revolution of space invaders, crafty revolutionaries, yarnbombers, downshifters, 'naked' fashionistas, pavement pimps, energy innovators and alternative currency pioneers. Ordinary people setting the agenda for long-term change, addressing injustices, inequalities and the damage caused to people and planet by our current systems.

What's more, I found that it was possible to take these ideas and make them work for me. I could make the transition from a despairing spectator to someone who actually accomplished something positive. I could be an activist in the way I wanted to be one, fighting a battle largely from the comfort of my own home – an armchair activist.

I would like to share with you a few ideas for how you too can be an armchair activist. Whether it's to do with what you eat, how you dress, how you travel or even how you bank, making the tiniest changes to your habits can have a positive impact, and if you stick with those changes for the long term, you can be a part of making great things happen – including ending global ecocide.

Forage, share and swap

Nettles were never what I'd had in mind when I'd begun looking for ways to eat local food. They were a weed, they were ugly, and they had a sting. Surely just looking at them was enough to tell me they would taste disgusting? But I'd met a lady who was determined to convince me otherwise. Gemma Harris runs a north London food group called Urban Harvest, which encourages people to harvest unwanted fruit and wild plants in their local area.

The idea is not to live entirely off food sourced in this way, but to make it part of your intake all year round, depending on what's available. Gemma explained that for her it's a crucial activist tool – and one that anyone should be able to make use of. 'As far as I can see, just about all the food we eat is a product of slavery or abuse or colonialism. When I say abuse I mean abuse of people, abuse of animals and abuse of the environment. Our whole food system is screwed up. So I see foraging as an important thing – it's about reclaiming all the waste around us, whether it's wasted food that people don't harvest or wasted food that people don't realise is good to eat. It's so much simpler to adapt what I eat than adapt the world.'

I could see what she meant. When you really thought about it, it simply seemed counter-intuitive to rely on imports while the bounty on our doorstep went to waste. 'We treat these plants as weeds and spend money and manpower getting rid of them,' said Gemma. 'But what if we used them as a resource instead?' It was this way of thinking that took us to the nettles.

In the Borough of Camden, London, is a green space. It's a grassy playing field – pretty underwhelming at first glance. I would never have expected to find food there. But Gemma was taking me round the edge, pointing edibles out every few steps: red valerian, a cherry tree, elderflower, a linden (or lime) tree, a blackthorn tree (which would later produce sloes), an oak, nettles and goose-grass. It was a proper education. You also needed to have an open mind. 'I think lots of people have a mental block about using them, and that's natural,' said Gemma. 'There's something in the human head that says "if they were that good everyone would be eating them". That's the barrier we have to break.'

Start a seed swap

If you've never heard of a seed swap before, you'd be forgiven for thinking it's a very lovely but pointless pastime for bored gardeners. But there's much more to it than that. Some people do just go along for fun, that's true. But there are also a whole host of people tackling big issues one small step at a time. One of these issues is corporate control of the seed market.

Pat Bowen of the seed swap Seedy Sunday told me, 'There are five major seed companies and they are monopolising seed production and controlling it by creating terminator seeds and hybrid seeds, which means that farmers can't keep their own seeds.' Terminator seeds are genetically engineered so that once a crop has been harvested, the seeds are sterile and can't be replanted for the next year. It's both a local and a global issue – because with many small-scale farmers unable to afford to buy new seeds every year, collecting and replanting seeds is an important part of the agricultural cycle.

But the implications of the corporate control over this type of resource don't stop there. It's about independent food sovereignty. 'For farmers and growers to be able to keep their own seeds just seems utterly fundamental,' said Pat. 'These companies – their aim is profit and control, and they don't appear to be thinking about resilience to climate change. They want seeds that work in a monoculture set-up and they also want to sell chemical fertilisers and pesticides because that's part of their industry, so they make seeds that depend on those things.'

'The kind of seed saving that people are doing at these sort of things are ideally those seeds that do best without pesticides. Farmers and growers have always bred seeds that are good for their locality and their conditions.'

Food sovereignty is a term that was coined back in 2007, when more than 500 groups representing a range of grassroots social movements, communities and organisations from more than 80 countries came together in Mali.

The resulting declaration defined it as 'the right of peoples to healthy and culturally appropriate food produced through ecologically sound and sustainable methods, and their right to define their own food and agriculture systems'. It says that food providers should be valued, and food should be seen primarily as sustenance for the community – that trading should be a secondary concern.

It dictates that we should work with nature, that control should be with local people and that knowledge and skills are built and passed on. It defends the interests and the inclusion of the next generation. And, ultimately, it's about reclaiming democratic control of our food system. It's food as a right, not a commodity.

Beg, barter, borrow

We all know we're buying too much, throwing away too much, and giving too little thought to the processes and people behind it all. Most of us would probably also admit that we could take action on it, if only we could be bothered. We know the facts – yet with shopping now possible from your home computer or on the go and adverts telling us to buy, buy, buy at every turn, there's plenty to tempt us.

But the more I thought about the situation, the more I realised I could be bothered. And I saw that it made sense for me to tackle over-consumption in my personal life. As far as I could see, you could scream at corporations and brands that the whole system was wrong, but unless we did something about our buying habits our words wouldn't carry much weight.

Whether I needed an item or had to get rid of something, I suspected that begging, borrowing and bartering could help. I wasn't planning to stand on the street corner asking for donations from random people (I didn't think I had the charm for that) but I did want to find a way to connect with others who had similar goals to me.

One of the resources I'd used before – and probably one of the best-known resources out there – was Freegle. It's a re-use network that makes it easy for people to pass on items that they would otherwise throw away, and a handy source of free stuff. If you're in need of something, you can go online and send out a request for it, and other members will get back to you if they can help. On the flip side, you can offer up anything that you might have finished with and hope someone wants it. It's free to join and free to use.

Now, I looked for other groups and sites that I might be able to connect with. That way, I'd be able to cut my consumption bit by bit. There are plenty of options out there, if you know where to look. Sites such as Swap Tree and Swap Shop are online trading marketplaces. There's the Collaborative Consumption movement, which brings together peer-to-peer schemes allowing people to work together and share resources. Plus there's the long-established, well-known networks such as Craigslist and Gumtree, and offline local groups like the ReUse network.

Interestingly, it wasn't always just about giving things away or swapping them for something else. There were also a number of sites, such as the Rent My Items, where people were renting out items for a fee.

Through these networks, I was beginning to understand that just because I thought something was useless didn't mean other people would agree, and it was far better to keep things in the system – and make sure they were used until they were worn out – than just chucking them away.

And I saw that this was an alternative system driven by passionate people. There were now businesses based around it, campaign groups promoting it and networks of individuals embracing it.

This is an edited extract from 'The Armchair Activist's Handbook' by Ruth Stokes (Silvertail Books). Further ideas for activism can be found at www.ruthstokes.com

PETER JEWEL

My Allotment

A bitter wintry morning, the ground soggy from several days' heavy rain, yet covered with a crisp frost, like icing. The white on the branches of the little apple tree stands out against the dull grey sky, and my breath condenses in the still air. A shiver runs up my spine – part cold, part anticipation – as I walk to my plot. In their neat rows, the cabbages, kale and chard look limp in the dampness. By the overflowing water butt the fox's sodden droppings, and on a bare branch a solitary magpie, squawking. It's 8.30 am on my allotment, and I'm the only one here working, all the other plots a silent empty patchwork. My winter landscape. I left my warm bed with the cat snuggled into the hollow left by my head. But I'd rather be here than almost anywhere, a place that I have created and nurtured, one of a small group of allotments bordered by the road on one side and the railway on the other, a little bit of flat suburban England on the edge of town. Three years ago I was offered an all-expenses-paid trip to Japan to give a talk at a friend's important anniversary. My immediate thought was: 'Oh no, I won't be able to go to the allotment!' and I had to think very hard before accepting.

For the allotment has become part of me. I remember standing on it one morning at the beginning of last autumn, by the beetroot and parsnips. My whole body and being felt rich and utterly at peace, and there was a growing sense of warmth that seemed to rise from the ground and permeate every sinew and nerve. I really belonged to the earth, was completely rooted. The warmth percolated up from the rich loam and went right through me like an energy-giving sap. I was full of a calm joy, fully connected, absolutely part of the world, the earth, the grass, and all the vegetables. The laden tree exemplified the sense of swelling fruitfulness and glowing fulfilment of the whole allotment. It was Samuel Palmer's Magic Apple Tree. When I was a small boy living in a small house in a London suburb, my father created three tiny gardens, for me and my two brothers, at the

end of his own vegetable patch. We each had a little fence and a gate, and I loved creating borders, sowing a few seeds, and watching some of them actually come up and produce real carrots or peas. Now as I stand in my prepared allotment all the delight and thrill of that small boy returns, and I find myself in touch with that wonderful sense of the possibility of growth. When I took the allotment over it was not like that – it was in a state of great neglect. Waist-high thistles and nettles covered much of the large plot, and as I gradually and painfully dug them out by hand I discovered the couch grass roots, feet deep in the ground. Years later, I still haven't got rid of them all. The digging was very hard work, but I resisted the temptation to hire a rotavator or use any chemical weedkillers, and very gradually what looked like rich, pristine soil was exposed, full of large, plump worms. The excitement of seeing beautiful beds of clear fertile earth! I had at last got the ground ready for planting, hoeing and raking to achieve a fine tilth, and this felt like a great achievement in itself. I had carefully prepared the canvas and was now rather nervously ready for the first brushstroke. It was very daunting too. I had no particular gardening skills or horticultural knowledge. Over the years, I had tended various gardens attached to houses I had lived in, and I had enjoyed doing that. I had sometimes bought and planted flowers, shrubs and even occasional vegetables chosen from garden stores. But this was very different. It would all be trial and error. And that felt fine – it was even part of the excitement. I had no desire to grow show vegetables or compete with the other allotment holders. I would gratefully accept any tips they might offer, and perhaps in time I would become a 'good enough' grower of vegetables myself.

One of the joys of having an allotment is the sense of camaraderie with other plot holders. I can think of no other human activity where one meets and works alongside people from completely different backgrounds, and all are accepted and valued for themselves.

People often offer each other some of their vegetables, or share seeds. Around my plot there are a Spanish husband and wife, whose plot is impeccable and who each year present me with some of their pepper plants; a company director who plants by the moon; a drama teacher from a local secondary school; an ex-policeman who grows wonderful leeks; and an Indian gardener who has a huge coriander patch and cultivates many other herbs. Two young women share a plot, and near them is a family with young children who dig away enthusiastically with their plastic spades. The IT specialist three plots away told me he used to belong to a health club that cost him nearly a thousand pounds a year. Now on his allotment he gets all the aerobic exercise he needs, plus the fresh air and a year's supply of fresh organic vegetables – and all for an annual rent of about £30.

Most people have a sense of the beauty of the natural environment, but it is often a selective one. They will walk in the Cotswolds or the Lake District, and take their holidays on the Cornish coast. They will fly to exotic locations around the world, and take photos of spectacular scenery. Travel documentaries and glossy brochures reinforce this sense that beauty is always somewhere else, somewhere not really connected to one's real life. We go there, see the sights, and then return. Next year, having 'done that', we find another beauty spot. On my allotment I have a very different sense that it is where I am right now, working on the soil of my small patch of ground, that is so beautiful and so fulfilling. Banal and very ordinary-seeming to most people who drive past without really looking, allotments are places where you have to slow down and open up to a different rhythm – the rhythm of the Earth, from which we have cut ourselves off, and to which we need to return to fulfil our human potential.

Many years ago I used to make a lot of homemade wine. A friend and his wife came to offer their help collecting dandelions, which make a delicious white. 'What next?' he asked, once we had picked a large pile of the flower-heads. 'We'll sit down in the sun and pull off the individual petals and put them in this bucket,' I said. 'But that'll take hours!' – he was horrified. 'Yes,' I smiled, and I think his wife understood: she smiled back and settled down. On an allotment many things take time; one needs to settle back into a different sense of time, to get back into balance with the pulse of Nature. Each year I witness the amazing miracle of growth, and still get as excited as I did as a little boy when I see the first shoots emerge. How incredible it is that from the small bean I planted several weeks ago a plant will emerge that grows to waist height and produces so many long pods of broad beans! That a straggly large-leaved plant producing masses of green or yellow courgettes that seem to get bigger and bigger in front of my very eyes should come from a little pip! Or that amazing cabbages or leeks will emerge from tiny seeds! One cannot fail to experience a sense of wonder and awe, and when the fruit or vegetable is picked at the end of the long process that began with the planting of the seed, there is a sense of joy in the completion. Then, a couple of hours later it is cooked and eaten, and the delight in its startling freshness and rich full flavour is something no supermarket commodity can ever match.

This delight continues through most of the year. Those long pods of broad beans, with seven or eight beans swelling inside, give way to the carrots with their filigree leaves and a hint of dark orange stump, and the red-veined leaves of the beetroot. Later comes the wonderful 'Cosse Violette' French climbing bean, purple flowers and stems and long purple pods, soaring upwards, while on the ground the straggly courgettes, some buttercup yellow, others light and dark green stripes, sprawl and swell. Throughout autumn the glossy dark leaves and bright yellow stems of the Swiss chard intermingle with the densely curled violet-green leaves of the curly kale, and – my favourite vegetable of all – the profusion of dark florets of the purple sprouting broccoli. Allotments are bright havens in a world where the destructive plundering of Nature by industrial companies and the despoiling of the environment by agribusiness are all around us. My heart screams out when I see cut hedges where the mangled, ripped and torn branches are the gashed wounds of a callous and brutal machine. Contrast that with the work of the traditional hedger whose sympathetically half-cut and carefully bent saplings are woven into a living fence that will grow organically – a source of pride and delight. It is exactly that sense of pride and delight that I feel in my allotment. Things of course go wrong – some seeds don't come up, blackfly and blight sometimes destroy my broad beans and tomatoes, slugs and snails are a perennial problem, whitefly can get everywhere, the weather sometimes makes things very difficult, and there are always the weeds, which survive and flourish when my vegetables don't.

But that is all part of the way things are in the natural world, like the sweat and aches of my body. I accept it all as it is, just as I accept the fox who tramples and digs up some of my plants. Once as I was sitting by my shed, he walked up to me, stopped a few feet away, and looked long and hard at me, almost nonchalant. He was scraggy and thin, but still very beautiful. I smiled at him, a momentary recognition, a connection. Then he was off, and I got up and carried on digging. I think of him now, in the winter cold. I hope he's survived. As I dig through the crisp frosty covering to the rich earth beneath, the damp greyness all around me, I notice that the first tiny tips of the winter onions are emerging from their globe-shaped bulbs, and there is a hint of green.

Peter Jewel is a counsellor and supervisor, with a special interest in the potential for growth. This essay was originally published by Resurgence & Ecologist in 2013 and was a winner of their nature writing competition.

Horse Power: The Future of Farming?

The countryside around the village of Chagford, on the edge of Dartmoor in Devon, is the stuff of picture postcards – rolling hills, thick forests, deep valleys, gushing streams, lots of farms. The winding, narrow lanes that criss-cross the region follow the contours of the land closely; when the hill is steep, the road is steep; where a stream or river runs its course the road simply cuts right through – quite literally.

Village notice-boards carry posters advertising field sports. Passing 4x4 vehicles are splattered with real mud. This is traditional rural England where country pastimes remain popular and meddling by outsiders is frowned upon.

Not quite so conservative as it appears

It's the sort of place that would have sent coach-loads of people to the huge countryside protest marches periodically held in London during Tony Blair's Labour government. But the notice-boards here are also dotted with posters hinting at a very different community. One announces a course in Goddesses – workshops where participants apparently use 'myth, journeying, movement and creativity'. Another has details on a local allotment scheme and how to get involved.

In the village centre there's a packed wholefood cafe and health food shop that sells lots of vegetarian and vegan food. There are adverts on the wall for organic smallholdings for sale in places such as Spain. Three people queueing up for food are talking about the spiritual retreat – and associated detox – that they've just completed locally. A lady with long, long dreadlocks is chatting to someone about festivals.

Community supported food

I'm in the cafe with Ed Hamer. He's a radical young farmer and the driving force behind a pioneering community-supported agriculture scheme – Chagfood, based at Easton Cross just outside Chagford itself. It's increasingly attracting attention because of its vigorous rejection of conventional, oil-based farming methods in favour of traditional horsepower.

Everyone in here seems to know Ed. Because of atrocious weather the planned Chagfood open day has just been postponed; people are asking when it'll be rearranged for – and those that don't will almost certainly have heard of him.

A financial commitment

Ed explains how Chagfood supplies seasonal fruit and vegetables to a growing number of local households on a weekly basis, with the recipients paying a annual subscription fee of up to £600 to secure their share of produce for the year ahead.

This unique upfront payment is partly what makes the venture stand out from more typical box schemes – where consumers generally pick and choose when and what to buy.

The financial commitment helps Ed, and co-founder and business partner Chinnie Kinsbury, plan and bankroll the year's cultivation. It also means – as is central to the ethos behind community-supported agriculture projects – that the risks and rewards of production are more equally shared between consumers and producers.

'In 2010, we supplied 25 weekly boxes from one acre of land; in 2011 it was 50 from two acres, last year it was 75 boxes from three acres,' he says; 'this year we are planning to increase this further... but not too much.' Shareholders receive a full box of produce between June and December – the bountiful months – and a smaller clutch of items in the leaner times between January and May.

Cutting the food miles

The venture started life in 2009 after a public meeting organised by think-tank the New Economics Foundation found that a significant cross section of the local community wanted to try and 'shorten the distance' between local food producers and consumers. Residents said they wanted access to fresh and affordable produce and so initial plans to establish a community-owned market garden were put in place.

Following the securing of a suitable site – a small plot rented out from a sympathetic farmer – a core group, Ed and Chinnie, supported by an enthusiastic body of friends and volunteers, spent much of the autumn and winter of 2009 preparing the ground to begin sowing their first crops.

The project then managed to secure financial backing from a number of sources, including the Big Lottery Fund's local food programme – enabling the purchase of essential tools and helping underwrite costs in the teething phase – which helped make the whole thing viable.

Community support

Ed is certain the venture would have happened anyway, even if there was some scepticism amongst the region's veteran – and sometimes weary – farmers. 'It was certainly easier having a history', says Ed, recalling his many months of misspent youth working on local farms. 'But in that first year a lot of farmers were sceptical.' However the scepticism transformed into open support within the year 'once they saw it working through'.

Chagfood wouldn't be possible without the physical assistance of the shareholders and other supporters. Because of the upfront outlay many subscribers have a lot more interest in being directly involved in helping with the planting, harvesting and other farm tasks, Ed says.

'Each week we have between 10–15 people helping out. It's about the community aspect and the cultural side of farming, a side that's been lost. We have harvest and spring festivals, and the kids are always involved.'

Horse drawn power

Now, impressively, with the scheme in its fourth year proper, Ed confirms that Chagfood is financially self-supporting with two wages (admittedly low, even by farming standards) being paid and essential operating costs covered.

The cost of the operation is kept low in part by the deployment of horse-power in place of diesel-thirsty tractors and other vehicles typically used in conventional farming. Chagfood uses Samson, a Welsh-cob-horse-cross-Dartmoor-pony, to carry out most of the cultivation and tilling of its fields – the original site at Easton Cross has just been joined by another nearby field leased from a local organic farm – and to transport its produce.

Wonderful contraptions

Until recently, Samson has worked the fields attached to a tillage device known as the Kassine, which originates in France where horse-drawn agriculture is more commonplace, especially amongst peasant farmers. Now, the arsenal at Chagfood's disposal includes another contraption called the Pioneer Homesteader. Ed imported the old fashioned yet sturdy-looking device from an Amish community in the US.

'These are hand-made,' Ed says, showing me the device as we shelter in a small shed that offers little protection from the driving rain. 'There's been 200 sold so far – this is the first one in Europe.' Like a Massey Ferguson tractor it straddles the bed and can take a variety of different tools, each for a specific job.

'It's the principal of mechanisation applied to horses,' Ed enthuses. The system gives him the best of all worlds – a relief from the back-breaking slog and zero fuel bills, while protecting all-important soil structure: 'There's less compaction on the soil and little running costs.'

Industrial agribusiness

Ed's enthusiasm for using a horse in place of a tractor or other machinery runs deeper than simple financial calculations. As well as being a farmer, he's co-editor of the radical *The Land Magazine*, and a founder of the campaign group Reclaim the Fields, which seeks to empower those seeking greater access to land across Europe.

He argues that conventional farming and agribusiness is fundamentally wrong because of its reliance on financial subsidies, and says that two of the biggest hurdles facing those wanting to farm are access to land and skills. He believes in stripping it all down – what Chagfood is doing is actually just growing food and selling it at a realistic price:

'It's the real cost of food, our costs are the same since we started, compared with the supermarket. We're able to tailor production to local demand. Local food schemes are more resilient; we're not plugged into the food infrastructure – we are connecting people to local food.'

Andrew Wasley is an investigative journalist specialising in food, environmental, and consumer issues.

BERNARD JARMAN

A Dare for the Life, Soul and Spirit of the Earth

For the last hundred years or so our planet has been considered to be a globe of rock rotating round the sun in a vast empty space, endless and barren save for occasional fragments of matter floating aimlessly by. Life on earth began, so it is thought, by some chance act of evolution that caused certain chemical substances to take on living characteristics and gradually evolve into the life forms we know today and that the prime driver of evolution was a multi-million year struggle for existence in which competing organisms sought to gain advantage over one another.

Perhaps a crucial change in perception occurred when the first astronauts were able to look back from space and see with human eyes how precious and unique our planet is and experience how nothing in the vast enormity of space can be compared with the wonder and beauty of this one great jewel of creation.

The Earth today is increasingly seen as being an interrelated web of living relationships. Every part of the Earth's geography and each organism living above or beneath its surface is essential for the well-being of the whole. It is mutual support rather than competition that appears to be the driving principle. The rain forests have been described as the lungs of the Earth and without the desert regions global rainfall circulation patterns could not function as they do. There is a fine balance between climate, vegetation and animal life across the world which is constantly adapting and readjusting itself. This implies that not only is the Earth a living organism but that there is an organising principle – the planet has its own unique identity or spirit.

The relationship between the Earth and humanity is close and inseparable. The current abstract conception of evolution, with its vast cycles of time, is but one way of understanding this Earth of ours. There are within all cultures of the world rich folk memories and legends that tell the story of how the Earth was

born and how human beings came to be. The images vary greatly and yet there is no contradiction between them. These creation myths express in an imaginative language accessible to everyone, a sense for the true origins of our existence. The common thread running through all these legends is the story of how human beings gradually emerged as the guardians and protectors of all created life. The so-called indigenous peoples of the Earth have always known this and consider themselves and the land they live in as one organism. In the well-known statement attributed to Chief Seattle in 1854 for instance we hear: 'Every hillside, every valley, every plain and grove, has been hallowed by some sad or happy event in days long vanished. Even the rocks, which seem to be dumb and dead and swelter in the sun along the silent shore, thrill with memories of stirring events connected with the lives of my people…'

And in the words of Genesis we read: 'And God said, let us make man in our own image, after our likeness and give him dominion over the fish of the sea and over the fowl of the air and over the cattle and over every creeping thing that creepeth upon the earth.'

In both examples the story is of human beings having or being given responsibility for the Earth. The Genesis version of being given 'dominion over' suggests power to control and exploit but it can also be interpreted to mean 'to care for and nurture'. After God created the world he rested and made the further progress of creation dependent on what human beings do with it. Indeed a discussion is currently underway amongst geologists as to whether our time should be given the name 'Anthropocene' to reflect a geological age that is dominated by human interventions. Today the future of our planet is very clearly in our hands. We can either decide to destroy what has been bequeathed to us or take care of it and start transforming it into something new.

Ever since human beings settled down and began tilling the soil, nature has been worked upon and transformed. Truly untouched wilderness is extremely rare. The cultural landscapes such as those of Europe, Asia and the Americas have been crafted by human hands over hundreds or even thousands of years. Thoughtless and one-sided development is rapidly destroying this heritage. Rewilding may be part of its redemption but only as part of a holistic approach that includes human-cultivated landscapes. Conservation and agriculture, too often seen as separate, belong together. The whole farm needs to be a diverse 'nature reserve' while at the same time being productive and meeting the needs of the human population. Agriculture ('agri-culture'), which literally means 'culture of the field', is about taking care of and respecting what already exists, but also creating a new culture of nature. It is an imagination that inspires organic and especially biodynamic farming.

A central principle of biodynamic farming is connected with the living nature of the Earth but also with its soul and spiritual aspects. 'A farm is true to its essential nature', said Rudolf Steiner in lecture II of his Agriculture Course, 'if it is conceived of as a self-contained individuality.' This means on an agricultural level that all the compost and manures required for fertilising the soil, as well as the feedstuffs needed to sustain its livestock, should originate from the farm itself. Although hard to achieve in an absolute sense this is the ideal towards which every biodynamic farmer aspires. Working towards this goal means that as the years go by, the soil, plants and animals on the farm adapt ever more closely to each other's needs. Their closer kinship can then strengthen the immune system of the whole farm, improve health and lead to greater biodiversity. The biodynamic approach also employs special measures to enhance the health and vitality of animals, plants and especially the soil. Soil is the basis of our existence and the creation of healthy and vital humus is arguably one of the most important challenges facing us throughout the world today.

A site-adapted, ecologically diverse and self-contained farm also creates fertile ground upon which to develop community life – not as in ancient times based on family and tribal ties – but on the free association of individual human beings interested in sharing responsibility for the land. Community-supported agriculture is a good example of how an ecologically aware farming system can lead to the creation of a mutually supportive economic structure and offer an alternative to the self-serving and ultimately ecocidal mechanisms operating in our so-called free market economy. A farm can be a focus for social and ecological renewal and through its seasonal community events and festivals, provide a cultural focus extending beyond the boundaries of the farm. Caring for the diversity of creation and growing sufficient to feed, clothe and house everyone on Earth is a goal that we can all share in as part of a positive campaign to save the Earth from the threat of ecocide.

Bernard Jarman is a biodynamic farmer and gardener.

The Power of Just Doing Stuff

Something is stirring. People around the world are deciding that the well-being of their local community and its economy lies with them. They're people like you. They've had enough, and, rather than waiting for permission, they're rolling up their sleeves, getting together with friends and neighbours, and doing something about it. Whether they start small or big, they're finding that 'just doing stuff' can transform their neighbourhoods and their lives.

This shift represents the seeds of a new economy – the answer to our desperate search for a new way forward – and at its heart are people deciding that change starts with them. Communities worldwide are already modelling a more local economy rooted in place, in well-being, in entrepreneurship and in creativity. In cities, villages, towns, islands, streets and regions, people are coming together. Possibly you've noticed it where you live. It can be seen in the local food movement, the explosion in 'pop-up shops', craft breweries, the rebirth of independent record shops, the growth of social enterprises, the flowering of community renewables, and in communities taking over and investing in their local football clubs.

As you come to feel more engaged in shaping your economic destiny, and become more aware that your actions can actually lead to change, you will see that much of the power to make change actually lies with you. It has the potential to alter how we educate our young people, how schools and colleges interface with their local communities, how they see their role in preparing young people for work – perhaps more about how to create their own work, rather than find traditional employment.

When communities take the initiative they show that the changes needed are not some kind of step backwards but are in fact unleashing huge creativity and entrepreneurship. In order to realise this potential, we need to not just remove the obstacles that stand in its way, but also be able to mobilise people to make it happen, to harness 'the power of just doing stuff'.

There are now about 1,300 registered Transition groups, active in 43 countries around the world, although we know there are many more. In Sweden for example, of the 170 active groups, only 4 or 5 are registered, and in Japan there are 4 registered but we hear of about 70 on the ground. The same is the case in other places too, so the figures may well be the tip of the iceberg.

I wrote 'The Power of Just Doing Stuff' because it felt like the maturing of Transition had reached a crucial point. Increasingly Transition groups are using the foundations they have built, of vibrant groups, of community support, of a dynamic vision for the future, to build new, localised and resilient economies. What we are seeing is a deepening and a maturing as well as growth in the number of initiatives. It's very exciting.

Initially it was very much founded on a concern about peak oil and climate change. It argued that when you look at those two as overlapping issues, what emerges is the need for decarbonisation and resilience-building alongside each other. Since then, the economic situation has also become a driver. What fascinates me most though is that when you ask people involved in Transition why they do it, they mainly talk about how it brings people closer together, how they feel part of the creation of a healthier human culture in the place they live.

Most recently, the concept of 'community resilience as economic development' has really come to the fore, the idea that the very process of making a community more resilient could also be what revives its economic fortunes, creates the livelihoods and businesses that we need to move forward, and meets our needs better than the current approach.

The challenges presented to Transition are huge. How on earth can Transition be a proportionate response to them? There is no guarantee that it can be. However, I think that what we are seeing emerging is starting to show a way in which it could. The core argument of 'The Power of Just Doing Stuff' is that, according to the Portas Review, 97% of all groceries sold in the UK are now sold through just 8,000 supermarket outlets. Let us say, for argument's sake, that the other 3% is the local and independent retail sector. The question for me is whether we seek to, as the government and corporations are currently doing, grow the 97% even further, or whether our future actually lies in growing the 3%.

We know that the 3% economy creates three times more jobs for every pound spent than the 97% economy, that it builds greater social capital, more resilient economies, is lower in carbon use, and even, according to a US study, results in higher voter turnout at elections. We already know that the Transition model, as a way for people to meet other people, organise and support each other and start making things happen, is very effective and works in most places. The next consideration is how we turn that into new enterprises, and support people so they have the right skills and confidence to think they can start new enterprises.

Then there are what we call 'economic evaluations', which have been done for Totnes and for Herefordshire, with Brixton's coming soon. These are a detailed mapping of the local economy and where the money goes, which allows, for the first time, an economic case for localisation to be presented. For example, we now know that in Totnes we spend £30 million on food every year, £22 million of that going to just two supermarkets. That's £22 million slipping through our fingers every year like sand. If we could shift just 10% of that to the local food economy, that's

£2 million a year. Suddenly localisation becomes a form of economic development. Nottingham University Hospitals Trust now sources 90% of its meat and 90% of its seasonal vegetables from within 30 miles, a £2 million injection into the local economy. That's not some sort of 'flight from progress', that's the innovative economy of the future.

Finally, when we have lots of enterprises coming through, and the kind of strategic context that economic evaluations provide, we have an economic approach that delivers a social return and an economic one. We are working to create an investment fund to bring in the kind of support that this needs. If we can get all these elements working really well, then maybe, just maybe, we will start to have something that is proportionate to the problem.

However it's important to say that Transition can't do all this on its own. We also need individuals, government, business, and local authorities playing a role, but what Transition offers is that vital piece in the middle – what we can do if we get together with the people around us and do the things that can only come from the ground up. Whether you have an interest in food, arts, energy, social enterprise, or simply meeting and getting to know members of your community, then Transition has something for you.

Rob Hopkins is founder of the Transition movement. This article was originally published by The Ecologist in 2014.

The Importance of Community

One of the great challenges of our time is to create and nurture sustainable communities, designed in such a way that our ways of life, businesses, economy, physical structures, and technologies do not interfere with nature's inherent ability to sustain life. Over the last few years, I have become more and more convinced that the focus on community itself will be critical in this endeavor. There are several reasons for that. To design sustainable human communities, we first need to understand how nature sustains life. Over billions of years, the Earth's ecosystems have evolved certain patterns of organization to sustain the web of life. Examples of these patterns of organization are: one species' waste is another species' food, matter cycles continually through the web of life, the energy driving the ecological cycles flows from the sun, and diversity assures resilience. Most importantly, perhaps, we need to understand that life, from its beginning more than three billion years ago, did not take over the planet by combat but by networking. These basic patterns of organization, or principles of ecology, can also be understood as principles of community.

Sustainability is not an individual property but a property of an entire web of relationships. It always involves a whole community. This is the profound lesson we need to learn from nature. The way to sustain life is to build and nurture community. A sustainable human community interacts with other communities – human and nonhuman – in ways that enable them to live and develop according to their nature. Today, the greatest obstacle to moving toward sustainability is the persistent illusion, maintained by economists and politicians, that unlimited growth is possible on a finite planet. Economic and corporate growth are pursued relentlessly by promoting excessive material consumption. A continual barrage of advertising tells us that buying more goods will make us happier. The most powerful antidote against this corporate onslaught is to find happiness in human relationships – in other words, in community.

I have long thought that building communities is important not only in our society at large but also within business organizations. This was confirmed to me when I came across the recent book by the American organizational theorist and management consultant Peter Block, titled *Community: The Structure of Belonging*. In this book, Block describes his philosophy, experience and methods for creating more accountable leadership and citizenship as well as the importance of 'place' that inspires people to build thriving, connected communities. Building community, for Block, means interconnecting people and systems emotionally, spiritually and psychologically with a sense of safety and belonging. He emphasizes the importance of designing the right space for these interactions to take place. Designing the right space is as important for cities as it is for human organizations. The loss of community in our modern cities is the central concern of landscape architect and urban designer Randolph Hester. In his book *Design for Ecological Democracy* Hester observes that nurturing a sense of community is not a goal in conventional urban design and that, as a consequence, most neighbourhoods have lost the ability to engage in deliberation and cooperation. In addition, he notes that most urban design practices separate us from the natural environment and render us ecologically illiterate. To overcome these twin problems, Hester proposes to use urban design to transform our inhabited landscapes into ecologically sustainable, community-oriented, and joyful places. At the core of Hester's approach is his concept of 'ecological democracy' – the attempt to foster direct citizen participation in ecologically oriented urban design.

In conclusion, moving toward a sustainable future will only be possible if we can transform our schools, business organizations, and urban neighbourhoods into vibrant communities.

Fritjof Capra is a physicist and systems theorist.

Love in Corporations

I believe that sustainable business will emerge out of a conversation between value and values, between profit and purpose.

I have a rather faded sarong that I have carried on my travels for 25 years, using it as a towel, a sheet or even, on occasions, a piece of clothing. I bought it in the north-east of Thailand from a business set up by some enterprising nuns to help local women make a living from their traditional weaving skills. The aim was to reduce the numbers of women driven by poverty to join the sex trade in Bangkok. The business – the Village Weavers Handicrafts – has been a great success and the last I heard was still going strong. It is hard to imagine any other type of intervention that would have been so effective, so sustainable in the long term and so empowering for these women.

I'm sure we can all think of small, inspiring businesses like this that have made a positive contribution to their communities. What is much rarer is large, inspiring businesses. When a business grows beyond a certain size, efficiency and growth seem to come to the fore and 'softer' priorities such as compassion, truth and social justice fade away into the background. The logic of the system takes over, often despite the best efforts of those supposedly in charge. At scale, the organisational structure becomes decisive. And our structures are now showing their age.

The fundamental legal form for business, the limited company, has been with us in its current form since 1856. It's remarkable to think of all the technological advances we have made in the last 157 years (such as putting men on the moon, the internet, splitting the atom) while we haven't changed the basic form of organisation for business, despite its drawbacks.

Its principal shortcoming is that those who finance the business are treated as owners, having the ultimate power to appoint and dismiss the board with no matching responsibility. This power without responsibility tends to encourage immorality and a lack of concern for the consequences of shareholders' actions. It also encourages the board to focus more on 'shareholder value' than on human or environmental values such as conservation and a reduction in waste and pollution. This top-down model, a hangover from a bygone feudal age, is also disempowering for those further down in the system. Isn't it time to liberate the modern-day serfs who toil away in our large corporations?

I started to think these thoughts 10 years ago when, as a corporate lawyer, I was handling mergers and acquisitions for a multinational retailer. I had always enjoyed my work and was comfortable amongst the trappings of power – the dark suits, the imposing corporate buildings, the teams of support staff for the top people, the huge salaries. Yet I was starting to feel uncomfortable. It was becoming impossible to ignore the environmental crisis, and the role played by large corporations in contributing to that crisis. Subscribing to *Resurgence* magazine only increased my discomfort! It kept raising questions I couldn't answer. And I didn't find a place within the corporation to raise my concerns.

Eventually I left the corporate world and went to work in the not-for-profit sector. At first this made for a refreshing change – everyone wore jeans and sweaters and talked a lot about values. Yet they also spent inordinate amounts of time worrying about diversity policies and arguing about whose values were best. I came to miss the dynamism, energy and creativity of business. Couldn't we combine the best of these two worlds, I wondered.

I am not the first person to ask this question. I came across 'social enterprises': small, dynamic enterprises aiming to use the power of business to achieve social or environmental aims. Yet I was intrigued to learn that there is no legal form for a social enterprise. They are a hotchpotch of charities, cooperatives and limited companies, none of which are quite suited for the job. Every structure has its own bias. I dreamed of experimenting with new structures, which led me to Riversimple.

Riversimple is a UK-based business that I am involved with. Our special talent is integration, and our first product is a very unusual type of car. Capable of 300 miles per gallon (energy equivalent), our demonstrator vehicle is powered by hydrogen and built from carbon composites. Its carbon emissions are three times lower than anything on the market and there is potential for much greater reduction in the future as green hydrogen appears. (We intend to have cars on the road in 2015.)

Our breakthrough with the technology comes from integrating existing components in a new way. We have done something similar with our legal structure. Our starting premise was simple: if you're a stakeholder, you should have a stake! We have appointed six trustees (custodians) to speak for six groups of stakeholders who are customers, staff, investors, suppliers, neighbours and the planet. These six custodians, each a separate legal entity, collectively appoint the board. Investors receive 'shards', similar to non-voting shares. We believe our model will scale very well.

As far as we are aware, this structure is unique, in particular the giving of a voice to the planet at the highest level of the business. Yet the underlying philosophy is not new. It is based on trusteeship, where assets are held 'in trust' by one group to be used by and for the benefit of others. Moving beyond ownership to trusteeship is critical if we are to achieve the level of selflessness needed to truly integrate multiple interests, and to think and act for the long term. Trusteeship was advocated by Gandhi (amongst others). The John Lewis Partnership is owned by a trust, as is *The Guardian*. And *Resurgence & Ecologist* magazine.

Looking wider, I see us as part of a movement of people developing Earth law, which includes Polly Higgins' work on the Law of Ecocide, and the Mother Earth law adopted in Bolivia.

I continue to take inspiration, 25 years on, from the nuns in Thailand. They created a business that was financially and socially sustainable, holding on to their deeper values while pursuing efficiency on a daily basis. It is out of that conversation between value and values, profit and purpose, power and love that new sustainable businesses will emerge to lead the way to a more just and caring society.

Patrick Andrews is a facilitator and governance adviser. He has contributed to 'Stories of the Great Turning', edited by Peter Reason and Melanie Newman (Vala Publications). This article was first published by Resurgence & Ecologist in 2014.

"Ecocide is the term for serious destruction to the environment – to nature. Simply put, it is damage to the air we breathe, the water we drink; the rivers and oceans we love to swim and fish in. It is also the serious destruction of the countryside we love to stroll in, the mountains, hills, rivers, forests and seas. It is devilishly hard to re-create an ancient forest or a mountain top that has been trashed by mining. The earth has enough slag heaps and ugly quarries. Ecocide is already a crime – in war-time but not in peace. We drew the line at Napalm, and Agent Orange, eventually. Now it is time to draw some more lines."
Joselyn Morton, journalist and campaigner with 'End Ecocide in Europe'

Business Harmony

Why must business become scientifically inspired and emotionally connected with Nature? Can business be a force for good? Should it strive for more than just limiting its harm? I think we intuitively know it can; yet it requires courage to break rank from the mainstream approach to business.

The prevailing business paradigm of maximisation, monoculture, self-interest and short-termism is weakening its own resilience, in turn sowing the seeds of its own demise. Our business concepts, values, perceptions and practices are being disrupted and systemically challenged. This 'perfect storm' of crises provides a situation for individuals and organisations to retrench or transform. Those who are able to adapt in these volatile times face nothing less than a shift to a new business paradigm: a way forward that seeks to enhance life on Earth rather than destroy it. Like the ancient Chinese proverb: in times of great winds some build bunkers, others build windmills.

Our approach to business has encouraged us to see ourselves as separate from Nature, and to view the world around us as something to be analysed and exploited for our own wants and needs. The sobering fact of the matter is that this approach (and its immense power to fuel problems as well as implement solutions) is neither balanced nor life-encompassing: it is reductionist and anthropocentric in its belief and behaviour. This reductionist view of the world has encouraged an alienation from Nature, leaving us unbalanced in our understanding of the real world – the world not just of stock market trends and commodity prices, but also of soil and sea, of cycles and seasons, and of ecosystems and environments.

Ray Anderson, former Chair and CEO of Interface, observed: 'We have been, and still are, in the grip of a flawed view of reality – a flawed paradigm, a flawed world view – and it pervades our culture putting us on a biological collision course with collapse. It is the paradigm that is reflected in our culture's infatuation with stuff and our willful ignorance of Nature.'

When Charles Darwin published his *Origin of Species*, the phrase 'survival of the fittest' was quickly co-opted and distorted by powerful elites to promote the idea that only the biggest, strongest and most powerful can survive. In reality, what Darwin found and described in his findings was that those organisms with the greatest ability to adapt to their local environment would survive when and where others would fail. He found that sensing, responding, adapting, and aligning with and within the local ecosystem were key to survival. Recent scientific discoveries, coupled with advances in systems thinking and quantum theory, continue to build on these findings, and uncover a more complex and holistic view of Nature, the workings of the universe, and the evolution of life.

So how does business go about shifting from a mindset of short-term profit maximisation that views the world as a collection of things to be consumed, to a worldview that has an energetic and material engagement with place and a symbiotic relationship with life? In short, how does the prevalent approach of business break its devastating illusion of being apart from Nature to realise that we are a part of Nature, even with our specialities?

This question of the moment can be answered through three Rs – Redesign, Reconnect, Rekindle:

1 Redesigning – new ways of operating and innovating beyond 'less bad' into 'doing good' (shifting from the take/make/waste economic paradigm to a regenerative approach that heals society and the web of life rather than destroying life in the name of short-term gain).

2 Reconnecting – reconciling our human relationship with life/ Nature and our own authentic human nature (re-establishing our vital bond with ourselves, our neighbours and the web of life of which we are a part, through education, authentic leadership and ecopsychology).

3 Rekindling wisdom – working with the grain of Nature and operating within the rules of life on Earth (enabling businesses and societies not merely to 'sustain' but to thrive in the years ahead by practising wise approaches to life that draw on symbiosis, ecological thinking, permaculture, systems-thinking and systems-being, business inspired by Nature and Indigenous wisdom).

In these challenging times for business, we must realise that to become truly sustainable, business life has to become scientifically inspired, emotionally connected and spiritually entwined with Nature and Gaia. Nature and business must be symbiotic and operate in mutualism for there to be anything resembling a successful outcome.

The sooner business realises the opportunities that come with being connected to and inspired by Nature, the better for humanity and the interconnected fabric of life.

Giles Hutchins is the author of 'The Nature of Business: Redesigning for Resilience', published by Green Books. www.thenatureofbusiness.org. This article was first published by Resurgence & Ecologist in 2014.

CARL HONORÉ

Eco-slow

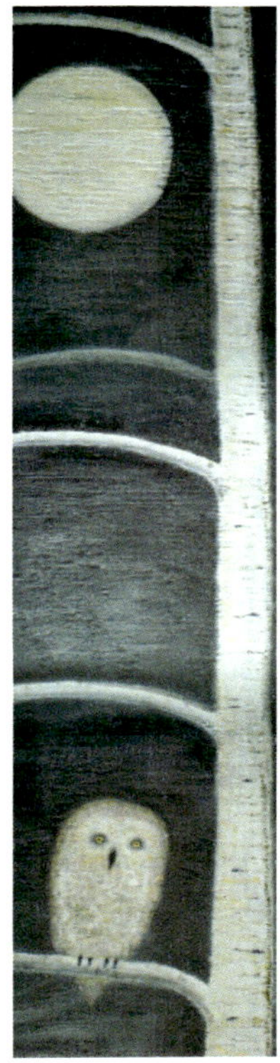

PETER ADAMS

The other day a woman walked into a doctor's surgery and issued a demand that summed up why the world is in such a mess. 'Look, I know I have a million things wrong with me, but I really don't want a lecture; I just want a pill that will make it all go away.' The doctor, an old friend of mine, waited for the woman to laugh at her own joke. But she didn't, because it wasn't a joke.

Of course, her craving for a quick fix is nothing new. Two thousand years ago, Plutarch denounced the army of quacks peddling miracle cures to the citizens of Ancient Rome. Today, however, the quick fix has become the default setting in every walk of life. Whenever a problem crops up in business, politics or society, in the environment, in our health or relationships, we reach for the nearest just-add-water solution. And it's taking a heavy toll.

Why? Because quick fixes seldom deliver on their seductive promise of maximum return for minimum effort. When it comes to the really hard problems in the world – combatting poverty, tackling disease, eradicating ecocide – there are no shortcuts or instant remedies. This is especially true when dealing with Mother Nature. Everywhere you look, quick fixes are failing to solve environmental problems – and often just making things worse.

One example: To clean up the oil spill caused by the Deepwater Horizon disaster of 2010, BP pumped more than seven million litres of a dispersant called Corexit into the waters of the Gulf of Mexico. Such chemicals help make the oil less visible and prevent it reaching the shore. A win-win fix, right? Wrong. Recent studies show that combining oil and Corexit yields a mixture that is up to 52 times more toxic than oil by itself. Which is seriously bad news for marine life in the Gulf of Mexico.

The good news is there's an alternative to our culture of the quick fix. It's called, not surprisingly, the Slow Fix. You may have heard of the Slow Movement, which challenges the canard that faster is always better. You don't have to ditch your career, toss the iPhone or join a commune to take part. Living 'Slow' just means doing everything at the right speed – quickly, slowly or at whatever pace delivers the best results.

When it comes to solving problems, a speedy solution can sometimes be just what the doctor ordered. There are times when you have to reach for the duct tape and cobble together whatever fix works right now. The Heimlich manoeuvre saves many lives. But for more complex problems, the best remedy is always a Slow Fix.

That means taking the time to: admit and learn from mistakes; work out the root causes of the problem; sweat the small stuff; think long term and join the dots to build holistic solutions; seek ideas from everywhere; work with others and share the credit; build up expertise while remaining sceptical of experts; think alone and together; tap emotions; enlist an inspiring leader; consult and even recruit those closest to the problem; turn the search for a fix into a game; have fun, follow hunches, adapt, use trial and error, and embrace uncertainty. This Slow Fix toolbox can be used to tackle any problem afflicting the environment. Just imagine if BP had sweated the small stuff by testing Corexit more thoroughly for side effects.

Yet forging smarter solutions for the environment will never be enough on its own. Each win for Mother Nature must be anchored in a deeper, seismic shift that puts nurturing the planet's ecology at the core of everything we do. Imagine a world where there is no need to take the risks that BP took hunting for oil deep in the Gulf of Mexico. In other words, we need a revolution in the way we live, work, travel, consume – and think. Making that happen will be the biggest Slow Fix of all.

It will not be easy to achieve. In these times of economic hardship, many people are more worried about paying their bills than nurturing the environment. But there are reasons to be hopeful. A new generation is coming of age that sees the world through an environmental lens. Companies and governments are under increasing pressure from the public to think and act green. Last November, for the first time ever, China made 'ecological progress' a pillar of its national development plan.

Putting the environment at the top of the agenda must go hand in hand with beating our addiction to the quick fix. In every walk of life, the time has come to resist the siren call of half-baked solutions and short-term palliatives, of band-aid cures and pills that 'make it all go away', in order to start fixing things properly.

The time has come to learn the art of the Slow Fix.

Carl Honoré is an award-winning journalist, author, and globetrotting ambassador for the Slow Movement. His first book, 'In Praise of Slow', examines our compulsion to hurry and chronicles a global trend toward putting on the brakes.

"Anyone who believes you can have infinite exponential growth on a finite planet is either a madman or an economist."
Kenneth Boulding (1910-1993) economist and poet

Defending Democracy

Transatlantic Trade and Investment Partnership has profound implications for British democracy.

Many years ago I had the pleasure of interviewing consumer activist and occasional presidential candidate Ralph Nader about the North American Free Trade Agreement (NAFTA). He told me that even though Congress was lining up to overwhelmingly back the treaty, he was convinced that very few of its members had bothered to actually read the text.

So he offered a prize for any member willing to publicly answer 10 simple questions about the treaty. Eventually the strongly NAFTA-supporting Republican Senator Hank Brown of Colorado accepted the challenge. Nader reserved the Senate Foreign Relations Committee room for the ordeal, and there, surrounded by reporters, and to everyone's amazement, Brown managed to answer each of the questions perfectly. When he'd finished, he turned to the cameras and declared that, having read the treaty, he felt he now understood it, and would consequently be voting against it.

The simple truth is that all too often national legislators simply don't pay attention to complex international agreements. At this stage, we don't have a huge amount to go on in relation to the Transatlantic Trade and Investment Partnership (TTIP), but if it goes through in the form that is expected, it has profound implications for the workings of British democracy, and merits very serious scrutiny.

On the whole, free-trade agreements are about lowering barriers to trade. However, between the EU and the US there are very few such barriers, so the main focus is likely to be on standards and regulations, and the goal will be to 'harmonise' them. It sounds very friendly, until you consider that big business is very

unlikely to be lobbying for standards to rise. Indeed, big-business lobby groups are quite openly calling for the removal – under TTIP – of whole swathes of regulations that hinder their activities.

Food is an obvious area because the US approach is very different from that of Europe, and of Britain in particular. It is very hard to imagine 'harmonisation' working in British interests.

For instance, the EU takes a different view from the US on GM food, a position by and large backed by consumers across Europe. In Europe, we believe that providing clear labelling of GM food is a consumer right. US agribusiness strongly disagrees.

Along with many other parts of the world, but not the US, the EU refuses imports of beef from cows fed a diet that includes the hormone Ractopamine. Given the widely documented health concerns, I suspect most consumers would support that position as well. Likewise concerning chickens treated with chlorine after slaughter.

Most worrying is strong opposition by US agribusiness to EU attempts to limit endocrine disrupters. Before 1997, it was estimated by US authorities that 1% of 8-year-old girls showed signs of entering puberty (known as precocious puberty). After 1997, following what remains the largest ever study into the phenomenon, that figure was revised to 1% of 3-year-old girls. The links between endocrine-disrupting chemicals and precocious puberty are not disputed.

Under the proposed TTIP, how would Europe's position on GM labelling, hormones and endocrine disrupters fare? It's hard to imagine Europe holding out for long against the US. It's far more likely that 'regulatory convergence' will mean chasing the lowest common denominator.

It's worth noting that – according to a number of Freedom of Information requests by the Corporate Europe Observatory – in the context of the TTIP, the Commission has met with civil society groups just 8 times. It has met corporations and their lobbyists 119 times.

Very few people would argue against removing and simplifying unnecessary regulations, and in particular removing barriers to entry for small firms. However, we cannot allow that to happen at the expense of our democracy, and the proposed investor-state dispute settlement (ISDS) mechanisms at the heart of this transatlantic agreement can only undermine democracy.

Under the ISDS mechanism, companies wanting to challenge a national regulation are able effectively to bypass the usual process and go straight to investment tribunals. Often hugely important outcomes rest on the shoulders of just three arbitrators – one chosen by the company, one by the state, and a third agreed by both.

It's hard to understand why we would even want such a system in the UK. After all, ISDSs are supposed to provide protection for investors dealing with shady countries. The UK MP Kenneth Clarke has explained that investor protection 'is designed to support businesses investing in countries where the rule of law is unpredictable, to say the least' .

When examples of such countries in the EU have been sought, none have so far been given. The ISDS looks less like a measure to protect businesses against failed states, and more like a measure to protect big business against democracy.

Such concerns are dismissed as conspiracy theories, but we don't need to rely on theory. There are plenty of examples in practice of companies undermining national policy using similar dispute mechanisms under different trade agreements – like NAFTA, for instance, which is now so unpopular in the US that only 15% of Americans want to remain part of it.

The most striking example relates to Canada, which was sued by Ethyl Corporation via one of these dispute mechanisms for banning the chemical MMT, an Ethyl product, which Canada considers to be a highly dangerous toxin. Canada had to settle; it paid millions in compensation and reversed its ban. The ban incidentally also applies in the US, on public health grounds.

Around the world there are countless other examples of companies extracting vast compensation or simply overruling national laws by using provisions in trade agreements: attempts to limit coal mining in sensitive areas in Indonesia; attempts to raise standards for coal power plants in Germany; attempts to impose oil-spill controls in South America; and so on.

The danger is that in their hunger for growth, enthusiasts for this treaty have, like Senator Brown, been too willing to overlook the details. Civil society cannot allow that to happen. One way or another, national legislators must apply scrutiny before signing off a deal that could fatally undermine our democracy.

For more information on the campaign against TTIP visit www.stopttip.net. Zac Goldsmith is the MP for Richmond Park and North Kingston and former editor of The Ecologist. This article was first published by The Ecologist in 2014.

MARTIN POWELL

JOHANNES STEUCK

Imagine a world where what a wise man once said,
Led to wealth from his words – not a price on his head.
Imagine a world where we were not misled,
Believers and dreamers as leaders instead;
For the good men talking are soon walking dead.

Imagine that it matters not which flag you stand beside,
Which country is your calling – where you currently reside,
Because what lies on the inside ties us together;
And when love is what finds us it binds us forever…

Martin Powell is a poet, activist, and lyricist.
www.martinpowellpoetry.com

Imagine

RUTH DAVEY

Imagine the well-being of seas and oceans always coming first. Commercial use would be permitted only if it were rational and truly sustainable. Industry would no longer have the right to ransack. Misuse would be a criminal act.

Suppose those in power were forced, by scientific evidence and public pressure, to redefine their thinking and revolutionise their approach to our ocean planet. Governments would work together and take decisive action to tackle these solvable problems. They would become accountable to the people they represent, who want clean and vibrant seas. The health of the marine environment would then always take priority over selfish interests and profit-making at any cost. Imagine over-fishing and destructive mining becoming a thing of the past; pollution and plastic waste diminishing and eventually disappearing; and wildlife flourishing – in coastal waters, ocean depths and on the high seas. Imagine that.

Deborah Wright is an author living in the West Country who wrote 'Conserving the Great Blue – Overturning the Dominant Ocean Paradigm', and is now working with Marinet for the adoption of this principle.

We acknowledge and thank all publishers who have given us permission to quote from a number of their publications.

We acknowledge and warmly thank all contributors whose work we were not able to include. We had a large response to our initial requests.

DESIGN: © CHRIS J BAILEY 2015

Books by Polly Higgins

Eradicating Ecocide
Earth Is Our Business
I Dare You To Be Great

We thank Ecolibrium®, Incorporated for permission to use the word 'Ecolibrium'.

Ecolibrium® is a woman owned, next stage consulting company based in Livingston, Montana USA, operating at the intersection of economic and environmental opportunity. We assemble interdisciplinary teams of experts to create successful business models anchored in sustainability. We specialize in helping our clients manage their environmentally, culturally and historically sensitive resources to optimize the return on investment from these resources while ensuring their preservation for the greatest enjoyment and long term benefit for all. The thrust of our work has been to provide clients improved profitability through sustainable practices prioritizing on integrated energy systems, new agricultural approaches, energy efficiency within the built environment, innovative land use and strategic eco-tourism hospitality venues. Business disciplines include natural and environmental sciences; social and economic research; decision planning and analysis; strategic marketing and communications; curricula development, training and education; architecture, engineering and construction management; communications technology; strategic partnership development; hospitality management; and sustainable energy systems. Contact Elizabeth Scholl, CEO: 406.579.2987 escholl@ecolibrium.com; www.ecolibrium.com

ECOLIBRIUM®
A BETTER ENVIRONMENT FOR BUSINESS.

"Our problems are man-made, therefore they can be solved by man. And man can be as big as he wants. No problem of human destiny is beyond human beings. Man's reason and spirit have often solved the seemingly unsolvable and we believe they can do it again."

John F Kennedy, US President

"The ecological perspective begins with a view of the whole, an understanding of how the various parts of nature interact in patterns that tend toward balance and persist over time. But this perspective cannot treat the earth as something separate from human civilization; we are part of the whole too, and looking at it ultimately means also looking at ourselves. And if we do not see that the human part of nature has an increasingly powerful influence over the whole of nature – that we are, in effect, a natural force just like the winds and the tides – then we will not be able to see how dangerously we are threatening to push the earth out of balance."

Al Gore, author and environmental activist

"Perhaps it has been too uncomfortable for those with vested interests to acknowledge, but we have spent the best part of the past century enthusiastically testing the world to utter destruction; not looking closely enough at the long-term impact our actions will have."

HRH Prince Charles

WWW.ECOLIBRIUMNOW.COM